MODELS OF VISUOSPATIAL COGNITION

MANUEL DE VEGA
MARGARET JEAN INTONS-PETERSON
PHILIP N. JOHNSON-LAIRD
MICHEL DENIS
MARC MARSCHARK

New York   Oxford
OXFORD UNIVERSITY PRESS
1996

Oxford University Press

Oxford   New York
Athens   Auckland   Bangkok   Bombay
Calcutta   Cape Town   Dar es Salaam   Delhi
Florence   Hong Kong   Istanbul   Karachi
Kuala Lumpur   Madras   Madrid   Melbourne
Mexico City   Nairobi   Paris   Singapore
Taipei   Tokyo   Toronto

and associated companies in
Berlin   Ibadan

Library of Congress Cataloging-in-Publication Data
Models of visuospatial cognition / Manuel de Vega . . . [et al.]
p.   cm. —(Counterpoints)
Includes bibliographical references and index.
ISBN 0–19–510084-0 — ISBN 0-19-510085-9 (paper)
1. Mental representation.   2. Space perception.   3. Imagery
(Psychology)   I. de Vega, Manuel.   II. Series: Counterpoints
(Oxford University Press)
BF316.6M63   1996   95-16782
153.7'52—dc20

1 3 5 7 9 8 6 4 2

Printed in the United States of America
on acid-free paper

Preface

As human beings, our reality is a visuospatial one. Physics, biology, and psychology combine to make visuospatial cogniton perhaps our most important form of information processing. Research (and intuition) has shown that visuospatial processes play a vital part in language comprehension for both abstract and concrete materials. We can rotate, fold, travel, and even zoom in and out on visuospatial images in our "mind's eye." For over two millennia, visuospatial strategies have been used to augment human memory, and they have played prominent roles in science as well as art. Even people who are totally, congenitally blind report mental representations and processes similar to those of sighted people.

How is it that we are able to perform all of these wonderful feats? How are visual and spatial information represented in the mind and in the brain? Why does visuospatial imagery play such a preeminent role in cognition, memory, and language? If the answers were known, there would be no need for this volume—but they are not. Theory and research on visuospatial processes have been a guiding force in the shaping of cognitive psychology over the past three decades. From verbal learning to connectionism and neuropsychology, the mechanisms of visuospatial cognition continue to present challenges to our understanding of the psychology of the mind

The present volume provides a seminar of sorts with prominent experts in the area of visuospatial cognition. Their counterpoints on visuospatial processes in cognition, memory, and language are already well-known through their extensive writings in the area. With the support of the University of La Laguna and its Faculty of Psychology (Tenerife, Spain), the Ministerio de Educación y Ciencia, and the Consejería de Educación del Gobierno de Canarias, we were able to come together and discuss a variety of relevant issues at the Fourth European Workshop on Imagery and Cognition at Puerto de la Cruz in the Canary Islands. We now are able to share the fruits of that discussion in a form that captures the content as well as the tone of that meeting. We hope that our progress toward answering the above questions has as much influence on others as it did on us.

M. M.
M. de V.

Contents

MODELS OF VISUOSPATIAL COGNITION

CHAPTER 1

Visuospatial Cognition:
An Historical and Theoretical
Introduction

Manuel de Vega and Marc Marschark

People process spatial information in at least two different ways. Most obviously, we have visual (perception) systems that pick up information from the environment about the visual properties of objects, spatial relations among them, and their motions within the environment. We also have mental representations that allow us to process visuospatial information in a more constructive and less data-driven way than that permitted by the visual system. Through the retrieval of visuospatial information from memory, we are able to "re-experience" or reconsider past perceptual experiences and plan in advance our future interactions with objects or navigation in familiar environments. Through the construction of mental representations, we can mentally combine visuospatial elements in new ways, perform or simulate (depending on one's theoretical preference) mental transformations on them, and engage in reasoning and problem solving involving visual and spatial information. These capabilities all go beyond ordinary visual perception, but they are still aspects of visuospatial cognition.

This volume is concerned mainly with visuospatial representation rather than visual perception, although the functional relations between perception and mental representation will be discussed in several contexts. To the extent that we are also concerned primarily with "typical" modes of visuospatial functioning, the visual and the spatial aspects of mental representation can be considered largely redundant. This is not to deny that there are spatial representations experienced by congenitally blind people, which in some cases seem remarkably visual-like (Cornoldi, De Beni, Roncari, & Romano, 1989). For the present purposes, however, "spatial" and "visuospatial" usually can be used interchangeably, and we do so in this chapter, even if others do not (for various reasons) in the chapters that follow.

Issues surrounding the mental representation of spatial information have been of major theoretical and empirical interest in cognitive psychology since its nominal beginning a quarter century ago. A complete review of the relevant work that has emerged from that field is neither possible nor necessary in this chapter. Instead, throughout the remainder of this book we will focus on some central issues that have been at the forefront of the area and that are of recurrent interest: the isomorphism of spatial representations, the functional relations between visual perception and visuospatial cognition, and the roles of spatial cognition in memory, reasoning, and language comprehension.

ISOMORPHISM REVISITED

Investigators interested in the role of mental imagery in human cognition have obtained a variety of empirical findings that are best explained in terms of an *isomorphism* between perceptual products and their mental representation (Shepard & Chipman, 1970). For example, mental images "retain" metric properties (e.g., size) of their referents. Paivio (1975), therefore, found that it takes longer to decide which of two words signifies the object that is larger in real life when they are similar in size (e.g., *zebra—bed*) than when they are dissimilar (e.g., *zebra—key*). Similarly, Kosslyn (1978) found that it takes longer to "find" details in images of small objects than in images of large objects. Both of these phenomena are examples of what is referred to as the *symbolic distance effect.*

Many of the more common demonstrations of analog qualities in spatial representation involve transformations of mental images such as mental rotation, mental folding, and mental assembly or disassembly. For example, when people have to judge whether two pictures differing in their spatial orientations are identical, reaction times conform to a linear function of the angular disparity between the stimuli (Shepard & Cooper, 1982). This finding suggests that subjects perform a continuous mental transformation—a *mental rotation*—of one of the stimuli in order to match the orientation of the other, and then they execute the comparison.

Other experiments have revealed similar results through the examination of *mental scanning.* In the typical mental-scanning task, subjects initially learn about a series of locations in a fictional or a real geographic area and then are asked to mentally "travel" between pairs of locations in their image. Reaction times in that task reflect the linear relation of distances between each pair of locations, regardless of whether subjects originally learn the locations by examining maps (Kosslyn, Ball, & Reiser, 1978) or via verbal descriptions of their locations (Denis & Cocude, 1989; Denis, this volume). These findings thus clearly indicate second-order isomorphism (Shepard & Chipman, 1970) at the level of on-line visuospatial functioning (or working memory), even if the issue of long-term memory remains to be dealt with elsewhere (see Marschark, Richman, Yuille, & Hunt, 1987).

Despite the apparent clarity of such results in favor of isomorphic spatial representations, the issue has remained controversial. With only a few exceptions, however, critics of the image-as-isomorphism view have mounted their attacks on theoretical rather than empirical grounds. Most frequently, these arguments have taken the form of claims that the phenomenal characteristics of visuospatial images can be better accounted for in terms of abstract symbols governed by an arbitrary syntax (e.g., via propositions or structural descriptions). Critics do not deny the subjective experience of mental imagery, but claim that the underlying format of images lacks any isomorphism with referents and that the analog qualities of images are thus epiphenomenal (e.g., Anderson, 1978; Pylyshyn, 1973, 1981). Images do not have any privileged format in this view, and all information, visuospatial or otherwise, is encoded in the same amodal format. Indeed, from the strong form of this position, it appears that neither images nor percepts can be considered to have second-order isomorphism.

There are, of course, other interpretations of the above phenomena that fall between the extremes of analog imagery and amodal propositional representation. Relative to mental imagery accounts of these findings, for example, the mental model approach to visuospatial cognition relies on a somewhat different notion of isomorphism. Johnson-Laird (1983, p. 419) described this relation as a "weak isomorphism" or "homomorphism" when he suggested that "[t]he structures of mental models are identical to the structures of the states of affairs, whether perceived or conceived, that the models represent" (see also Johnson-Laird, this volume). From the mental model position, descriptions involving logical quantifiers (e.g., "Some men own cars") lead subjects to build sets of tokens that stand for the objects described (i.e., for cars and men). Relations among the tokens are then used to represent the relations among the objects described in the description.

This sort of representation differs considerably from a propositional encoding, which would translate the superficial verbal description into representations in terms of an arbitrary mental language (e.g., "For some x, if x is a man, then x owns a y, where y equals car"), but it also appears far from an analogical representation in the imaginal sense. For example, the mental models approach, unlike the mental imagery account, does not presume that all parameters represented in mental models are "concrete" and visuospatial. Some nonvisual, relational information, such as causal links, intentions, and logical connectives, also are represented in mental models. Therefore, the isomorphic assumption is more relaxed than for the mental imagery position, although mental models still have a more isomorphic character than the arbitrary structure of structural descriptions (Johnson-Laird, this volume).

PERCEPTION AND MENTAL REPRESENTATION

Fully recognizing that visuospatial perception and visuospatial imagery are different at one (obvious) level, it is nonetheless likely that they share some underlying neurological and psychological mechanisms. Most generally, vision derives from an on-line exteroception system that extracts information from the images of the external world activated on the retina (Marr, 1982). Perceptual images of spatial scenes are thus constructed in a bottom-up fashion in terms of edges, surface textures, and shadows. Visuospatial representation of the mental variety, in contrast, derives from the top-down (conceptually based) retrieval, or generation of virtual images that are used in the context of explicit or implicit task demands. At a more specific level, visuospatial perception and visuospatial imagery typically differ in their accuracy, grain, longevity, and transformability.

So, where should we look for the shared components of visuospatial perception and mental representation? Neither "high-level" processing nor early stages of visual processing are good candidates for such mechanisms. The early, bottom-up stages of visual perception appear to be informationally encapsulated or modular, in the sense described by Fodor and others, and consequently cannot be influenced by the higher-order cognitive processes involved in visual imagery. Note that this does not mean that visual perception cannot be affected by higher-order cognition. There have been many demonstrations of viewer expectations or prior language affecting how a visuospatial stimulus is interpreted (e.g., in ambiguous figures) (see Intons-Peterson, this volume). Interpretation, however, occurs at a later rather than an earlier stage in vision (see Cornoldi, Logie, Brandimonte, Kaufmann, & Reisberg, 1995).

At the "other end" of the system, semantic processing typically involves general purpose, central executive processes that are involved in the interpretation and assessment of experience. Almost all cognitive functions interface at this level, including vision, language, memory, and self-generated representations; and it is unlikely that clear links between perception and imagery can be observed there. Rather, levels of cognition most likely to be informative with regard to the functional equivalence of perception and imagery lie in intermediate stages of visual processing (Finke, 1980, 1989). Johnson-Laird (1988) and others have suggested that Marr's (1982) *2½-D sketch* might be the most appropriate level of comparison, and Kosslyn (1980) proposed that the medium for building mental images is a two-dimensional array that shares some properties with the visual field of perception.

Some convergent evidence supports the suggestion that imagery and perception share a common underlying mechanism interface at some stage. For instance, when subjects perform concurrent tasks of perceiving and imagining in the visuospatial modality, either interference (Craver-Lemley & Reeves, 1992; Perky, 1910) or facilitation (e.g., Farah, 1989; Finke, 1989) can be observed, depending on the task. In addition, Shepard (1984) described similar time-angular disparity functions for mental rotation (imagery) and apparent rotation (perception), suggesting that both phenomena are probably governed by the same built-in "mental kinematic mechanism." Finally, studies involving cerebral blood flow and event-related potentials have shown that activity in the occipital cortex is similar when subjects see objects and imagine them (see Farah, 1988; Intons-Peterson, this volume).

Despite the evidence outlined above, there remain some important limitations on the overlap of perception and imagery, even when considered at similar levels of analysis. One problem in interpreting relevant research is that subjects in imagery tasks may be relying on their tacit knowledge about visual processes, and thus they may simulate (intentionally or unintentionally) results that are not directly dependent on analog representations (Pylyshyn, 1981; cf. Intons-Peterson, this volume). The role of knowledge in visuospatial representation is an important issue, and the other three contributors to this book devote some attention to it (see also Intons-Peterson & Roskos-Ewoldsen, 1989; the final chapter of this volume). However, unlike Pylyshyn (1981), who claimed that evidence for the use of tacit knowledge argues against analog visuospatial representation, the present contributors find that the two phenomena are quite compatible.

A related limitation on the linkage of perception and visuospatial imagery derives from studies that have examined subjects' abilities to "reconstrue" visual images (e.g., Chambers & Reisberg, 1985; Cornoldi et al., 1995; Intons-Peterson, this volume). The most straightforward reconstrual studies have examined whether people are able to reinterpret their images of ambiguous stimuli in the same way that they perceptually reinterpret the stimuli themselves. The Jastrow duck-rabbit figure, for example, allows two different interpretations or readings. Regardless of one's initial interpretation, visual inspection usually allows the viewer to make the other interpretation as well. The interesting question is whether a similar reinterpretation or reconstrual can be made solely on the basis of a visual image when the figure is removed, or whether both interpretations might be available if the initial figure were not initially interpreted one way or the other (see Cornoldi et al., 1995, for arguments and evidence).

Chambers and Reisberg (1985) argued that images of such figures are never ambiguous in the same way as the original figures because they are interpreted at the moment of their generation. In their view, no reconstrual is possible if the image itself is created as an interpretation of something. If this were the case then images would be just symbols and their perceptual quality would be epiphenomenal. Consistent with this view, Chambers and Reisberg showed that, across several experiments, none of their subjects were able to reverse their mental images of ambiguous figures. Subjects were, however, quite accurate in drawing the original ambiguous figures from memory, and they easily were able to reinterpret their own drawings (but see Intons-Peterson, this volume).

The complete failure of subjects in reconstruing images in the Chambers and Reisberg study was a striking result. However, it is now clear that the situation is not quite so simple. Kaufmann, Wenevold, and Murdock (1992), for example, found that 28 percent of art students were able to perform reconstruals of ambiguous stimuli, and Hyman and Neisser (1991) reported that giving subjects conceptual cues increases the likelihood of reconstruals. In her chapter in this volume, Intons-Peterson considers some recent studies in the larger context of visuospatial cognition, yielding important insights into the locus and implications of the reconstrual effect.

MEMORY AND VISUOSPATIAL COGNITION

Long-Term Memory

Perhaps the most intuitively obvious, and certainly the best documented role of mental images in human cognition, is their enhancement of memory performance for verbal materials. Paivio (1971, 1983, 1986) took advantage of this intuition and empirically explored the cognitive functions of visuospatial imagery using a variety of verbal learning paradigms. His extensive research led to the formulation of the *dual-coding model,* which has served as the primary explanatory tool for imagery researchers for over 20 years. Two findings, in particular, have been taken as indicators of a central role for visuospatial imagery in long-term memory, consistent with the dual-coding framework. The *concreteness effect* refers to the robust finding that concrete words (i.e., words that refer to concrete referents) generally are easier to remember than abstract words. From the dual-coding model, this result derives from the fact that concrete words are more likely than abstract words to evoke mental imagery, thus leading to their being encoded in both verbal and imaginal systems, whereas abstract words are more likely to be encoded only in the verbal system. These two systems are seen to be separate but interconnected such that at retrieval "two codes are better than one." The other finding is that instructions to use imagery improve memory for verbal materials as compared to standard memory instructions that do not entail mental imagery: the *imagery effect.* Again, the dual-coding explanation is that imagery instructions increase the likelihood of dual verbal and imaginal encoding in long-term memory relative to standard instructions.

The dual-coding interpretations of both concreteness effects and imagery effects have been challenged by findings demonstrating that imagery alone is not sufficient to enhance memory performance in either free or cued recall (e.g., Marschark & Hunt, 1989; Marschark & Surian, 1992). Marschark and Hunt (1989), for example, presented subjects with lists composed of concrete and abstract cue-target word pairs, and then tested incidental memory using either cued or free recall of target words. Concreteness effects were obtained in cued recall but not in free recall. That finding was interpreted as indicating that it was easier to establish relational links between concrete words than between abstract words, thus facilitating cued recall. For free recall, the relational clues between cues and targets (within pairs) would be irrelevant and relational links between pairs would be at a minimum. In any case, when relational information was absent or disrupted by either encoding or retrieval tasks, Marschark and Hunt failed to obtain concreteness effects.

Other experiments have shown that imagery instructions in paired-associate learning also may be insufficient to improve memory performance in some situations, thus weakening the dual-coding model. Instead, it appears to be the integrative, relational processes that often accompany the generation of images—but may also occur in nonimaginal tasks—or some combination of relational (integrative) and distinctive (imaginal) processes that is responsible for enhancement of memory (de Vega, 1978; Marschark & Surian, 1992). When either the integrative or distinctive operations are prevented, neither item concreteness nor intentional use of imagery improves memory.

Research concerning the role of mental imagery in the comprehension and memory of complex verbal materials, such as texts, also has suggested that imagery alone may not be as strong a predictor of memory as we once believed. Indeed, when the materials are otherwise well controlled, concrete paragraphs generally are not better remembered than abstract paragraphs (e.g., Marschark, 1985). In a review of the literature on the role of imagery in memory for texts, Denis (1988) found that the locus of imagery effects in text memory lies in the organization and recall of lower-level elements (words and phrases), but that imagery is not involved in the thematic organization of the text. Looking ahead, we will see that comprehension and memory of complex verbal materials likely relies on building and updating some sort of schema or conceptual model of the situation described, which involves not only visuospatial information, but also thematic relations about protagonists, their intentions, and so on. These mental schemas provide readers with a rich and flexible structure of the global meaning of the text and play a central role in both comprehension and memory.

The moral of this section, thus far, is that some effects traditionally attributed to the mnemonic power of visuospatial imagery appear to have been caused by confounded factors (e.g., in the case of cued and free-recall experiments), and others do not occur in cases in which they would be predicted from a simple dual-memory framework (e.g., with complex text materials). Marschark and his colleagues have elaborated an alternative framework in which relational and distinctive information (independent of the perceptual quality of images) are the critical factors explaining most of the effects considered as evidence of dual-coding (Marschark & Surian, 1989, 1992). Consequently, the necessity of postulating the existence of two modality-specific codes in long-term memory has been questioned by several current memory researchers.

Working Memory

The studies considered earlier on mental rotation, mental scanning, and mental comparison originally were taken as evidence of the role of imagery in an imaginal system that included long-term memory (Paivio, 1986). It is now clear, however, that essentially all of the experiments that have successfully explored the analog-perceptual qualities of images have employed tasks involving the on-line use of imagery in working memory and need not have any bearing on the nature of long-term memory codes (see Baddeley, 1986; Intons-Peterson, this volume; Marschark et al., 1987).

With the dual-coding model in mind, however, a relevant question emerges: Are there two separate working memory systems corresponding to the imagery and the verbal modalities? Baddeley's (1986, 1988) answer is affirmative. Working memory, in his view, involves a *Central Executive* aided by at least two subsidiary systems, an *Articulatory Loop* involved in storage and processing of verbal material, and a *Visuo-spatial Sketchpad* that performs a similar function for visuospatial material.

The support for a specialized visuospatial working memory comes from the selective interference observed in the context of dual-task paradigms. For example, concurrent visuospatial tracking interferes with a primary task that involves storage of the relative positions of numbers in a square matrix, whereas memory for similar verbally encoded material is less affected by tracking (see Logie, 1989, for a review). Such a system also is consistent with essentially all of Paivio's (1971, 1986) results that have been taken as evidence for the dual-coding model. Alternatively, this system could be viewed in terms of Kosslyn's (1980) computational imagery model, which included a visual buffer (the "two-dimensional array") in which images are generated and refreshed on the basis of information from long-term memory.

Accepting that working memory is divided into visuospatial and verbal subsystems, another question arises: Do these subsystems work cooperatively or competitively? The traditional answer from the dual-coding model is that both the verbal and imaginal systems cooperate in memory, and consequently a dual encoding in both systems produces more persistent memory traces. However, some evidence indicates that verbal codes can interfere with visual representations. Schooler and Engstler-Schooler (1990) showed subjects a videotape featuring a salient individual. Later, they asked some subjects to describe the individual's face. Subjects who performed that verbal task performed less well on a subsequent face recognition test than did control subjects who did not engage in verbalization. The locus of the interference was clearly at the retrieval stage rather than at the encoding stage, indicating that it was an *overshadowing effect* of a later verbalization on an intact spatial code.

Brandimonte, Hitch, and Bishop (1992) found similar interference of verbalization on imagery memory, but at encoding rather than at retrieval. In their experiments, subjects were engaged in a mental substraction task involving visual stimuli, in which they were asked to mentally take away a part of the image in order to discover an "implicit" object in the reminder. When subjects verbally named (encoded) the discovered pattern, their performance in a visual memory task was impaired as compared to conditions in which verbal encoding was prevented by a concurrent, articulatory suppression task. These results suggest that there are two alternative manners of encoding visual material in working memory, visuospatial and verbal, both of which can influence subsequent visual imagery performance. Some of the implications for such findings are considered later by Denis, Intons-Peterson, and Johnson-Laird, although from somewhat different perspectives (see also Cornoldi et al., 1995).

REASONING AND SPATIAL COGNITION

All of the studies cited thus far were intended to reveal the nature of visuospatial mental representations, exploring their format and their interface with perception. In fact, much of the research on memory for word lists was motivated initially by the goal of elucidating the properties of imagery in cognition rather than increasing our knowledge of memory per se. Spatial representations, however, also have been of interest to researchers exploring other fields of human cognition, particularly reasoning and language. Over the last two decades or so, these areas have led to the framework of mental models, initially developed by Johnson-Laird and his colleagues to explain reasoning and problem solving (Johnson-Laird, 1983, Johnson-Laird & Byrne, 1991). Later, that framework was extended to the field of language comprehension (Bower & Morrow, 1990; de Vega, 1994; Garnham, 1987; Sanford & Garrod, 1981) with considerable success.

In the fields of both problem solving and language comprehension, many researchers have long been dissatisfied with the assumption that language processing essentially entails a formal, syntactic computation derived from words to produce mental symbols (i.e., propositions). Instead, it has been evident that, in most cases, some representation of reference must take place during comprehension. In syllogistic reasoning, for example, people do not rely on content-free rules applied to an abstract representation of premises, but usually represent the "world state" referred to by the premises; and these representations, mental models, influence the course of reasoning (Johnson-Laird & Byrne, 1991). Language comprehension outside of such tasks similarly involves not only the processing of the linguistic message at phonological, lexical, and syntactical levels, but also the building of the referent or "model of the situation" (e.g., Bower & Morrow, 1990; de Vega, 1995; Garnham, 1987; Sanford & Garrod, 1981).

Mental models, like mental images, seem to depend in part on the representation of spatial information. As we have already seen, both approaches entail representations that have some isomorphic spatial features, and both agree that spatial representations play an important role in human cognition, mediating language comprehension and production, reasoning and problem solving, and creativity. Therefore, it is worth considering whether "images" and "models" can be unified into a single theoretical framework or, conversely, whether they are necessarily two distinct representational systems for spatial information. One might suspect, at the outset, that images and models involve different systems, because images are more closely linked to the visual features of a situation, whereas mental models involve not only isomorphic information but also abstract entities and relations. A detailed analysis of this issue is provided later in this volume by Johnson-Laird.

One striking aspect of syllogistic reasoning, especially if one considers the use of some kind of visuospatial representation therein, is that people are very prone to errors. This characteristic notwithstanding, some theoreticians have maintained a belief in a rational competence (e.g., a set of inference rules, predicate calculus, and so on) underlying human reasoning. From that view, performance factors like misunderstanding of premises and linguistic biases would be responsible for errors, much as the fallible language production system is assumed to be responsible for apparent errors (i.e., ungrammatical utterances) produced by generative grammars. The rational model, however, fails to explain many of the layperson's errors in reasoning and does not provide a complete account of the underlying rules that account for a person's success.

A more realistic account of reasoning than the rule-based approach is inherent in Johnson-Laird's (1983; Johnson-Laird & Byrne, 1991) mental model framework. That view emphasizes the way people represent the referents of premises and how these representations constrain reasoning. Consider this inference problem from Johnson-Laird and Byrne (1991):

(1) The black ball is directly behind the cue ball. The green ball is on the right of the cue ball, and there is a red ball between them.

(2) Therefore, if I move so that the red ball is between me and the black ball, the cue ball is to the left of my line of sight.

It might be possible to establish a set of rules to produce the inference (2). Most people, however, report that they solve this problem by imagining or modeling the spatial relations described by the premises. In many cases like this, "reasoning" is thus a matter of gaining "understanding" by generating a mental model of the premises. Syllogistic reasoning, of course, may involve much more complicated situations, such as when subjects test their mental models in trying to falsify them. The mental model framework has been successful in predicting the empirical difficulty of syllogisms, based on the number of mental models involved in reasoning, while approaches based on the complexity of inference rules have fared less well (Johnson-Laird, this issue). This is not to say that visuospatial representation is involved in all reasoning, and in his chapter, Johnson-Laird shows this clearly not to be the case.

LANGUAGE AND SPATIAL COGNITION

The critical insight of the mental models framework for language comprehension is that comprehenders must build representations of the referent of the text (the objects, characters, events, and processes described) in addition to the representation of the text itself (Bower & Morrow, 1990; Garnham, 1987; Sanford & Garrod, 1981). One illustration of how mental models might work in comprehension is provided in an experiment reported by Glenberg, Meyer and Lindem (1987). Subjects in that study read short texts in which a target object was described as spatially associated to the protagonist (e.g., "John put on his sweatshirt") or as spatially dissociated from the protagonist (e.g., "John took off his sweatshirt"). Later in the text, when the protagonist was described as moving to a different location, subjects were tested with an identification probe in which they judged whether or not the target word ("sweatshirt") had been included in the text. Results showed faster responses after reading the associated rather than the dissociated version of the text, indicating that in the former condition the target was more accessible in readers' memories. This greater accessibility was attributed to the represented structure of the situation rather than to the surface features of the text (which was identical in both versions of the task except for a single verb) or their propositional encoding.

Mental models also appear to mediate the processing of anaphoric (pronoun) reference during language comprehension. Assigning a pronoun to its antecedent sometimes depends on a mental model of the situation rather than on the syntactic clues of gender and number. This alternative is particularly apparent when there are several potential antecedents that syntactically match the anaphor. For example, de Vega (in press) had subjects read short descriptions involving two target objects, one placed inside and the other outside of a building. A protagonist was described either as entering or leaving the building, and an embedded sentence described the protagonist as interacting with an indeterminate object referred to by a pronoun whose number and Spanish gender matched both targets. The question was whether subjects would be able to select the appropriate antecedent relying on the protagonist's spatial position inside or outside the building. Consider this example:

(3) Julie likes to walk in the area of the museum. The museum has a famous exhibition of Egyptian mummies that are very well preserved. In the square in front of the museum there are many pigeons which come there to be fed by people.

Critical sentences:

(4) Julie went into the museum from the square and smiled with pleasure when she saw them again.

(4') Julie went out from the museum to the square and smiled with pleasure when she saw them again.

Immediately after reading sentence (4) or (4'), subjects received one of the possible antecedents of the pronoun ("mummies" or "pigeons") in a speeded identification task. Reaction times were significantly faster when the target was consistent with the protagonist's position than when it was inconsistent. Thus, after reading sentence (4) subjects responded faster to "mummies" than to "pigeons," whereas after reading (4') that pattern was reversed.

Mental models are so compelling in language comprehension that sometimes subjects solve anaphors despite mismatches between the syntactic markers of the pronoun and the antecedent. This is the case of conceptual anaphors like:

(5) After college, my sister went to work for IBM. They/it made her a very good offer.

Subjects who read the anaphor "they" are faster and rate it as more natural that those who read "it," and this difference occurs despite the fact that the latter— but not the former—syntactically matches the antecedent (e.g., Gernsbacher, 1991). The reader's model of the situation explains this linguistic anomaly, as subjects activate the collective set implicit in the antecedent IBM (a group of people who work at IBM).

Other experiments in which subjects learned verbal descriptions of three-dimension environments have shown that, in such circumstances, subjects are able to elaborate protagonist-centered perspectives and to compute the position of objects as the protagonist is "reoriented" in the narrative (Franklin & Tversky,

1990). Moreover, de Vega (1994) has shown that readers are able to keep track of the perspective of two different characters with different points of view of the same environment.

Mental models thus seem to underlie human reasoning and language comprehension. However, the emphasis of those research areas is somewhat different. Whereas the focus in reasoning research has been on the number of models activated by a given correct or incorrect approach to a problem, comprehension studies are more interested in the dynamic, incremental nature of models that are enriched and updated from moment to moment during comprehension.

For its part, language production is a less developed branch of psycholinguistics than comprehension, and the interface between spatial cognition and the production of messages is far less understood. This interesting area is now being actively explored by several researchers (see Denis, this volume). Robin and Denis (1991), for example, examined how people describe mental images and their "equivalent" visual configurations. Their results showed that subjects' reports were governed by the same principle of economy regardless of whether they were describing their images or their perceptions. In addition, subjects showed considerable flexibility in their strategy use as a function of stimulus complexity in both modes. The direction that this research will, or should, take in the future is unclear. Several suggestions are offered in the coming chapters, however, and we now turn to those and other issues of common interest.

PERSPECTIVES ON VISUOSPATIAL COGNITION

In the following chapters, three rather different views of visuospatial cognition are considered. As will become clear in the discussion that follows them, there seem to be more points of agreement than disagreement in the conclusions reached by Michel Denis, Margaret Intons-Peterson, and Philip Johnson-Laird about the fundamental nature of mental representation. How they go about reaching their conclusions and the type of arguments that they find convincing, however, differ considerably. As a result, each one of the contributors has made some assumptions, and perhaps some conclusions, that the others find unnecessary if not misguided. Rather than attempt to mediate those differences, we allow the contributors to deal with those issues themselves, both in terms of their chapters and in their discussion to follow. Similarities in the ways that these investigators think about their problem areas derive from their common interest in the format and function of visuospatial representation. Differences in the content of their chapters primarily reflect differences in the substance of their research in seeking answers to the fundamental questions of human cognition.

Michel Denis, for example, considers the functional interface between imagery and language. Denis has developed a paradigm that explores how speakers generate verbal descriptions of spatial configurations to induce the construction of cognitive maps in listeners. This paradigm reveals that speakers with high visuospatial abilities demonstrate more efficient strategies in their descriptions than do subjects with low visuospatial abilities.

Linking language and imagery in another way, Margaret Intons-Peterson brings together two theoretical and empirical traditions in imagery research: the (verbal) memory branch, which started with Paivio's early research with verbal learning paradigms, and the (perceptual) spatial branch, concerned with the perception-like properties of mental images. Intons-Peterson attempts to integrate both traditions into a single model of spatial representation that accounts for the role of both verbal and nonverbal processes in visuospatial representation.

Philip Johnson-Laird considers the verbal-nonverbal distinction from yet another perspective. He discusses the psychological status of three kinds of representations: propositions, mental models, and mental images. Rather than arguing for a single form of representation, however, Johnson-Laird presents evidence that all three may serve important cognitive functions, representing different sorts of information in different ways. In describing how people go about syllogistic reasoning, he demonstrates that individuals can rely on all three levels of representation. Ultimately, however, Johnson-Laird argues that most human reasoning is based upon the building of one or several mental models of the premises that serve functions traditionally ascribed to either verbal or imaginal representations.

Consistent with the *Counterpoints* model, the final discussion provides a forum in which the three contributors are able to comment on each other's perspectives and provide rebuttal, where appropriate. The discussion also provided an opportunity for "higher-level" consideration of points of agreement and disagreement. In the best tradition of scientific pursuits, portions of the discussion come from a face-to-face roundtable held by all five of the contributors involved in this volume. Perhaps the most exciting aspect of that meeting were the emerging insights that seemed to rise up out of the ashes of empirical differences. Not all of those insights were points of agreement among the contributors, however, and other perspectives not represented here provided points of mutual consensus and dispute. The result was a synergistic if multifaceted understanding of visuospatial representation and its central role in human cognitive functioning.

REFERENCES

Anderson, J. R. (1978). Arguments concerning representations for mental imagery. *Psychological Review, 85,* 249–277.

Baddeley, A. D. (1986). *Working memory.* Oxford: Oxford University Press.

Baddeley, A. D. (1988). Imagery and working memory. In M. Denis, J. Engelkamp, &

J. T. E. Richardson (Eds.), *Cognitive and neuropsychological approaches to mental imagery* (pp. 169-180). Dordrecht: Martinus Nijhoff.

Brandimonte, M. A., Hitch, G. J., & Bishop, D. V. M. (1992). Influence of short-term memory codes on visual image processing: Evidence from image transformation tasks. *Journal of Experimental Psychology: Learning, Memory, and Cognition, 18*, 157–165.

Bower, G. H., & Morrow, D. G. (1990). Mental models in narrative comprehension. *Science, 44*–48.

Chambers, D., & Reisberg, D. (1985). Can mental images be ambiguous? *Journal of Experimental Psychology: Human Perception and Performance, 11* (3), 317–328.

Cornoldi, C., De Beni, R., Roncari, S., & Romano, S. (1989). The effects of imagery instructions on total congenital blind recall. *European Journal of Cognitive Psychology, 1*, 321–331.

Cornoldi, C., Logie, B., Brandimonte, M., Kaufmann, G., & Reisberg, D. (1995). *Stretching the imagination: Representation and transformations in mental imagery.* New York: Oxford University Press.

Craver-Lemley, C., & Reeves, A. (1992). How visual imagery interferes with vision. *Psychological Review, 99* (4), 633–650.

Denis, M. (1988). Imagery and prose processing. In M. Denis, J. Engelkamp, & J. T. E. Richardson (Eds.), *Cognitive and neuropsychological approaches to mental imagery* (pp. 121-132). Dordrecht: Martinus Nijhoff.

Denis, M., & Cocude, M. (1989). Scanning visual images generated from verbal descriptions. *The European Journal of Cognitive Psychology, 1* (4), 293–308.

de Vega, M. (1978). La representacion de la informacion en la memoria a largo plazo: Una evaluacion experimental de la teorias duales y proposicionales. *Analisis y Modificacion de Conducta, 4* (7), 103–128.

de Vega M. (1994). Change of character and change of perspective in narratives describing spatial environments. *Psychological Research, 56*, 116–126.

de Vega, M. (1995). Backward updating of mental models during continuous reading of narratives. *Journal of Experimental Psychology: Learning, Memory and Cognition, 21*, 373–385.

Farah, M. J. (1988). Is visual imagery really visual? Overlooked evidence from neuropsychology. *Psychological Review, 95* (3), 307–317.

Farah, M. J. (1989). Mechanisms of imagery-perception interaction. *Journal of Experimental Psychology: Human Perception and Performance, 15* (2), 203–211.

Finke, R. A. (1980). Levels of equivalence in imagery and perception. *Psychological Review, 87* (2), 113–132.

Finke, R. A. (1989). *Principles of mental imagery.* Cambridge MA: MIT Press.

Franklin, N., & Tversky, B. (1990). Searching imagined environments. *Journal of Experimental Psychology: General, 119*, (1), 63–76.

Garnham, A. (1987). *Mental models as representations of discourse and text.* New York: John Wiley.

Gernsbacher, A. M. (1991). Comprehending conceptual anaphors. *Language and Cognitive Processes, 6*, 81–105.

Glenberg, A. M., Meyer, M., & Lindem, K. (1987). Mental models contribute to foregrounding during text comprehension. *Journal of Memory and Language, 26,* 69–83.

Hyman, I. E. & Neisser, U. (1991). *Reconstructing mental images: Problems of method.* Emory Cognition Project, Technical Report #19, Emory University, Atlanta, GA.

Intons-Peterson, M. J., & Roskos-Ewoldsen, B. B. (1989). Sensory-perceptual qualities of images. *Journal of Experimental Psychology: Learning, Memory, and Cognition, 15,* 188–199.

Johnson-Laird, P. N. (1983). *Mental models.* Cambridge: Cambridge University Press.

Johnson-Laird, P. N. (1988). *The computer and the mind. An introduction to cognitive science.* Glasgow: Fontana Press.

Johnson-Laird, P. N., & Byrne, R. M. J. (1991). *Deduction.* Hillsdale, NJ: Erlbaum.

Kaufmann, G., Wenevold, E., & Murdock, M. C. (1992, December). *Reconstrual of images.* Paper presented in the Fourth European Workshop on Imagery and Cognition, Puerto de La Cruz, Spain.

Kosslyn, S. M. (1978). Measuring the visual angle of the mind's eye. *Cognitive Psychology 10,* 356–389.

Kosslyn, S. M. (1980). *Image and mind.* Cambridge, MA: Harvard University Press.

Kosslyn, S. M., Ball, T. M., & Reiser, B. J. (1978). Visual images preserve metric spatial information. Evidence from studies of image scanning. *Journal of Experimental Psychology: Human Perception and Performance. 4,* 47–60.

Logie, R. H. (1989). Characteristics of visual short-term memory. *European Journal of Cognitive Psychology, 1* (4), 275–284.

Marr, D. (1982). *Vision.* San Francisco: W. H. Freeman.

Marschark, M. (1985). Imagery and organization in the recall of prose. *Journal of Memory and Language, 24,* 554–564.

Marschark, M. & Hunt, R. R. (1989). A re-examination of the role of imagery in learning and memory. *Journal of Experimental Psychology: Learning, Memory, and Cognition, 15,* 710–720.

Marschark, M., Richman, C. L., Yuille, J. C., & Hunt, R. R. (1987). The role of imagery in memory: On shared and distinctive information. *Psychological Bulletin. 102,* 28–41.

Marschark, M., & Surian, L. (1989). Why does imagery improve memory? *European Journal of Cognitive Psychology, 7* (3), 251–263.

Marschark, M., & Surian, L. (1992). Concreteness effects in free recall: The effects of relational and distinctive information. *Memory & Cognition, 20,* 612–620.

Paivio, A. (1971). *Imagery and verbal processes.* New York: Holt, Rinehart and Winston.

Paivio, A. (1975). Perceptual comparisons through the mind's eye. *Memory & Cognition, 3,* 635–647.

Paivio, A. (1980). On weighing things in your mind. In P. W. Yusczyk & R. M. Klein (Eds.), *The nature of thought.* Hillsdale, NJ: Erlbaum.

Paivio, A. (1983). The empirical case for dual coding. In J. C. Yuille (Ed.), *Imagery, memory and cognition* (pp. 307–332). Hillsdale, NJ: Erlbaum.

Paivio, A. (1986). *Mental representation: A dual-coding approach.* New York: Oxford University Press.

Perky, C. W. (1910). An experimental study of imagination. *American Journal of Psychology, 21,* 422–452.

Pylyshyn, Z. (1973). What the mind's eye tells the mind's brain: A critique of mental imagery. *Psychological Bulletin, 80,* 1–24.

Pylyshyn, Z. (1981). The imagery debate: Analogue media versus tacit knowledge. *Psychological Review, 88* (1), 16–45.

Robin, F., & Denis, M. (1991). *Description of perceived or imagined spatial networks.* In R. H. Logie & M. Denis (Eds.), *Mental images in human cognition.* Amsterdam: North-Holland.

Sanford, A., & Garrod, S. (1981). *Understanding written language: Exploration of comprehension beyond the sentence.* Chichester: John Wiley.

Schooler, J. W., & Engstler-Schooler, T. Y. (1990). Verbal overshadowing of visual memories: Some things are better left unsaid. *Cognitive Psychology, 22,* 36–71.

Shepard, R. N. (1984). Ecological constrants on internal representation: Resonant kinematics of perceiving, imagining, thinking, and dreaming. *Psychological Review, 91* (4), 417–447.

Shepard, R. N., & Chipman, S. (1970). Second-order isomorphism of internal representations: Shapes of states. *Cognitive Psychology, 1,* 1–17.

Shepard, R. N., & Cooper, L. A., (Eds.). (1982). *Mental images and their transformations.* Cambridge, MA: MIT Press.

CHAPTER 2

Integrating the Components of Imagery

Margaret Jean Intons-Peterson

What is imagery? At the moment, I define it as sensory-perceptual memory with spatial extent. That is, I propose that we learn to label as imagery those memories that have salient sensory-perceptual and spatial features. This chapter surveys support for the components of this definition. It also examines two major lines of research that have shaped current views of imagery. Thus, the chapter begins with a brief historical overview of the definition's genealogy plus observations about why some potential components have been omitted. This evaluation, then, will consider evidence for what imagery is not as well as what it is. Next, I will offer a framework for imagery that embraces linguistic components, rather than minimizing them, and will examine some research in light of implications of the framework.

Questions about imagery echo from the distant past, often with persistent currency. Is imagery a separate cognitive system? Are images simply faint reflections of percepts or sensations? Most important, what are images? Do they represent bona fide phenomena, unique and distinct from other processes? Accompanying these questions are doubts about the concept of imagery. Such reservations come from different quarters, with philosophers occasionally denying the existence of images and psychologists offering occasionally dismissive explanations for the experiences of imagery.

These denials may seem strange because people often report that their personal experiences of images are vivid and compelling. Such creative individuals as Einstein, Kekulé, Mozart, and Watson (e.g., McKim, 1972; Miller, 1984; Shepard, 1978) describe their imaginal experiences in graphic, fascinating detail. Most of us resonate to these anecdotal reminiscences as we mentally count the corners of a block-letter E or the number of windows in our living room. These introspections of imagery are not restricted to a group of unusually talented individuals; they constitute frequently experienced, persistent, often persuasive psychological phenomena. To many psychologists, these experiences demand an explanation if psychology is to offer a comprehensive understanding of the human mind (see Kaufmann & Helstrup, 1993). As noted, however, at least some philosphers are not convinced. They claim that an image must represent an object. Because images cannot be seen or demonstrated objectively, these philosophers argue that images do not exist (e.g., Ryle, 1949; Shorter, 1952). Indeed, Dennett declared that the dismissal of mental images would be "a clear case of good riddance" (Dennett, 1969, p. 141).

Some psychologists grant the introspective experience, but prefer appeals to deep propositional or amodal structures as representations that underlie both imagery and language (e.g., Anderson, 1978; Pylyshyn, 1973, 1980, 1981, 1984). Presumably, these propositional representations and the processes that act on them are so tightly coupled that they cannot be disentangled (e.g., Anderson, 1978). Moreover, Pylyshyn claims that imagery may reflect tacit demand characteristics arising from task requirements and the subject's knowledge of the world. Furthermore, responses in imagery paradigms may be unintentionally biased by experimenters who understand the hypotheses under test (Intons-Peterson, 1983). It is true that many imagery paradigms invite subjects to generate images that are ill-defined and for which the subject may have no clear standards. Such vague situations are vulnerable to these criticisms, but most recent work is designed to minimize these potential confounds.

Still other psychologists question whether effects such as those of concreteness and verbal imagery are products of rather general features of relational (shared) and item-specific (distinctive) information in high- and low-imagery verbal materials (e.g., Marschark & Cornoldi, 1991; Marschark, Richman, Yuille, & Hunt, 1987). This is a strong possibility, as we shall see.

As suggested by the foregoing, imagery may be explained in terms of other types of processing and capabilities. These processes include perception, memory, expectations, linguistic influences from the phonological to the pragmatic level, and neurological mediation. In this chapter, we consider evidence from these and related sources, exploring image-language reciprocities from simple to complex situations, from sensory levels to creative production. The chapter takes its cue from the definition of imagery as a sensory-perceptual memory with spatial extent, probing the reality of various aspects of the definition and the concomitant role of language.

Although numerous experimental methods have been devised to pursue imagery, two tracks have been particularly prominent. I call them the memory (linguistic) and spatial (perceptual) traditions, partly following Ulric Neisser, who, in 1972, described imagery as being at the intersection of perception and memory: "If memory and perception are the two key branches of cognitive psychology, the study of imagery stands precisely at their intersection" (p. 233). These two tracks represent distinctly different methodological traditions. The memory-linguistic tradition has been dominated by the use of verbal materials to elicit imagery as a variable that affects learning and retention. In contrast, the spatial-perceptual tradition focuses on efforts to induce and measure manipulations of mental events that correspond rather closely to visual or auditory perception. Almost guaranteed by the diversity of these approaches, imagery has remained an elusive, even an evanescent phenomenon.

HISTORICAL REVIEW

In addition to grounding subsequent discussion, the brief historical review distinguishes among features that seem essential to understanding imagery and those that do not. To further these aims, the experiments and positions cited were chosen to illustrate relevant points. Hence, the history is highly selective and noncomprehensive.

The Memory (Linguistic) Branch

The work of Allan Paivio (e.g., 1971, 1986) and his colleagues affords a classical example of this branch of investigating imagery. Drawing heavily on traditions established in the verbal-learning literature, this research typically manipulated the characteristics of words or phrases, using ratings of concreteness, imageability, meaningfulness, to vary the level of imagery likely to be induced by the materials. The use of this approach was deftly strategic, for in addition to its general appeal as a way to understand the differential power of various classes of words, it restored the study of imagery to professional respectability after a long eclipse (Holt, 1964). Paivio probably needed to capitalize on the *Zeitgeist* then current in the area to capture the attention of the scientific community.

However, this approach had an obvious flaw, for it lacked documentation that images had (or had not) been invoked by the various manipulations. Subsequent analyses have suggested that the operation of factors such as distinctiveness and relational properties of component items and even an amodal conceptual representation may explain many of the phenomena formerly ascribed to imagery. In this section I have relied heavily on the reviews by Marschark and Cornoldi (1991) and Marschark et al. (1987).

Unsurprisingly, Paivio (1971, 1986) developed a model that incorporated both imaginal and verbal components. In essence, his dual-code model postulated two major forms of encoding—imaginal and verbal. Some materials are more likely to be coded in one form than in the other. For example, pictures and images are likely to be coded imaginally; words are likely to be coded verbally. The two forms may interact, so that pictures and images may be named or labeled, thereby acquiring a verbal code, just as words, phrases, and sentences may be encoded in a more graphic form.

This model predicts that concrete words probably would be coded both imaginally and verbally, which should make them more memorable than abstract words. Abstract words would be coded verbally, but are less likely to be coded imaginally, particularly if short-exposure durations minimize pictorial (imaginal) recoding. Similarly, instructing subjects to imagine the referents of words should result in greater opportunities for dual coding of the words than not instructing subjects to imagine the referents. These and related predictions precipitated an avalanche of research, as investigators rushed to test them. Early tests supported the predictions. Indeed, the finding that verbal materials rated as concrete or easy-to-imagine typically are easier to remember than verbal materials rated as abstract or hard-to-imagine remains one of the most robust in the memory literature. Memory "experts" (e.g., Lorayne & Lucas, 1974) routinely recommend the use of imagery as a memory aid.

Despite these common successes and the demonstrable effectiveness of imagining to-be-remembered items, discordant results began to emerge. Concrete materials are not always easier to remember than abstract ones. For example, Marschark (1985; Marschark & Paivio, 1977) found that sentence memory improved with concreteness when the sentences were presented in a random order, but not when the sentences were ordered topically. These results suggest that concreteness is beneficial when materials lack other organizational (relational) structure, such as a theme. When the material is well organized, concreteness does not enhance memory.

Neither do instructions to use imaginal processing invariably facilitate retention. Perrig (1988) found the imagery instructions aided prose memory in only 36 percent of the studies he reviewed. Moreover, effective imaginal processing seems to be restricted to otherwise unstructured material (Paivio & Csapo, 1969; Snodgrass, Burns, & Pirone, 1978). In these studies, instructions to process materials imaginally did not necessarily show an advantage over control instructions when the task required output of a serial sequence. In summary, the advantageous effects of imagery for multiple items are most apparent when order does not matter.

Another difficulty is that the possession of high imagery does not necessarily aid retention. Efforts to demonstrate reliable differences between high and low imagers have yielded ambiguous results (for reviews see Marschark & Cornoldi, 1991; Marschark et al., 1987; Paivio, 1986).

Nevertheless, the memorial successes associated with concrete or highly imageable materials and with instructions to imagine the referents of to-be-remembered materials do not explain the processes underlying either the common successes or the occasional failures.

One line of explanation for the diverse results deals with timing; another deals with the interrelations of the materials to be remembered. The timing explanation derives from the assumption that the generation of an image to a verbal cue takes time. Although image-generation times vary somewhat, 3 seconds is typical for concrete words and 5 seconds, for abstract words (see Paivio, 1986). Hence, any model that assumes a serial process of linguistically coding verbal material and then imagining a referent of the linguistic coding must predict that brief presentation times will reduce or eliminate opportunities for imaginal encoding—and will, therefore, diminish the concreteness effect.

This prediction was refuted in an experiment by Paivio and Csapo (1969), who presented stimuli at two rates, 0.5 items per second and 0.19 items per second (or roughly ½ or ⅕ items per second), both of which should have been too fast for image generation, according to Paivio (1986). The items (pictures, concrete, and abstract words) were tested in two sequential memory tasks (memory span and serial learning) and in two item-memory tasks (free recall and recognition). For our purposes, the critical outcome was that, at the slower (but still fast) rate, concrete words and pictures were remembered better than abstract words for all tasks, even though imagining the referents of the concrete words should have been hard to complete in the available time. At the faster rate, we would expect even fewer differences. As expected, the retention of concrete and abstract words did not differ on the sequential memory tasks (although both were remembered better than the pictures), but the three types of stimuli did not differ on the item-memory tasks. Obviously, Paivio's modality-specific model did not predict concreteness effects with a presentation rate as fast as 0.5 seconds per item.

The modality-specific model yields another prediction about time, namely that if the time allowed per item exceeds about 5 seconds, concreteness effects should disappear because there is ample time to name and imagine the referents to both concrete and abstract words. Indeed, concreteness effects disappeared when items were presented for 10 seconds in free-recall study or when the items were presented at a 5-second rate but shown twice before recall (Marschark & Surian, 1992). In contrast, however, a study (Bugelski, Kidd, & Segmen, 1968) of key-word mnemonics, which used presentation rates of 2, 4, or 8 seconds per item, found imagery mnemonics to aid memory more than a control with the 8- and 4-second-per-item presentation rates, although not with the 2-second rate (consistent with the first prediction). Clearly, a dual-code-type model's predictions about timing and its effects on concreteness have received mixed support.

Another line of explanation is that variables other than concreteness and imageability contribute to the results. Imageability correlates with a number of variables, including age of acquisition, concreteness, familiarity, frequency, image latency, meaningfulness, and vividness (Cornoldi & Paivio, 1982; Di Vesta, Ingersoll, & Sunshine, 1971; Paivio, 1986; Rubin, 1980), but these variables have not proved as successful as imageability (see Paivio, 1986, for a review).

The modality-specific, dual-code approach may be recast to allow for the differential processing of relational and item-specific information for the materials. The general notion is that memory for a component of an episode depends on the relation of the component to other elements (relational information) and its own distinctive attributes (e.g., Einstein & Hunt, 1980; Humphreys, 1978; Marschark, 1985, 1988; Petersen, 1974). This alternative view affirmatively accommodates Marschark's (1985) findings that concreteness improved sentence memory only when the sentences were presented in a random order. He explained these results by assuming that, at the time of retrieval, concrete sentences tend to be more distinctive (have more distinctive features) than do abstract sentences. Other things being equal (i.e., random presentation of the sentences rather than a logical progression, which would encourage relational processing), the greater distinctiveness of the concrete sentences will confer an advantage on them over the abstract sentences. This benefit may be overridden and the concreteness effect eliminated when the inter-sentence relations foster processing of relational, rather than distinctive, information.

Marschark and Cornoldi (1991) develop their ideas further, noting that

[i]mages may still play a role in the comprehension of prose, but will operate at the level of working memory [Kosslyn, 1980]. At this level, images will likely involve isolated aspects of a larger episode, such as the physical appearance of the protagonist, or to units larger than a single sentence, such as a scene described in a paragraph or chapter, rather than the units typically scored in studies of prose memory. (Marschark et al., 1987; Perrig, 1988, p. 155)

A related view is that information in long-term memory involves cognitive, amodal representation. Consider the construction of the meaning of a sentence from its component words. The meanings of the words may be represented within the lexical system or in a generalized conceptual system that is not restricted to language. To distinguish between these two possibilities, Potter, Kroll, Yachzel, Carpenter, and Sherman (1986) substituted pictures for words (which named them) in sentences (the rebus sentences) in one condition and maintained a standard word presentation in another condition. In all cases, the words of the sentences were shown at a rate of 10 or 12 words per second (rapid serial visual presentation, RSVP) to maximize possible disruption to the comprehension process produced by the insertion of pictures into the sentences. Potter et al. (1986) argued that if pictures in sentences are understood by first naming the picture as a means of accessing the lexical entry, naming the pictures of the rebus sentences should take longer than naming the matched words in the regular sentences. Recall, however, would not differ. If the alternative hypothesis is correct, so that the meanings of words and their matched pictures are represented in an amodal conceptual system, access would be about the same for both pictures and words. Thus, the two would show similar naming latencies and recall. The data supported the latter view. Potter et al. (1986) extended the generality of their work by modifying their general paradigm to vary the length of the sentences and the position of the critical pictures and words. Across these various conditions, the data strongly supported the general conceptual view.

Importantly, *in isolation,* words are named some 200 milliseconds (ms) faster than matched pictures, but pictures are understood slightly faster than the same words (Potter & Faulconer, 1975). Taken together, these data also implicate context as an important determiner, with lexical representations providing a "pointer to a nonlinguistic conceptual system, and it is in that system that the meaning of a sentence is constructed" (Potter et al., 1986, p. 281).

In brief, the developing perspective suggests that retention is enhanced by relational encoding of materials when organized retention is tested or by greater item distinctiveness for recall of individual items. Concreteness and imagery instructions are effective to the extent that they aid relational or distinctive encoding. It follows that concreteness effects are not necessarily attributable to the induction of images. Marschark and Cornoldi (1991) contend that images, per se, operate only within working memory. From my perspective, concreteness may enhance featural information in long-term memory that is subsequently retrieved into working memory, but does not, itself, induce imaginal processing. The features in working memory patently affect subsequent processing, including comparisons and manipulations, in working memory, a view compatible with the spatial or perceptual branch of imagery.

The Spatial (Perceptual) Branch

The memory or linguistic branch of imagery relied heavily on linguistic contributions to imagery, as suggested by its name. The spatial (perceptual) branch focused on the relation between perception and imagery. This relation could be functional, structural, or integrative. Each relation is considered in this section.

About the same time as the dual-code model was gathering momentum, Roger Shepard (e.g., 1975) directed a more perceptually oriented attack on the investigation of images. His initial strategy was to devise a situation that relied on mental rotation for successful execution. Although this and most related situations were described verbally (some linguistic input was required to explain the task and to retrieve information from long-term memory) the emphasis was on the manipulation of images, their rotation or transformation, as well as on the relation to perceptual processes.

To a substantial extent, the models arising from this perspective argued that imagery was akin to perception, and many experiments were conducted to examine the parallelism. Most of these models focused on mental manipulation, with little attention paid to verbal or linguistic contributions from the instructions or the materials. The rest of this section examines some evidence for perceptual-imaginal parallelism and for the influence of linguistic contributions on imagery. This parallelism raises theoretical issues at the functional, structural, and interactive levels (for reviews see Finke, 1985; Finke & Shepard, 1986; Intons-Peterson & McDaniel, 1991).

Perceptual-imaginal parallelism

The question of perceptual-imaginal parallelism pervades most of the models to be discussed in the rest of the chapter. In general, the reviews cited above conclude that the two show parallel characteristics some of the time.

The functional level

At the functional level, these models (e.g., Shepard, 1975) hold that images preserve the *relations* among components of objects and among objects and their context. These relations may represent a one-to-one correspondence of an image with an external object, or they could be preserved in the sense that the image has a functional representation that is closer to the object, say a square, than to other objects, say a rectangle. Shepard argues that images bear the second relation, or second-order isomorphism, to percepts, rather than the first, first-order isomorphism.

This view implies that the process of mental rotation of a rigid object should resemble that of perceiving a rotating object in the world. Shepard and his colleagues (see Shepard & Cooper, 1982, for a review) conducted conceptually relevant tests for which the central task for the subjects was to judge whether a misoriented stimulus, when rotated, would match a target stimulus. For example, the subjects might see, briefly, a capital letter presented in its standard appearance or as a mirror reversal at 0°, 45°, 90°, 135°, 180°, 225°, 270°, and 315° orientations from the vertical upright. After the offset of the letter, subjects were to indicate whether the letter was the same as the target letter. Shepard and his associates hypothesized that if imagery bore a second-order isomorphism to perception, the time to respond would increase as a function of the angular separation from the upright. Their classical results corresponded to this expectation. Reviews by Finke (1985), Finke and Shepard (1986), and Intons-Peterson and McDaniel (1991) cite other supporting examples.

It is possible that the results described above might have been mediated by subvocalizations, verbal self-instructions, or other demand characteristics, including those induced tacitly by characteristics of the stimuli themselves. Indeed, these potential confounds plague much of the research on imagery, and they must be taken seriously. There are other reasons to heed them. As already noted, an alternative explanation of imagery is that the concepts and relations supposedly encoded in imagery are more parsimoniously explained as propositional in nature (Anderson, 1978; Pylyshyn, 1981). Indeed, Pylyshyn argued that true imagery should be "cognitively impenetrable." That is, it should not be explainable as the product of linguistic devices, for such devices or components could be propositionally encoded. Because I will contend that language plays a very important role in imagery, it is important to address these possible confounds.

We begin with the possibility of *subvocalization*. Subvocalization, like overt vocalization, should increase the likelihood of propositional encoding (or the reliance on a form of interlingua). Two recent approaches are relevant. Both of them adopt the strategy of testing domains that are difficult to describe in words, namely odors and timbre. Lyman and McDaniel (1990) obtained similarity judgments of ten perceived (sniffed) odors and the same odors imagined from odor names. The dimensions of odors are notoriously difficult to describe verbally. After obtaining all possible paired comparisons of odor-odor, odor-image odor, image odor-odor, image odor-image odor, with the orders of presentation counterbalanced over the subjects, Lyman and McDaniel obtained a multidimensional scaling solution. It accommodated the data, yielding goodness-of-fit indices for the three-dimensional solution of $R^2 = .793$, stress $= .153$, and S-stress $= .246$. The locations of the imagined odors in two-dimensional space were close to those of the perceived odors for nine of the ten odors. The exception, chocolate, showed an unexplained divergence. In brief, then, judgments of the similarity of imagined and perceived odors tended to support a lightly qualified form of imaginal-perceptual parallelism.

The other approach uses auditory stimuli. Adapting the methodology of Posner, Boies, Eichelman, and Taylor (1969) to audition, Crowder (1989) worked with judgments of pitch identity when tones were played by different instruments (and therefore had different timbres) and when the tones were imagined as being played on different instruments. He demonstrated pre-experimentally that timbre matches facilitated pitch judgments. The regular experimental task was to indicate whether two tones had the same or different pitch when the tones had the same or different timbre. Timbre distinctions, the supposedly irrelevant variable, also are difficult to capture verbally. In the imagery condition, subjects were given the name of an instrument (guitar, trumpet, or flute). They then heard a sine wave tone and were to imagine that pitch played by the cited instrument. In both the heard and imagined conditions, timbre matches facilitated detection of pitch identity, relative to timbre mismatches. Thus, this paradigm also delivered evidence of imaginal-perceptual parallelism.

Not so in another variation of the paradigm. When Pitt and Crowder (1992) substituted spectrally identical synthesized tones generated to have an abrupt or a gradual onset for the timbre manipulations that Crowder (1989) used, they found that pitch identification was faster with perceived onset matches than with onset mismatches, but no such differences appeared with imagined stimuli. Perhaps subjects have difficulty imagining dynamic characteristics of sound, even though they are able to imagine more static components.

Surprenant (1993) pursued this possibility, using vowels and stop consonants as her stimuli. Her methodology was similar to that used by Crowder (1989) and Pitt and Crowder (1992), except that, across several experiments, she counterbalanced the task used as the basis for judgments and as the irrelevant dimension. Hence, subjects had to judge whether one stimulus was the same as a second one, when the stimuli assumed two levels on the relevant dimension and two on the irrelevant dimension. Subjects were told to ignore the irrelevant dimension. Surprenant used two dimensions, pitch (high or low) and letter identity (stop consonants or vowels). The vowels had longer steady states than did the stop consonants, which were more dynamic. In the perception conditions, judgments were faster when the sounds matched on both physical dimensions than when they did not. The same was true for judgments involving imagined vowels, but not for imagined stop consonants. Subsequent clarifying experiments targeted the steady-state versus dynamic nature of the sounds as the basis for the different results. Apparently, static sounds are relatively easy to imagine, whereas dynamic sounds are not, probably because of incompatibility between the rapid time changes of dynamic sounds and the slower pace of imaginal processes.

Differences among the materials used in these two approaches are difficult to ensnare verbally, and they certainly defy the kind of rapid compression and translation into a verbal format that would be demanded by a subvocalization explanation. The fact that subvocalization does not hold sway with these experiments does not invalidate its potency with more readily nameable stimuli, but the evidence markedly weakens arguments for subvocalization, per se, as an omnibus explanation for imaginal results.

What about tacit knowledge? The tacit-knowledge contention holds that the stimuli evoke general knowledge about the world (e.g., Pylyshyn, 1984). According to this explanation, the results described above may not entail essential relations between imagery and perception, but, rather, they may reflect general knowledge about the world. But do images convey general knowledge about the world, as the tacit perspective maintains? The answer is clearly yes. For example, in one experiment, I (Intons-Peterson, 1980) showed college students pairs of sounds, such as *popcorn popping, whisper*. Their task was to mentally adjust one sound to match the loudness of the other. No mention was made of the use of imagery to this control group. Another (imagery) group was asked to imagine the referents of the phrases and to mentally adjust one auditory image to match the "loudness" of the other auditory image. Even though the same pairs were judged, matching times were much longer for the first (control) group than for the second (imagery) group, an outcome that clearly disputes a tacit-knowledge claim of highly similar response times for the two groups. In general, the greater the difference in loudness, as judged by a separate standardization group, the longer it took to achieve a match.

Parenthetically, I note that this experiment yielded an unexpected result: Many subjects said that they had to visualize the image before they could "hear" it. Thus, they "saw" popcorn popping before they could "hear" the pops. No such claims were made by the control subjects, even though they were recruited from the same population and presumably had comparable experiences. In summary, tacit knowledge does not appear to explain differences between imaginal and control performance.

In another explicit attempt to recruit real-world knowledge into imagery, Bev Roskos-Ewoldsen and I (Intons-Peterson & Roskos-Ewoldsen, 1989) asked college students to imagine carrying balls over varying distances. The balls were described as having the same 3-inch diameter, but they varied in supposed weight from a 3-ounce balloon to a 3-pound rubber ball to a 30-pound cannon ball. On the one hand, if images contain or recruit information about the real world, we would expect mental travel times to increase with the supposed weight of the ball even though the distance mentally traveled remained constant. On the other hand, if images do not carry such additional information, the mental travel times should be independent of the hypothetical weight of the objects. The data were clear: Hypothetically heavy objects took longer to transport mentally than did hypothetically lighter ones.

Furthermore, mental travel times were systematically longer when subjects memorized the map before mental travel and then had to traverse the remembered mental map than when they had the map before them as they performed the mental travel. These results imply that images may recruit real-world knowledge, either implicitly or explicitly. This knowledge, however, does not necessarily produce performance that mirrors perceptual counterparts, as is assumed by the tacit or demand characteristics argument for explaining imaginal-perceptual similarity.

Evidence gathered to assess the functional approach of the spatial (perceptual) branch of historical imagery inquiry surely informs us that images depict spatial extent (the rotation studies) and are subject to linguistic influence from the phonological level (Surprenant, 1993), and to expectancies induced by real-world knowledge (Intons-Peterson & Roskos-Ewoldsen, 1989).

We turn next to what has been called the structural version of the spatial-perceptual branch of research (Finke & Shepard, 1986; Intons-Peterson & Mc-Daniel, 1991).

The structural approach

This approach posits a closer parallel between imagery and perception than the functional one: It approximates first-order isomorphism between structural and surface features. Kosslyn (1980) proposed that images occur in a visual "buffer," akin to what might be presented on a television screen. The buffer has an array-type format with coordinates. These coordinates make it possible to assemble parts into a whole. They index geometric properties about the image, including its spatial extent.

These assumptions led to experiments on visual scanning (e.g., Kosslyn, Ball, & Reiser, 1978), in which subjects learned a map containing landmarks situated at varying distances from each other. After learning the map, the subjects heard the names of two landmarks. They were to imagine starting at the first-named landmark and then to scan in a direct line to the second. Upon arrival at the second, they pressed a button. The scanning times were directly related to the length of the distances. When subjects received the same training, but were not told to scan mentally, their response times were flat, rather than showing the increase with distance exhibited by the group receiving the imaginal scanning instructions. These results suggest that mental scanning has spatial characteristics similar to those expected when we track an actual moving object, but they do not speak to the presence or absence of either a visual buffer or even of a first-order isomorphism between imagery and perception.

The interactive level

The relation between imagery and perception can be even more tightly construed. For example, Farah (1985), Finke (1980), and Weber and Brown (1986) have proposed that the two use the same neural pathways. Finke (1980) suggests that the common use of pathways occurs not at the sensory level but at higher perceptual levels. These views predict a closer perceptual-imaginal parallelism than was observed in the studies already reported.

Some similar messages come from recent explorations of cerebral functioning. In the following, I consider results with normal, intact adults because this work addresses more directly the issues being presented in this chapter than do studies of brain-damaged individuals.

Goldenberg, Podreka, Steiner, and Willmes (1987) auditorily presented lists of meaningless, abstract, or concrete words to their subjects, followed by a recognition test. Half of the subjects hearing concrete words were told to image the references; the other half received no such instructions. During the test list, subjects were to flash a lamp held in one hand if they thought a test item had appeared on the previous list. Regional cerebral blood flow was measured during rest and during the experimental procedures.

First, consider the recognition task. Imagined concrete words were recognized significantly more often than words of any of the other conditions. Concrete words without imagery instructions, abstract words, and meaningless ones were recognized at about the same (lower) rate. Meaningless words were falsely recognized reliably more often than imagined concrete words. No other differences occurred in the recognition task.

Next, consider the cerebral blood-flow measures. Smallest space analyses used to study the pattern of correlations among regions as functions of the various word conditions showed

> that the left hemisphere is predominantly engaged in the processing of verbally elicited mental images. However, regardless of whether imagery was used intentionally or not, the imagery system was composed of regions of both hemispheres. The explicit instruction to use imagery led to a marked leftward shift of hemispheric activity but at the same time the functional system comprised more right hemispheric regions than without an imagery instruction. The difference in hemispheric asymmetries is thus to be attributed to different modes of interhemispheric collaboration. Possibly, these modes are determined by the intentional control of visual imagery or by the amount of attention paid to mental images rather than by visual imagery per se. We found the imagery system to be composed of regions of the medial occipital and inferior temporal lobe. (Goldenberg et al., 1987, p. 483)

The comparisons of tasks must be interpreted cautiously, however, because different subjects were assigned to the various word-instruction conditions.

Farah, Weisberg, Monheit, and Peronnet (1990) used event-related potentials (ERPs, with 16 recording sites) instead of cerebral blood flow to track image-related cerebral activity. Subjects read either concrete and abstract words or they read and generated images of concrete words. They reported that waveforms for the various conditions were quite similar for the first 450 ms and then began to diverge, with the imagery condition showing more positivity than the no-image baseline condition, particularly in the left occipital and posterior temporal areas. Similar results emerged in a study with 22 placements when the subjects listened to spoken words. Farah et al. (1990) interpret their results as indicating that imagery is not an amodal process because "the ERP effect of mental imagery can be localized to visual processing areas" (p. 312), and that "an ERP correlate of imagery that has visual cortical localization cannot be accounted for by tacit knowledge" (p. 312). The latter conclusion does not necessarily follow if we allow cognitive penetration in imagery.

The number of subjects tested per condition tended to be quite small in these studies of cerebral responses to imagery situations, another reason for caution in interpreting the results. Nevertheless, the primary messages seem to be that instructions to imagine concrete words invoke cortical patterns across at least the posterior occipital and temporal lobes that differ from those initiated by concrete words without such instructions or by abstract words. It is not clear whether these changes reflect differences inherit in imaginal processing or additional attention (and elaboration?) paid to the to-be-imagined words. This latter point could be addressed by studies of imagined abstract words, which, as far as I found, have not been reported. The fact that reading plus imagining concrete words produced different patterns than reading the words (and the auditory counterpart) delivers the additional suggestion that perception and imagery do not necessarily induce parallel cerebral events.

Another indication of caution for the interactive view of imagery and perception is that the presentation of a visual prime that either matched or did not match an image constructed from four directional sentences (Intons-Peterson, 1993) was not incorporated into the image, as would be expected if imagery were tightly coupled to perception. This experiment is considered in more detail in a later section.

My goal in this section of the chapter was to examine how the two historical routes have fared, the insights into the imagery process they now afford, and to explore the intersection of the two routes or lines of imagery research.

These traditional spotlights on imagery are successful in some respects and not in others. Within the verbal-learning approach, for example, the dual-code or modality-specific model does not handle relational effects well, even though such effects have a significant bearing on the imageability of materials and on the retention of the items (e.g., Marschark & Cornoldi, 1991). The model does not encompass the kinds of mental manipulations that dominate research in the other tradition. Most important, it may not invoke imaginal processing. The manipulation model does not hardily accommodate such results as concreteness or imageability effects nor the differential times predicted to mentally transport objects of the same size but different weights (Intons-Peterson & Roskos-Ewoldsen, 1989). It does not explain the occasional lack of parallelism between imagery and perception (Intons-Peterson & McDaniel, 1991). Nevertheless, a satisfactory model of imagery demands both verbal and spatial approaches to encompass available data.

In the rest of the chapter I will develop the motivation for the amalgamation of the two perspectives, including recent research indicating that (a) even a highly visual task such as imaginal subtraction is largely determined by linguistic attributes such as nameability, (b) the strategies employed in imaginal classification differ when linguistic and perceptual components are manipulated, and (c) neuropsychological evidence implicates linguistic and spatial processes of both hemispheres of the brain.

A KNOWLEDGE-WEIGHTED FRAMEWORK

Images, I propose, are sensory-perceptual memories with spatial features. That is, when a memory has marked and obvious sensory-perceptual features and spatial extent, we are likely to label the introspective experience as that of having an image. The sensory-perceptual and spatial features constitute the signature of what we call an image. The sensory-perceptual-type of image identifies the predominant type of sensory processing. Most of the time, the experience involves a spatial extent of the concomitants of visual processing and is called a "visual image." At other times, the predominant experience is that of auditory extent, and we consider the mental event as that of "auditory imagery." Gustatory, tactile, and other types of images also exist, of course. The hallmarks of an image are, therefore, that of a memory—the experience of an event after its physical offset—and that the memory contains both sensory-perceptual and, in the case of visual and tactile images, at least, spatial features. By contrast, non-imaginal memories would not be introspectively described as ones we could "almost see," "almost hear," "almost feel," and so forth.

These memories, those labeled as imaginal or as nonimaginal, are retrieved from long-term memory. They may be initiated by sensory or perceptual experiences, or by linguistic input.

To repeat, a memory labeled as imaginal may be initiated by either a sensory-perceptual event or information retrieved from long-term memory. I assume further that, as with other memories, the information retrieved will consist of cues or features central to the concept represented by the memory. Thus, when retrieving a memory of a dog, the canonical features will include four legs, fur, and so forth. Recruitment of these essential or canonical features will, in turn, tend to activate other features associated with them. Hence, if fur is activated, color, coarseness, and other features of fur also may be activated. These ancillary or extra features embellish the canonical image and may influence subsequent imaginal processing. Thus, I construe the initial representation as consisting of a canonical form of information plus ancillary information. The retrieved representation must contain sufficient sensory-perceptual and spatial elements to exceed a threshold for classifying the resultant as an image. This threshold will differ from person to person, a situation that produces individual differences in claims to experience or to not experience imagery.

The search conducted to retrieve information from long-term memory is guided primarily by the propositions of the conceptual structures underlying verbal specification of the task. Once in working memory, the array may be combined, manipulated, compared, and so forth.

I note, parenthetically, that these concepts can be combined as a set of primitive functions for the computation of and reasoning with imaginal representations by drawing upon array theory or upon an assumption of hidden nodes in a connectionist framework. As Glasgow and Conklin (1992, p. 112) suggest,

Computational imagery involves techniques for visual and spatial reasoning, where images are generated or recalled from long-term memory and then manipulated, transformed, scanned, associated with similar forms, increased or reduced in size, distorted, etc. In particular, it is concerned with the reconstruction of image representations to facilitate the retrieval of information that was not explicitly stored in long-term memory. The image representations generated to retrieve this information may correspond to real physical scenes or to abstract concepts that are manipulated in ways similar to visual forms.

Thus, they note, the knowledge representation scheme partitions computational imagery into visual and spatial reasoning, each with its own independent mode of representation. The visual component addresses the appearance of an image, *what* it looks like. The spatial component locates the imaged object in space, *where* it is relative to its context or surround. Because each of the representations is derived from long-term memory, the model also provides for such a component. In their model, Glasgow and Conklin depict the spatial representation of an image as a symbolic array that preserves its spatial and topological properties. Visual representation is depicted by occupancy of the cells of the array, an occupancy array. Their knowledge-representation scheme for computational imagery is based on formal array theory (More, 1979).

The connectionist instantiation could be simplified by treating representations retrieved from long-term memory and perceptual events as input or expanded by including the search and extraction of meaning from these inputs as an early hidden layer.

Linguistic aspects, at various levels, may affect imaginal processing. Clearly, instructions or intentions to access images of particular items are likely to be verbally guided (see Denis, this volume). Here, the linguistic components may define the content of the concept being instantiated in the image. Ancillary features activated as part of the image-generation process also may have semantic effects. Instructions to imagine a dormant purple poodle surely elicit an image different from that of instructions to imagine a dancing green Saint Bernard.

Linguistic contributions to imagery may be at various levels, from the language used to describe the task, to linguistic materials intended to manipulate the likelihood that images will be generated (as through the use of items rated as concrete or abstract, or as easy to imagine rather than hard to imagine). Imagery also may be affected by naming, by either the experimenter or by the subject. As an example of the latter, consider Carmichael, Hogan, and Walter's (1932) famous work in which the label given to an ambiguous object biased drawings made later by the subjects.

Linguistic features may function as retrieval cues, as cues that facilitate subsequent retrieval of an image. They also may interfere with image generation, as when the verbal information is at odds with the image.

Finally, it is possible that linguistic information, even at an early stage, such as the initial acquisition of an image, may interfere with image generation by limiting the resources available to the subject.

This view is diametrically opposed to that of Pylyshyn (1981), who argued that images should be cognitively impenetrable (knowledge-independent) if we are to distinguish them from propositions. This controversy has been phrased as a question of whether imaginal representation is analogical or propositional. In fact, the distinction may be more apparent than real, for propositionalists (e.g., Anderson, 1976, 1978; Pylyshyn, 1973, 1980, 1981, 1984) seem to be arguing about the contents of imaginal representation (the propositional view), whereas proponents of an analogical perspective (e.g., Kosslyn, 1975; Moyer, 1973; Paivio, 1986) focus on utilization of the contents (Marschark et al., 1987). Moreover, a propositional view cannot readily explain figures that emerge from novel construction (e.g., Finke, 1990; Finke, 1993; Finke & Slayton, 1988; Roskos-Ewoldsen, 1993). In contrast, I propose that cognitive penetrability, in the sense of linguistic features, contributes substantially and integrally to imagery. It is the integrality of linguistic features to image construction and manipulation that distinguishes my framework from Paivio's (1971, 1986) model. I believe that most imaginal memories draw upon linguistic elements at some stage, hence the label "knowledge-weighted."

The framework delivers some predictions about when imaginal and perceptual performance will and will not be parallel. As noted elsewhere (Intons-Peterson & McDaniel, 1991; Intons-Peterson & Roskos-Ewoldsen, 1989), sensory and imaginal processes seem more likely to foster similar performance when the tasks are unfamiliar, and to produce differences when the tasks are familiar. These relations flow quite seamlessly from the knowledge-weighted model, for we would expect images of familiar objects or tasks to elicit a richer, more elaborated set of ancillary cues than images of less familiar objects and tasks.

As already noted, various linguistic levels affect imagery, from the phonological (recall Surprenant's, 1993, findings that subjects could imagine the steady-state portions of sounds, but not the more dynamic ones) to the development of expectancies (as shown in the Intons-Peterson & Roskos-Ewoldsen, 1989, research with mental transport).

The next section of the chapter examines some key assumptions of the framework, such as support for the contentions that images have sensory, perceptual, and spatial features, and that they are sensitive to linguistic influence from the phonological to semantic levels.

Sensory Features

Evidence for sensory-perceptual involvement in imagery comes from a number of sources. Obviously, the hypothesized relation predicts the co-occurrence of differential sensory-perceptual recruitment and indices of imagery. Particularly compelling are the recent neuropsychological studies (e.g., Farah et al., 1990; Goldenberg et al., 1987) showing cerebral activity in the occipital and temporal lobes when normal, intact subjects are asked to imagine referents of concrete words after hearing or reading the words, conditions that foster the use of imagery. These patterns differ from those induced by exposure to concrete words without instructions to imagine the referents, and to abstract and meaningless words, conditions that are less likely to induce imagery.

At a behavioral level, Segal and Fusella (1970) reported that the presentation of a physical auditory stimulus while subjects were imagining a visual one or vice versa interfered with detection of a probe compared to a control condition in which only a single modality of presentation was tested. Segal and Fusella did not consider the possibility that same modality imagery could facilitate detection of the probe if the two were compatible. Hence, Peterson and Graham (1974) pursued this possibility, in addition to repeating Segal and Fusella's cross-modality manipulations. They obtained same-modality facilitation and cross-modality interference when one sensory modality was imaginal and the other modality was manipulated physically. Clearly, images are sensation-modality penetrable.

What about more perceptual concomitants of imagery? For example, do images show such perceptual effects as reconstruals of ambiguous figures? Do images reflect the goodness of their perceptually initiating figures and the component parts of these figures? These questions define the next section.

Perceptual Features

Classical ambiguous figures, such as Jastrow's (1900) duck-rabbit, offer another medium for showcasing the effects of perception and language on imagery. If imagery parallels perception, we would expect subjects to be able mentally to reconstrue such figures. Note that this type of experimentation addresses only canonical features because, in the imaginal condition, subjects are shown the entire perceptual figure and asked to imagine it later. It also addresses the issue of parallels between imagery and perception.

In 1985, Chambers and Reisberg startled imagery researchers (including themselves) when they found that their subjects could not identify a second appearance of traditionally ambiguous forms when the forms were imagined. These strange results prompted an onslaught of research as investigators tested various theories about the reasons for the results. One possibility was that not enough information was given to the subjects about possible changes.

For example, Hyman and Neisser (1991; Hyman, 1993) gave both abstract and conceptual cues about what to examine. The abstract cue was "[c]onsider the front of the thing you were seeing as the back of something else," and the conceptual cue was "[c]onsider the front of the head of the animal you just reported as the back of the head of some other animal." In general, the conceptual cue prompted more reversals than did the abstract cue. These data suggest that subjects may be able to reverse imaginal ambiguous stimuli if they receive explicit hints about "viewing" their images.

Language also may establish expectancies. For example, only after imagers were told the top of a rotated image (map) of the state of Texas were they able to perceive the image as a representation of Texas (Chambers, 1993; Reisberg & Chambers, 1991; Reisberg & Logie, in press). This research with a rotated image of the state of Texas indicates that knowledge-related expectations may determine whether subjects are able to detect a particular shape in their image. These kinds of perceptual expectations (guidance) may arise from such subtle cues as presentations of other figures with the same or different orientations. For example, M. A. Peterson (1993, see also Peterson, Kihlstrom, Rose, & Glisky, 1992) argued that the demonstration figures may induce expectation-establishing reference frames. Peterson (1993) describes three types of perceptual reinterpretations:

> First, there are reversals that entail a reference-frame realignment. By "reference-frame alignment," I mean the reassignment of the top-bottom and/or front/back directions in a figure.. . . Second, there are reversals that entail a reconstrual of the parts of the figure, but no (or little) reference-frame alignment.. . . Third, there are reversals that entail a redetermination of figure and ground relationships and hence, a repartitioning of the shape's contour. In figure-ground reversals, the part structure of the figure changes from one minute to the next. . . . (pp. 153–155)

The Necker cube and the Mach book on the top row of Figure 2.1 illustrate reference-frame realignments. With the Necker cube, the reversal occurs as the assignment of front and back switches. With the Mach book, top and bottom realignments switch. The snail-elephant and the wife–mother-in-law figures on the second row involve a reinterpretation or reconstrual of the parts. Little or no change of reference frame is required. The third row depicts figures requiring both reconstrual and reference-frame realignment. Consider the duck-rabbit. The duck's bill becomes the ears of the rabbit, and the front of the duck's head is reinterpreted as the back of the rabbit's head. The top (vertical) orientation remains the same for both interpretations. The middle figure in Row 3, the goose-hawk, requires the same reinterpretations. The third figure in Row 3, the chef-

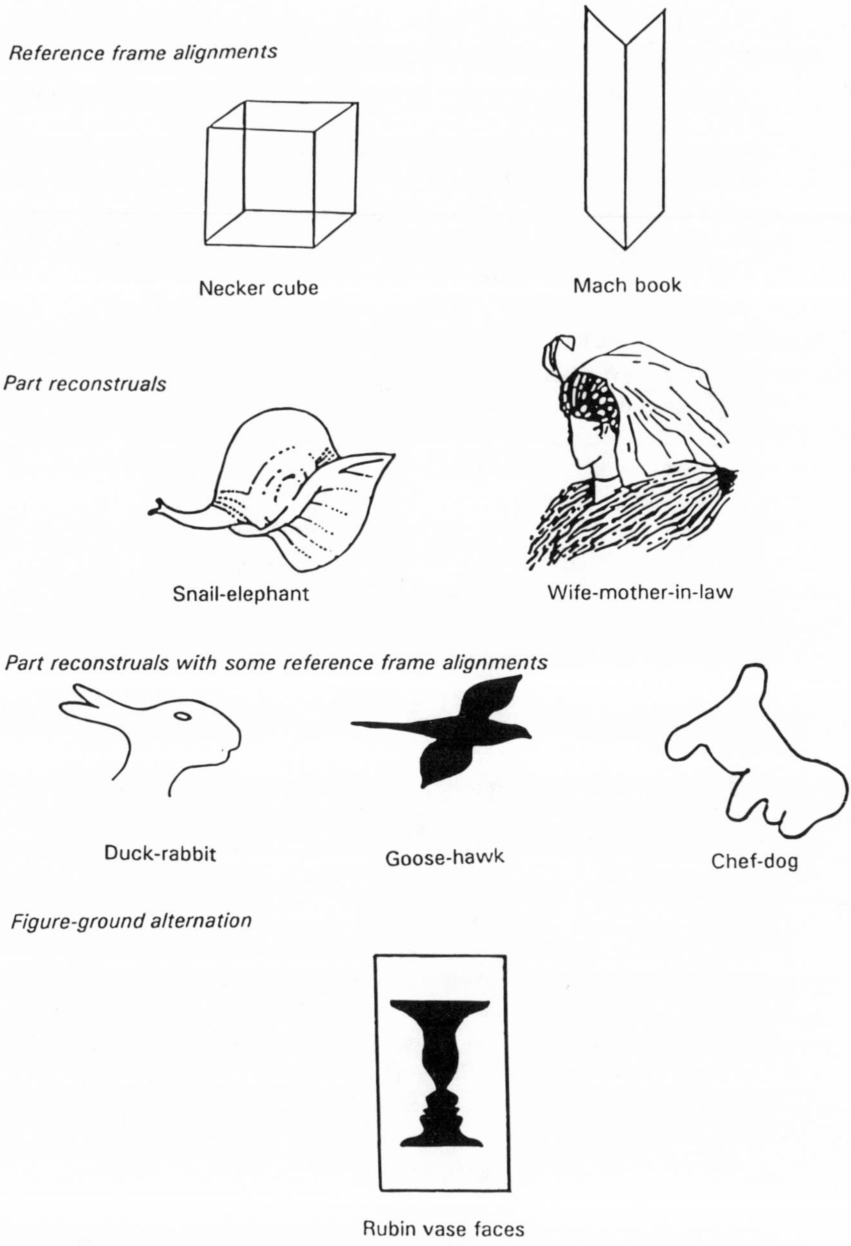

Reference frame alignments

Necker cube

Mach book

Part reconstruals

Snail-elephant

Wife-mother-in-law

Part reconstruals with some reference frame alignments

Duck-rabbit

Goose-hawk

Chef-dog

Figure-ground alternation

Rubin vase faces

Figure 2.1. Some ambiguous figures and the ways they reverse.

dog, also requires both reconstrual and reference-frame alignments, but it also entails reinterpretation of the top of the figure. Finally, figure-ground reversals, as in the Rubin vase-faces figure shown at the bottom of Figure 2.1 require reinterpretation of the entire figure and ground relations.

These ideas could explain the Reisberg-Chambers' (1991) Texas map experiment in the following way. The likelihood of correctly rotating and identifying a shape varies as a function of the angular disparity between the typical orientation of a shape and its orientation at presentation. This view is bolstered by observations that the latency to name disoriented shapes increases with the angular distance between typical and misoriented presentations (Jolicoeur, 1985, 1988; Tarr & Pinker, 1989). The assumption here is, of course, that naming latency and mental rotation involve similar processes, processes that underlie the recognition of disoriented shapes.

Another explanation is that subjects may develop expectations for reference-frame reversals and reconstruals. These expectations then may minimize the likelihood of correctly identifying a reinterpretation of the image. Specifically, M. A. Peterson and her colleagues (1993; Peterson et al., 1992) argue that the particular demonstration figures used to illustrate the experimental task may have led Chambers and Reisberg's (1985) subjects to expect inappropriate reversal strategies. Chambers and Reisberg used the Necker cube, the Mach book, and the Rubin figure-ground stimuli as demonstration figures. The Necker cube and the Mach book involved reference-frame realignments, and the third entailed a figure-ground redetermination in contradistinction to the reconstrual and reference-frame realignments characteristic of the target figure, the duck-rabbit.

To test this possibility, M. A. Peterson (1993; Peterson et al., 1992) compared reversals of the duck-rabbit after presentation of one of four demonstration conditions. One demonstration figure, the goose-hawk, involved the same front/back reversal as the duck-rabbit and should, therefore, promote a successful reinterpretation strategy. Two other demonstration figures were taken from the Chambers-Reisberg (1985) studies: the chef-dog and the Rubin figure-ground. The chef-dog involves both a reference-frame realignment and a part reconstrual. Hence, it might induce some successful reversal strategies, but fewer than the goose-hawk figure. Even fewer successful reversal strategies for the duck-rabbit would be induced by the figure-ground reversal, for its reversal follows quite different principles than does the duck-rabbit reversal. The fourth condition was a no-demonstration figure control.

Before any hints were given, subjects successfully reinterpreted the duck-rabbit figure following the goose-hawk 35 percent of the time. They did so 10 percent of the time after chef-dog, 6 percent after figure-ground, and 10 percent after no-demonstration figure. Obviously, the hypotheses of M. A. Peterson and her colleagues (Peterson, 1993; Peterson et al., 1992) were supported: The more the reversal of the demonstration figure used principles needed to reverse the duck-rabbit figure, the higher the percentage of successful reinterpretations. In addition, even with the two Chambers-Reisberg (1985) demonstrations and with no-demonstration, the success rates exceeded those of Chambers and Reisberg's (0%) rate. Other recent explorations of imaginal reversals of the duck-rabbit figure with unselected adult samples (Hyman & Neisser, 1991) have found rates of successful reversal similar to those of Peterson.

The reasons for these different results are not clear, but they suggest occasional nonzero base rates for reversals of imaginally construed ambiguous figures. Even with nonzero base rates, the reversal of these mentally constructed figures is far below the near universal reversal of their perceived counterparts. Once again, perception and imagery are related, but not fully parallel.

Could this lask of parallelism be language-induced? Implicit language effects in the work by Hyman (1993), Hyman and Neisser (1991), and M. A. Peterson (1993; Peterson et al., 1992) might have introduced ancillary effects or expectations via simple verbal labeling. This possibility was vitiated by M. A. Peterson's (1993) demonstration that subjects rarely gave the name of the reversal when cued with the name of the other form of the figure.

The research with ambiguous figures suggests that subjects are able to reconstrue the figures imaginally, but only when their interpretation, understanding, or expectation is for the appropriate reference frame only when the image is compatible with language-guided knowledge of the world. Reisberg and Logie (1993) take a different perspective as they argue that reference frames (interpretations) limit what can be learned from images. The limitations can be overcome, Reisberg and Logie contend, by cooperation with motor patterns (efferent input) to the sensory (affective) mode. This view stems from Chambers and Reisberg's observation that subjects could detect the alternative interpretation in drawings they produced after failing to reinterpret their images, and from evidence that subjects could satisfactorily reconstrue auditory ambiguous items if they were able to subvocalize (Reisberg, Smith, Baxter, & Sonenshine, 1989). In this latter research, subjects heard or imagined rapid repetitions of a word such as *stress*. In the perceptual condition, the subjects perceived the customary reversals from *stress* to *dress* and back again. So did subjects who imagined repeating the word *stress,* as long as their subvocalization was not suppressed by chewing or clamping their mouths shut. When their subvocalization was suppressed, the imaginal subjects did not detect the transformation.

Reisberg and Logie (1993) propose that the "inner voice" of subvocalization provides motoric (efferent) input to guide the afferent input of the "inner ear," and that a similar mechanism may underlie one form of visual imagery, notably spatial imagery. To use their picturesque language, in spatial imagery, the "inner scribe" may guide the "inner eye." To my way of thinking, these descriptions represent additional evidence that images have perceptual features and that imaginal processing is modifiable by language-induced expectations.

Other indications that imagining actions aids retention come from Engelkamp (1986, 1991) and Saltz and Donnenwerth-Nolan (1981). They contend that spatial-motoric imagery is dynamic, whereas the other form of visual imagery is static. Anderson and Helstrup's (1993) failure to find that externalization of visual images by drawing facilitated performance more than simply imagining compilations of objects is somewhat embarrassing to this view, but Anderson and Helstrup's creative-manipulation task may have invoked so many motoric components that the addition of drawing had little effect.

As Reisberg and Logie (1993) suggest, neuropsychological evidence may divulge cortical patterns that differentiate perceptual and imaginal processing. They cite the work of Georgopoulos, Lurito, Petrides, Schwartz, and Massey (1989) with monkeys. This research indicated that, with a mental-rotation task, neural activity in the parietal cortex preceded voluntary movement. In fact, the neural activity corresponded to the direction of movement needed to align the cue. Apparently, nonhumans display preparatory parietal activity suggestive of mental imagery before they respond. The exact dependencies between the preparatory neural events and the response remain a mystery.

Perception has other characteristics that might be manifested in imagery if imagery depends on perception. One characteristic is "judged goodness." Patterns judged good seem to be more unified, to cohere better than patterns judged less good (e.g., Kolinsky, Morais, Content, & Cary, 1987; Palmer, 1977; Reed, 1974; Reed & Brown, 1979; Reed & Johnsen, 1975; Thompson & Klatzky, 1978). If higher-order perception affects imagery, imaginally constructed representations of perceived patterns should show the same pattern.

These predictions were extended to imagery by Beverly Roskos-Ewoldsen (1993) as part of her exploration of the detection of imaginal emergent patterns. She first taught her subjects the line-number pairs of lines drawn between dots of a 9-dot array (see top of Fig. 2.2). Then subjects learned one 3-line pattern, followed by a second 3-line pattern by constructing the patterns from their line numbers. The perception group drew the lines on a 9-dot array; the imagery subjects imagined them. Then one of three 3-line test probes was presented. The probes tested an old part, an emergent part (constructed from the combined 6-line pattern), or a noncomponent part. Subjects had to ascertain whether the probe came from the total pattern. Prior to experimentation, all of the 3-line patterns and the composite 6-line patterns had been rated independently for goodness. These ratings were used to manipulate goodness of the component parts and of the overall 6-line pattern.

Roskos-Ewoldsen predicted that because parts judged good are synthesized into a pattern more rapidly than parts judged poor (Attneave, 1955; Hochberg & McAlister, 1953; Palmer, 1977), the processing of good parts would be less demanding than with poor parts, allowing more processing to be available for observation of emergent parts. Thus, the detection of emergent parts should be

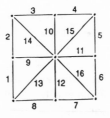

Pattern

Part Set A   **Part Set B**

A 1   A 2   B 1   B 2

Test Probes

Non-
Old   **Emergent**   **component**

Figure 2.2.   Samples of Roskos-Ewoldsen's initial array, a 6-line part, two 3-line parts, and test probes.

facilitated more by good than by poor parts. In contrast, good patterns tend to be internally coherent (Garner & Clement, 1963; Peterson, Rawlings, & Cohen, 1977), and therefore resistant to fractionation, including the detection of emergent parts. Thus, the detection of emergent parts should be impeded by the goodness of the overall pattern but facilitated by the goodness of the two parts.

Roskos-Ewoldsen (1993) used two measures, recognition accuracy and correct response times. Although some conditions did not show differences as functions of goodness taken collectively, her results supported the predictions, with somewhat more support from the imagers than from the drawers.

Note that these results can explain an oft-cited report (Pylyshyn, 1979; Reed & Johnsen, 1975) that subjects have difficulty detecting parts in patterns. Most of Reed and Johnsen's patterns would have been judged as good. As such, the patterns would have been difficult to segment and hence resistant to decompositional parsing. These same parsing difficulties may have been responsible for the slower mental rotation times for Pylyshyn's figures rated low in goodness (using Palmer's 1977, criteria) compared to those rated higher in goodness.

This research on what I consider the acquisition of a canonical image documents the effects of perceptual judgments of goodness. As hypothesized, perceptual origins influence imagery, although the evidence suggests that perceptual and imaginal performance occasionally differs. Neither parallel nor perpendicular, the similarity of imaginal and perceptual performance is often oblique and variable.

Spatial Extent

I suggest that, in addition to their sensory and perceptual features, memories called "images" also depict spatial extent. Three lines of research converge on this conclusion: work with the congenitally blind, imaginal-scanning results, and demonstrations of the cerebral distribution of imaginal processing.

The congenitally blind are able to perform imaginal tasks usually considered to be visual in nature (see Ernest, 1987, for a review). Presumably, if imagery relies exclusively on sensory underpinnings, individuals with sensory deficits should be unable to perform imaginal tasks. This is not the case. For example, Marmor and Zaback (1976) demonstrated that congenitally blind people can successfully perform mental-rotation tasks. Furthermore, the spatial resolution required for successful performance on an imaginal task such as mental rotation implicated spatial extent or similar amodal underpinning as an enabling mental substrate. See Zimler and Keenan (1983) for supporting results.

Imaginal performance also may be aided by sensitivities in other senses. For example, Paivio and Okovita (1971) reasoned that congenitally blind people might be more likely than sighted people to remember words rated as high in auditory imagery, compared to words rated as high in visual imagery. Indeed, the blind recalled words with high auditory imagery better than words rated as low in auditory imagery, but they did not differ on words rated as high or low in visual imagery. Sighted people were more sensitive to ratings of visual than of auditory imageability of words. There are no guarantees that these subjects attempted to form images, however, so these results are suggestive at best.

This is not to say that the congenitally blind perform in the same way as sighted individuals. The blind appear to have more difficulty constructing sequentially presented components into an image, particularly an interactive one, than do sighted subjects (De Beni & Cornoldi, 1988).

The tight association between physical separation of items on a to-be-remembered map and times to mentally scan from one to another object (e.g., Denis & Cocude, 1992; Kosslyn et al., 1978) also bolsters the contention that visual images have spatial extent. This correlation can be reduced considerably by giving verbal information about distance that differs from that implied by the map (Mitchell & Richman, 1980; Richman, Mitchell, & Reznick, 1979) or by inducing experimenters to believe the opposite relation will appear (Intons-Peterson, 1983). In general, these modifications reduce the effect, but do not eliminate it.

The research conducted by Denis and Cocude (1992) further extends our knowledge of the development of spatial extent. They found that the expected time-distance relation became more pronounced when subjects constructed their mental maps from well-structured verbal descriptions (descriptions that corresponded, in sequence, to positions on a clock face) than when they heard the same descriptions given in a random order. In addition, performance improved with six rather than three exposures to the descriptions, even though subjects could remember the descriptions after three presentations. These results suggest that imaginal resolution may be sharpened with additional repetitions of relevant information or that additional exposures focus attention.

Spatial maps may also be constructed from narratives (e.g., Denis, 1991a, 1991b; de Vega, 1991; Franklin & Tversky, 1990; Tversky, 1991). Documenting the spatial nature of these maps, researchers typically find that subjects are faster and more accurate at locating objects in front of or behind them than in locating objects to the left or right (see Tversky, 1991, for a review). It is interesting that the subjects construct mental maps even when not instructed to do so. Obviously, the use of imagery or some kind of mental layout seems to be commonplace.

Perhaps most compelling is the anatomical dispersion of cerebral activity when subjects are asked to imagine the referents of concrete words (see Farah et al., 1990; Goldenberg et al., 1987). This cerebral dispersion impressively instantiates the topologically distributed nature of at least images of concrete nouns.

These results strongly imply that images evoke spatially distributed neural activity with sensory and perceptual features. Collectively, they argue for definition of imagery advanced earlier, namely that images are memories with sensory-perceptual and spatial components. Is this definition sufficient? Must all three components be present for a memory to be called an image? Are memories with these components sometimes denied as images? These questions remain unanswered at the present.

I also claim that imagery is cognitively penetrable. That is, imaginal memories are guided by and are subject to linguistic influences at various levels from the phonological to semantically defined expectations. Indeed, demonstrations of the pervasive effects of language on imagery motivate the next section of the chapter. These demonstrations frequently use either an interference or a construction paradigm. In the interference paradigm, the notion is that some form of language will interfere with imaginal performance, whereas in the construction paradigm, the issue is whether subjects can accurately construct an image from language-delivered cues.

I begin with interference paradigms and the proposal that the phonological recoding posited to occur when images are retrieved from long-term memory will interfere with performance of a subsequent visual-image task.

Imagery, Memory, and Interference

Working from Alan Baddeley's (1986) model of memory, Maria Brandimonte, Graham Hitch, and Dorothy Bishop (1992a) proposed that verbal or phonological recoding of information being transferred to long-term memory and back into working memory for subsequent processing would interfere with performance of a visual manipulation task. They hypothesized that if such verbal recoding were minimized by the use of articulatory suppression, performance on the visual manipulation task would be superior to that when no articulatory suppression was used. They tested these hypotheses with an imaginal subtraction task, such as the one depicted in Figure 2.3. Subjects in the long-term memory (LTM) group began by memorizing a series of six original composite pictures. The test phase that followed this learning phase required the subjects to retrieve the first composite. Then a figure (part of the original composite) was shown. It was to be

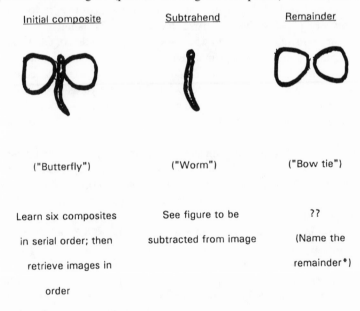

Initial composite	Subtrahend	Remainder
("Butterfly")	("Worm")	("Bow tie")
Learn six composites in serial order; then retrieve images in order	See figure to be subtracted from image	?? (Name the remainder*)

*In the Intons-Peterson version, subjects in the Name condition either named or described the remainder; subjects in the Draw condition drew the remainder.

Figure 2.3. An example of an imaginal subtraction task (long-term memory condition).

subtracted mentally from the image of the original. Finally, subjects were to name the resulting image (remainder). This process was repeated for each of the original composites.

Presumably, these subjects would recode the original composites phonologically and this recoding would interfere with subsequent processing of the imaginal subtraction task unless recoding was suppressed by articulatory suppression. These assumptions were tested by having some subjects engage in articulatory suppression (saying "la, la"), whereas other subjects did not. The group with articulatory suppression was expected to name more remainders than the group without articulatory suppression.

Brandimonte et al. (1992a) also tested a short-term memory (STM) group. This group saw an original composite for 2 seconds, then saw the to-be-subtracted (subtrahend) figure, and named the remainder. This process was repeated for each of the trials. The STM group did not engage in articulatory suppression because it presumably did not recode the original composites.

The results corresponded to the predictions: The LTM group with articulatory suppression correctly named about the same number of remainders as did the STM group, and these two groups named significantly more remainders than did the LTM group without articulatory suppression. Do these results reflect the role of phonological or verbal recoding interference with performance of a visual manipulation task?

My colleagues and I (Intons-Peterson, Hinshaw, Yarnall, Angotti, & Zhang, 1993) were not convinced, largely because some aspects of the design concerned us. Specifically, the requirement of naming the remainder introduced verbal elements into the final task so that it was no longer one of simple visual manipulation. Moreover, the only allowable response was the name of the remainder. This restriction meant that subjects who had a correct image of the remainder but lacked a name for it could not convey their knowledge. In brief, naming might have underdescribed performance. The procedure of having LTM subjects learn a sequence of original composites would induce implicit naming, as Nelson and his colleagues (Nelson, Brooks, & Borden, 1973; Nelson, Reed, & McEvoy, 1977) reported.

Finally, we noted that articulatory suppression introduces a resource-demanding dual task into the situation. Because subjects have to cope with these demands, they may engage in additional rehearsal of the task components as their articulation becomes automatic (as it does quickly). If so, the superior performance of the LTM group with articulatory suppression might reflect additional verbal-phonological rehearsal rather than the reduced opportunities that Brandimonte and colleagues (1992a) had assumed.

Accordingly, we modified the design in a number of ways. First, we used two types of tests. In one, we asked subjects to name the remainder, as Brandimonte et al. (1992a) had done. In addition, however, we told the subjects that they should try to name the remainder, but that if they could not do so, they could describe what they remembered. In the other test, subjects drew the contents of their memory.

The naming results were scored in two ways. First, we counted only names that corresponded to names provided by the norming subjects (these names accounted for most of the names given). Second, we added correctly described remainders to the correct names. The use of correct names mimics the scoring used by Brandimonte et al. (1992a), and it should deliver the same pattern of results. It did. For easy-to-name original composites, remainders were named correctly more often in STM without articulatory suppression and LTM with articulatory suppression than in LTM without articulatory suppression.

Brandimonte and colleagues would interpret these results as indicating that articulatory suppression reduced verbal or phonological recoding in the LTM condition, which otherwise interferes with performance of a visual manipulation task. They did not expect phonological recoding to occur to a significant extent in the STM conditions; hence, articulatory suppression should not have an effect. As they found, we also observed no significant differences in STM when articulatory suppression was or was not present while the original composites were shown.

For similar reasons, Brandimonte et al. (1992a) did not expect articulatory suppression to have a differential effect on LTM when the original composites were difficult to name. In this case, not much recoding would occur. They did not find reliable differences for this comparison; neither did we. To this point, our naming data replicate their results.

We also tested a condition not assessed by Brandimonte et al., namely the effects of articulatory suppression in the STM condition with hard-to-name composites. Even though they did not test this comparison, the logic of their arguments would have predicted no difference. That is, because recoding should be minimized by both the STM condition and the difficulty of naming the original composites, the presence of articulatory suppression should not advantage this condition more than its absence. Curiously, our STM subjects named the remainders reliably more often without articulatory suppression than with it when the original composites were hard to name.

Even though the naming results generally corresponded to the predictions of Brandimonte et al. (1992a), an alternative view also seemed reasonable. This view made the following assumptions.

1. The visual manipulation task elicits strategic processing. Just as Tversky (1973) demonstrated, subjects are likely to encode, elaborate, and otherwise strategically process information to facilitate ultimate performance. In the procedure of Brandimonte et al. (1992a), this ultimate performance was naming, whereas our ultimate task was visual recognition. Naming should induce sub-

jects to name during execution of the task more than visual recognition would.

2. Serial learning of pictures elicits implicit naming, as shown by Nelson and his colleagues (Nelson et al., 1973; Nelson et al., 1977). Thus, when LTM loading occurs via the serial learning of pictures, subjects are likely implicitly (or evenly explicitly) to name the pictures.

3. Articulatory suppression introduces an interfering, resource-demanding dual task. When articulatory suppression involves the repetition of simple syllables, such as "la, la," it rapidly becomes automatic, at which time subjects can resort to naming if desirable to achieve task-appropriate processing. The absence of articulatory suppression relieves interference, but may not encourage naming.

Thus, for a naming task, the serial learning of composites plus naming during articulatory suppression increases the probabilities of accurately retrieving the composite for subsequent processing in a manner appropriate to the final task. The net result is that LTM with articulatory suppression should have an advantage over LTM without articulatory suppression; and STM, which relies mainly on visual-perceptual factors, should be relatively unaffected by the presence or absence of articulatory suppression.

The drawing data showed the expected pattern. We again used a strict criterion to score these data. The drawing had to contain the distinctive features in the correct configuration to be scored as correct. More remainders were correctly drawn without articulatory suppression than with it. Furthermore, the advantage of no articulatory suppression to articulatory suppression was greater for the STM than for LTM conditions, for both easy- and hard-to-name composites.

Now consider the second scoring of the naming data. As mentioned above, the subjects were asked to name the remainder but were allowed to describe the remainders if a name (label) did not occur to them. These descriptions were subjected to the same kinds of critical evaluations as names and the drawings. When correct descriptions were added to correct names, the pattern resembled that of the drawings. In all conditions, performance was somewhat better without than with articulatory suppression. This difference was statistically significant for only the STM condition with hard-to-name composites.

I interpret the overall results as verifying that the use of only a strict naming task underdescribes what subjects retain in memory from their execution of the imaginal subtraction task. Obviously, we replicated the results of Brandimonte et al. (1992a) with the naming task, but not with the drawing task or when correct descriptions were added to correctly named remainders.

We propose that the replication with the naming task occurred because the naming task (a) is sensitive to only limited aspects of memory, (b) interjected verbal elements into the visual manipulation task, and (c) encouraged naming during articulatory suppression. Added to these effects was the implicit naming elicited by serial learning of the original composites in the LTM condition. Because the naming task encouraged task-appropriate processing during the acquisition stage of each trial, any earlier naming during serial learning of the original composites and articulatory suppression would favor the LTM condition with articulatory suppression over conditions.

The naming plus description results differed markedly from those of the naming task alone, even though the two sets of results came from the same subjects. When correct descriptions were scored as correct, in addition to correct names, articulatory suppression reduced, rather than improved, performance, for both STM and LTM conditions. These results provide a graphic demonstration of the need to use sensitive tests of memory and of the dangers of basing conclusions on limited memorial assessments.

The drawing data also demonstrated the disadvantages of articulatory suppression, even though the LTM condition would have involved implicit naming of the original composites. In no condition did articulatory suppression facilitate performance, thereby challenging the view that articulatory suppression would reduce the interference of verbal or phonological recoding in LTM on a visual processing task.

In subsequent work, Brandimonte, Hitch, and Bishop (1992b) explored the possibility that verbal labeling might interfere with the generation of visual images if verbal labels were placed under the stimulus composites (Experiment 2). Articulatory suppression was not manipulated. As Brandimonte and her colleagues predicted, naming of the remainder was disrupted by the labels. These results are easily accommodated by our view. Once again, the task was restricted to naming the remainder. The labels provided would not necessarily have corresponded to those given by a standardization group because the average agreement for names of the non-nameable figures was only 21 percent, although the average nameability for the nameable figures was 73 percent. The experimenter-provided labels may well have interfered with any names supplied by the subjects to help them learn the original series of composites. This situation would be expected to produce more interference than having label-less original composites.

A more definitive test of the effects of naming would be to have one group of subjects generate their own names for the items and speak the names aloud. This situation should yield the exact reversal of the effects of articulatory suppression: Performance should be better in the absence of articulatory suppression than in its presence with naming than without either articulatory suppression or naming.

First, the instructions are verbal. They require semantic analysis, and, often retrieval of information from long-term memory, plus manipulation of that information to execute the instructions. Presumably, the recoding of image information from LTM and back into STM for subsequent visual processing invokes at least some phonological recoding, regardless of whose view is adopted. Language, including labeling, also may interfere with imaginal performance.

Just as language may interfere with image-based verbal tasks (Peterson & Graham, 1974; Segal & Fusella, 1970) verbal labeling also may facilitate performance. Specifically, when pictures have to be recalled serially, verbal labeling may render the pictures and their interrelations more distinctive. Moreover, verbal labels function as cues in subsequent search.

In general, the easier to name, the more accurate and faster visual processing; this is because, we argue, the names cue retrieval of the original composites for subsequent processing. This argument is bolstered by significant differences in the likelihood of naming the original composites shown in our normative study. This result is hardly surprising, for the composites named by most subjects were chosen as the "easy-to-name" ones and the composites rarely named by subjects were designated as "hard-to-name" composites. Further examination of the frequency of naming of the original composites for object and letter remainders, of the subtrahends, and of the object and letter remainders themselves yielded significant differences for the original composites, but not for the subtrahends or remainders.

Naming also functions in another way. It aids the retention of visual information by adding context or similar cues to the representation. It enhances the likelihood of a successful search for the composite (as predicted by associative models, such as Raaijmakers and Shiffrin's Search of Associative Memory, SAM, 1981) or by a match (e.g., connectionist mapping).

In the preceding arguments, we have not differentiated among phonological recoding, and implicit and explicit naming. It should be obvious that the phonological recoding assumed to accompany transmission of information to and from LTM may or may not be strategic in nature. To the extent that this kind of processing is strategic, it adds features of different levels to the items. These ancillary levels could range from phonological ones to complex associative and semantic ones. The current results do not differentiate among these levels.

The preceding results indicate that some linguistic levels, implicit and explicit verbalization, affect imaginal performance, an important demonstration of the cognitive permeability of imagery. In the next section we consider a more dynamic use of language, the issue of whether accurate images can be constructed from descriptor sentences. A second query is whether an external physical prime will be incorporated into the image.

Imaginal Priming

As already noted, the task of constructing images from descriptor sentences is complex. In the work to be described in this section (Intons-Peterson, 1993), we had subjects construct an image from four descriptor sentences. The information contained in the descriptor sentences must be decoded in long-term memory and the appropriate instructions executed to construct the image. An initial query is whether subjects can perform the task. If laboratory approaches to imagery tap the resources we introspectively use to imagine and mentally manipulate our constructions, the task should be easy to do when undistracted by competing resource demands. Certainly, our model does not predict that the ability to generate and manipulate mental images is constrained by the length or dynamism of linguistic instruction, given that the imager understands the instruction. Also at issue is whether a physically presented prime (a figure identical to or different from the final correct image) would be incorporated into the developing image, as predicted by models that posit imaginal-perceptual sharing of visual pathways (e.g., Farah, 1985; Finke, 1980; Weber & Brown, 1986).

Before describing more details, let us consider some of the relevant issues. The first is that, as we shall see, external physical events may be used to verify the products of imaginal generation or may alert subjects to an upcoming imaginal task. According to views that visual perception and visual imagery recruit at least some of the same pathways, the interactive view of imagery (Farah, 1985; Finke, 1980; Weber & Brown, 1986), we would expect the prime to be incorporated into the developing image. This did not happen: Although we used various types of tests, we found no evidence that the primes were incorporated into the images. These external codes thus constitute a visual code separate from the imaginal code, although they affected strategic processes applied to imagery.

In our research, each sentence (delivered by a computer) instructed the imager to manipulate the developing images in specific ways. For example, the subject might hear, "Image a circle. Add a horizontal line so that it divides the circle into even halves." When they had executed this instruction, they pressed the space bar to advance to the next descriptor sentence. They then might hear, "Remove the bottom part of the circle below the horizontal line." After signaling for the next descriptor, the subjects might hear, "Now put a capital letter *J* directly below the horizontal line." Next, the subjects saw four alternatives. Their task was to select the one closest to the resulting image. Notice that this procedure affords almost unlimited time to the subjects to carry out the directions.

The answer to whether subjects could perform the task was clearly yes, for subjects selected the correct alternative on 82.5 percent of the trials of this type of descriptor set. This set had previously been judged as easy to imagine. Other sets were judged as medium or hard to imagine. An example of the latter type is, "Image a capital letter *D* as in Debby. Rotate it 90° to the right. Put a pointed number 4 directly above it. Now remove the horizontal segment of the 4 to the right of the vertical line." Subjects chose the correct alternative in 80 percent of the medium sets and 68 percent of the hard-to-imagine ones. Thus, when unencumbered by other demands, subjects performed easily and well above chance on this task.

Suppose a priming figure was flashed for 150 ms immediately before the fourth descriptor sentence and that the prime corresponded to the final or target image. What would happen? Or suppose that the prime depicted another (foil) alternative. What then? If primes were incorporated into the developing image, as should occur if both recruit the same visual pathways, the image would be modified away from the correct one by both primes (because a fourth descriptor sentence would state another manipulation). Thus, both "appropriate" and "inappropriate" primes would yield poorer performance than a no-prime control. Not so. Appropriate primes tended to facilitate performance, whereas inappropriate primes interfered with the no-prime controls of easy sets but aided the medium and hard sets. Why would inappropriate primes confer a benefit? One reasonable explanation is that an inappropriate prime might prompt retrieval of previous sentences and a reconstruction of the image. If so, we would expect particularly long response times for inappropriate primes with hard sets. The data obliged.

These results suggest that a physical prime affects image construction, but not by incorporation into the image. They yielded another insight as well. The time to process each descriptor sentence increased over the four sentences in each set, even in the no-prime condition. Moreover, the time for image generation increased from the easy-to-imagine to the medium-to-imagine to the hard-to-imagine sets. These results suggest that the image is being refreshed as it is constructed (Kosslyn, 1980) and that the developing image is being evaluated for meaningfulness. As with the more static images, the times to generate them appear to increase with the number of components (steps) and, in this case, with the ease of imagining them. These results resemble those for predominantly verbal processes.

The role of a physical prime on a developing image was explored further in another experiment. Here, appropriate, inappropriate, and no primes were introduced either before the initial descriptor sentence or after the last descriptor sentence. Easy and hard images were tested. Again, the view that imagery and perception share the same late sensory-perceptual pathways (Farah, 1985; Finke, 1980; Weber & Brown, 1986) predicts that presentation of a prime before the initial descriptor sentence should misdirect the image-generation process regardless of whether the prime is appropriate or inappropriate. Primes might not be incorporated into the image-generation process itself, however.

Alternatively, primes could influence an image by alerting the subjects to features likely to be included in the upcoming descriptors. This view suggests that presentation of primes prior to any description should be more advantageous for both appropriate and inappropriate primes than for the no-prime control. When the prime preceded the first descriptor, both the appropriate and the inappropriate primes delivered facilitation compared to the no-prime control, an outcome that contradicts the incorporation hypothesis and is more compatible with a feature-alerting view. When the prime followed the last descriptor, the situation was quite different: Appropriate primes yielded facilitation, and inappropriate primes produced interference, both compared to the no-prime control. In brief, inappropriate primes produced facilitation when the prime preceded the descriptor sentences, but interference when it followed the descriptors.

The incorporation hypothesis was investigated again in a third experiment in which subjects drew their final images. Appropriate, inappropriate, and no primes preceded all direction sentences or occurred just before the fourth and final descriptor. No drawings included evidence of prime intrusion or incorporation. Also noteworthy was the fact that subjects were able to generate accurate images most of the time, even when they received an inappropriate prime. Hence, the influence of the prime must be external to the developing image, even if the two recruit some of the same visual processes or pathways.

This external influence may operate through a prime-matching process. According to a prime-matching hypothesis, if the prime and the image match, the subject selects the corresponding test alternative. If they do not match, the subject rejects the alternative closest to the prime. Because mismatches may signal errors in image construction, when they are encountered, subjects may try to reconstruct both the descriptors and the image using information from the prime as a cue. Late primes should be retrieved more readily than early primes. A consequence is that fewer errors should occur following late than early primes. This kind of "strategy-verification" hypothesis was not tested optimally by the within-subjects designs of the first three experiments, so a fourth, between-subjects, experiment was conducted.

In the last experiment, subjects were assigned to the six cells of the 3- (type of prime: appropriate, inappropriate, no prime) by-2 (temporal position of prime: before first descriptor sentence, after the fourth descriptor) design. As predicted by the strategy-verification hypothesis, more correct alternatives were chosen after late (86%) than after early (81%) primes and for easy (91%) than for hard (76%) sets (ease of generating the image was a within-subjects variable). The type of prime interacted with the temporal position of the prime, also as predicted. When the prime followed the fourth sentence, appropriate primes were associated with more correct choices (.94) than by no primes (.86) or inappropriate primes (.78). When the prime preceded the first descriptor sentence, there were no differences as a function of the type of prime.

In general, for early primes, either appropriate or inappropriate primes typically yielded more correct selections than did no primes, whereas for late primes, appropriate primes delivered more correct choices than did the no-prime control (facilitation), and inappropriate primes produced fewer correct choices than did the no-prime control (interference). How can we explain these results?

The results speak to at least five hypotheses. The first is the incorporation hypothesis, that the prime is incorporated into the image itself, a view espoused by some investigators on the assumption that imaginal and visual processes use the same pathways (Farah, 1985; Finke, 1980; Weber & Brown, 1986). This hypothesis was most clearly disputed by the absence of such inclusion in the sensitive drawings of Experiment 3. I interpret this result to indicate that subjects are able to focus on image generation, excluding extraneous input while images are being generated and that images may be reasonably independent of related activity after image formation. It is as if the unique circumstances surrounding image generation confer distinctive cues so that subjects can easily distinguish among the imaginal code, the parent verbal code, and the visual code of the prime.

With respect to the overarching model, these results suggest that subjects can distinguish among the various levels of input (the auditorily presented instructions, canonical and ancillary codes of the images, etc.), and processing characteristics. The associated encoding-context (ancillary) cues also may help to explain why imagery appears to parallel perception only some of the time (Finke & Shepard, 1986; Intons-Peterson & McDaniel, 1991; Intons-Peterson & Roskos-Ewoldsen, 1989). Both imaginal and perceptual cues and their associated contexts are potentially retrievable. The likelihood of retrieving either or both depends on the task at hand.

Another hypothesis is prime-expectancy. Subjects are likely to select the test-trial choice that approximates the perceptually compelling prime, regardless of the appropriateness of the prime to the task. The influence of the prime would depend on its proximity to the test trial; hence, primes should govern test-trial choice more for late than for early primes. This hypothesis was supported to the extent that both appropriate and inappropriate primes were more likely to be selected after late appropriate and inappropriate primes. It was not supported in the sense that it failed to predict the systematic selection of appropriate alternatives almost as often after early inappropriate primes as after early appropriate primes.

A third hypothesis was that subjects learn the critical features of the images from the primes. Such a feature-learning hypothesis necessarily predicts that early primes should be more beneficial than later ones, a prediction disconfirmed by the data.

A hypothesis already mentioned—alerting signal—is similar to the feature-learning one, except that it holds that primes alert subjects to the coming information, making them more attentive. Such a hypothesis argues that any prime, regardless of its appropriateness, will be more beneficial than no prime and that early primes should help more than late primes. The evidence conformed to the first, but not to the second, prediction. In particular, the hypothesis did not predict the relatively poor performance for trials with late inappropriate primes.

Obviously, taken alone, the alerting hypothesis cannot handle all of the data.

A final hypothesis, also already described, is that, consciously or unconsciously, subjects use the match between prime and image to guide test-trial selection. In effect, they impose test selection conditions on the prime-image match. If the match is close, they then select the test alternative that matches the prime-image match. If the prime and image mismatch, they select a test alternative that differs from the prime. The former strategy leads to selection of the correct (appropriate) alternative following appropriate primes, and the latter strategy leads to rejection of an incorrect (inappropriate) alternative following inappropriate primes. The effect of the latter strategy is to reduce the number of test alternatives from four to three, thereby increasing the probability of choosing the correct alternative on these trials from one in four to one in three. The results of Experiment 4 were consistent with the strategy hypothesis, given late primes.

Obviously, no single hypothesis accommodates all of the data, but a combination of the alerting and strategy verification hypotheses does well. This combination holds that external priming events, encountered before descriptor sentences, alert the subjects to the upcoming information, regardless of its appropriateness to the subsequently generated images. The alerting function is responsible for the tendency for performance to be better following appropriate and inappropriate early primes than following no early prime. The subsequently encountered features of the prime are matched, probably unconsciously, with those of the image developed from the descriptor sentences. Test-trial choice follows, as described above. These strategies represent an integration of verbal (Paivio, 1986) and visual codes (Kosslyn, 1980) contributing to imagery, consistent with my framework.

Development of the visual-imaginal code from the verbal codes of the instructions was interesting because it took increasingly long times to execute the instructions as the images became more developed. It may be, as Kosslyn (1980) has suggested, that images need to be refreshed periodically as the image is formed. It also may explain why some features could be lost as the image is refreshed, leading to poorer performance with sentence sets describing hard-to-image images compared to those describing easy-to-imagine images.

Finally, consider the implications for priming. In our work, the verbal codes were lexical and semantic, whereas the primes were visual, a situation that parallels some work in the semantic-lexical priming literature, except that primes are words in most of the research.

Spreading-activation views of priming (Favreau & Segalowitz, 1983; Posner & Snyder, 1975) hold that the processing of a word activates related lexically, orthographically, and phonemically similar units. An extension to our paradigm suggests that the words of the descriptors access lexical representations, which then activate related terms—i.e., ancillary cues. If the representations constructed from the words are highly similar to those delivered by the visually presented primes we would expect the primes and the developing image to share some of the same pathways. In short, this view coalesces with the incorporation view that was not supported by the data.

Alternatively, primes might contribute to the development of expectancies (e.g., Becker, 1980; Neely, 1977; Posner & Snyder, 1975) and postlexical processing (e.g., Balota & Lorch, 1986; de Groot, 1984, 1985; Forster, 1979, 1981; Neely, Keefe, & Ross, 1989; Norris, 1986; Seidenberg, Waters, Sanders, and Langer, 1984). This perspective accords more satisfactorily with the data.

Like much current experimentation, this research employs the memory (linguistic) tradition of using verbal instructions to induce images that are then manipulated in the spatial (perceptual) tradition. The results yield the following insights about imagery.

One, to the extent that the constructed image recruits visual pathways, both its representation and processing do not meld with that of the processing of a visually presented prime. This apparent independence may inform us that even supposedly visual images do not activate visual pathways or that the image- and prime-activated processes have enough different features to allow them to remain distinct and to minimize interference. The former interpretation seems unlikely, given existing neuropsychological evidence; the latter seems plausible.

Two, imaginal construction has memorial properties. This feature has long been known, but it merits emphasis. Images can be constructed from parts. These parts, or the representation of the establishing language, can support subsequent additions. It is possible that the image needs occasional refreshing, as Kosslyn (1980) suggested, but the image under construction is retained over at least 10 to 20 seconds.

Three, the information available in memory about an image was very accurate when assessed by drawings. Other measurement techniques, such as multiple-choice tests, may be either less sensitive or more likely to interfere with reproduction of the contents of memory.

Four, although we found no evidence to indicate that primes were incorporated into the images, the features of the primes clearly affected final detection of the correct image. I take this result as additional evidence that images are a subspecies of memory.

Imaginal Recomposition and Categories

In the next section I report an experiment that bridges the gap between features that affect simple perception such as the number of component parts, and more complicated forms of perception and classification, such as the type of partitioning and blocking by categories. To the extent that images are memories, they should reflect standard memorial patterns.

In our view, the time to generate an image should increase with the number of component parts. Thus, if pictures of simple objects were divided into few (2 to 3) or many (4 to 6) parts, the time to mentally reconstruct and identify an object from its remembered fragments should increase with the number of parts. Moreover, performance time should be longer in the mental reconstruction case than in the physical reconstruction one because mental reconstruction requires retrieval of information from long-term memory.

Construction time should vary with another conceptual condition, the type of partition. As Tversky (1989; Tversky & Hemenway, 1984, but see Murphy, 1991) showed with perceived objects, meaningful (logical) divisions are easier to reassemble mentally than are random divisions. We asked whether the same conceptual, semantic effect would appear in imagery, as it should under our model. Finally, we predicted that, like perceptual classification, presentation of fragmented pictures representing objects blocked by category would facilitate identification of the objects more than unblocked (random) presentation of the fragmented pictures.

To investigate these predictions, we obtained initial ratings of the ease of identifying the object depicted by pictures taken from the Snodgrass and Vanderwart (1980) norms. The pictures were chosen to represent different categories, such as clothing, household items, animals, toys, and food. Each picture was fragmented in four ways, corresponding to the cells of a 2×2 design (number of components: few or many; type of partition: meaningful, random). The number of components in the "few" classification ranged from two to three. The number of components in the "many" condition ranged from four to six. The central purpose of this exercise was to identify four instances of three categories that were about equal in difficulty. Three categories were chosen: animals, clothing, and household items, each represented by four exemplars. The animal category was represented by pictures of a dog, frog, pig, and turtle. Clothing pictures showed a dress, hat, shoe, and sock, and household item pictures were a broom, chair, lamp, and table.

In the perceptual condition, each fragmented picture was shown until the undergraduate subjects identified it by typing in its name or pressed the space bar to advance the program if they could not name it. Response times were measured from the onset of the fragmented picture until the initial key press of the response. The imagery condition was handled the same way, except that each fragmented picture was shown for 3 seconds before the screen was blanked. Subjects were assigned randomly to the perceptual or imagery groups and to blocked or unblocked presentation of the fragments from a category. The number of components (few, many) and the type of partition (meaningful, random) were within-subject variables.

As expected, the imagery subjects took more than twice as long as the perceptual subjects to identify correctly the whole (mean correct response times were 6.47 and 3.00 seconds, respectively). Moreover, the differential increase in correct response time from few to many parts was considerably greater for the imagery subjects (5.18 to 7.75 seconds) than for the perceptual condition (2.61 to 3.39 seconds), producing a reliable interaction. This differential was significant even for the perceptual subjects. Thus, identification times increased with complexity for both the imaginal and perceptual conditions, but the increase was greater when the subjects had to retrieve the parts from memory prior to reconstruction.

To the extent that the type of partition affected retrieval, as expected on the basis of Tversky's (1989; Tversky & Hemenway, 1984) results, we predicted that expected meaningful partitions would be reassembled faster than would random partitions. Again, the data cooperated. Identification times were shorter for meaningful partitions than for random ones. This pattern appeared for both the imagery and the perception groups, although the perception subjects were slightly more accurate and faster than the imagery groups.

Table 2.1 presents the relevant means. The interactions between number of components and the type of partition were not significant for accuracy, but were for response times, for both groups. These interactions reflected the fact that the type of partition increased solution times only with many components. With a few fragments, the use of a random partition added only a short increase in response time. The more important observation is that in this case the patterns for the perception and imagery groups were largely parallel. Apparently, even information about the functional nature of parts affects imaginal construction. This is true, even with few components.

As expected from research on classification, blocking the pictures by categories improved performance, indicating that subjects can learn to classify imagi-

TABLE 2.1.   Mean number of figures correctly named from the parts (maximum = 4) and correct response times in seconds (in parentheses) by the perception and imagery groups as functions of the number of components and type of partition of the figures

	Perception group		Imagery group	
	Number of components			
Type of partition	Few	Many	Few	Many
Meaningful	2.45	1.53	2.33	1.39
	(2.69)	(2.98)	(5.45)	(6.43)
Random	2.06	1.05	1.98	.94
	(2.53)	(3.79)	(4.91)	(9.09)

nally constructed components even though they were never told about the categorical variable, so the manipulation amounted to an implicit test.

Let us take stock at this point. The data support the essential components of the definition, namely that images reflect sensory-perceptual elements with a spatial extent. Images are language-sensitive. This sensitivity extends from the phonological level to the conceptual-semantic level examined by the effects of meaningful versus random partitions of images. In each case, language plays an important role, as predicted by the knowledge-weighted model, among others.

In the knowledge-weighted model, images consist of canonical plus ancillary features, presumably learned. One way to probe such learning is to determine whether subjects can learn an imaginal classification problem, the kinds of strategies used, and the features of the parent patterns ultimately abstracted.

Imaginal Classification

The ability to classify, to create order out of the chaos of our world, is a major accomplishment. Although the models of classification are many and varied, the concept of similarity contributes in some way to all of them. The definition of similarity also varies considerably, but for purposes of this chapter I will take a generic approach of assuming that concepts and items are similar to the extent that people judge them to be similar. Obviously, physical similarity is often used to classify objects (e.g., Job, Rumiati, & Lotto, 1992), just as conceptual similarity is used. I propose that imagery is consulted as part of the classification process when the objects are not physically present at the time of classification.

To continue, when we are deciding whether an object we saw at Aunt Agatha's house was a cup, glass, or bowl, we retrieve an image of the object for comparison with a generic (canonical) image of the various categorical possibilities. The ideal way to test this proposition is to eliminate opportunities to generate images and ascertain whether subjects could learn to categorize novel objects. This approach hardly seems feasible with intact humans. Hence, I tried another approach, that of having subjects learn parts of a category prototype, which, when imaginally conjoined, would correspond to the prototype or parent pattern. In fact, subjects correctly learned to associate parts from two parent patterns. Then they were transferred to test trials designed to assess what was learned.

To be more precise, the subjects began by learning to associate numbers with the lines of the Rumelhart-Siple (1974) rectangle shown in the left-most portion of Figure 2.4. After successful reproduction of all of the lines and their corresponding numbers, they began the learning phase. Their task in this phase was to learn to associate pairs of numbers with response categories A or B. The pairs of numbers represented all of the pairwise combinations of the four numbers comprising each of the "parent patterns" (see lower portion of Fig. 2.4). Imagery subjects were instructed to imagine the lines corresponding to the numbers. No

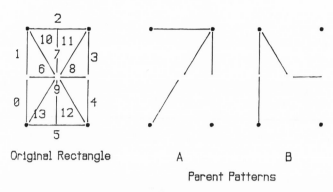

Original Rectangle   A   B

Parent Patterns

Figure 2.4. Rumelhart-Siple rectangle used to train number-line correspondences in imaginal classification and two sample parent patterns.

such instructions were given to a verbal strategy group or to the perception group.

Next, all subjects were transferred to the test trials. Again, their task was to assign the pattern to the most appropriate category, A or B. The test patterns (see samples in Fig. 2.5) were designed to check retention of the learning trials, to test generalization to three and then four lines from each parent, and to assess the type of strategy being used. This last aim was accomplished by devising test patterns that would be answered one way if the subjects were using a overall shape, or global strategy, and another way if the subjects were using a dimensional strategy. A global strategist would respond on the basis of overall similarity, whereas a dimensional strategist might analyze the number of lines associated with each parent category or with neither category and then respond by averaging the number of lines associated with each category.

For example, consider Category B (Fig. 2.4). If the mirror images of the four lines are presented, a global strategy would predict assignment to Category B, presumably because the overall envelope of Category B's mirror image remains more similar to the envelope of exemplars associated with Category B than to the envelope of exemplars associated with Category A. Moreover, the mirror image of Category B was prejudged to be more similar to B than to Category A. A dimensional strategy predicts assignment to Category A. The latter prediction reflects the fact that the mirror image of the Category B parent contains two lines previously associated with Category A and two nonassociated, or irrelevant, lines.

The test trials also were used to assess imaginal, perceptual, and verbal strategies. For imaginal and perceptual classification conditions, the test trials presented lines only. No numbers were given. Our contention was that successful performance on the test trials required the imagery subjects to convert their pre-

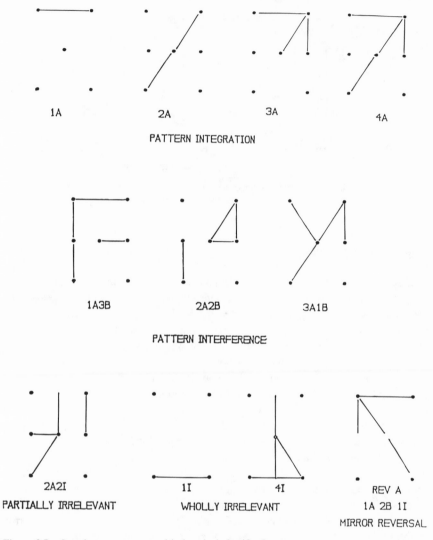

Figure 2.5.   Sample test patterns used in imaginal classification.

viously learned numerical equivalents into images of the lines. Without this conversion to lines, subjects would not be able to assign the test patterns (composed of from one to four lines) to the correct category above a chance level. Some of the test-trial lines had not been presented during the learning phase. These novel test patterns provided an empirical estimate of chance.

The perceptual group had no exposure to the learning trials. Instead, these subjects had pictures of the two parent patterns in front of them as they assigned the test patterns. The pictures named each category. The test trials for the verbal (numerical) strategy group presented the number equivalents of the lines. These approaches enabled us to examine the strategy patterns being used when imaginal, perceptual, and verbal-numeric aspects of classification were examined.

In general, subjects in all three of the groups performed very well when the test patterns presented one, two, three, or four lines (e.g., the 1A, 2A, 3A, and 4A patterns of Fig. 2.5) from a parent. In fact, the groups correctly assigned test patterns with single lines almost as often as they assigned test patterns with all four lines from the parent. When the test patterns presented one, two, or three lines (numbers) from one parent and three, two, or one line (number) from the other (e.g., 3A1B, 2A2B, 1A3B, Fig. 2.5), all groups assigned the patterns on a proportionate basis (e.g., patterns with 75%, 50%, and 25% of its lines from Category A were assigned to Category A about 75%, 50%, and 25% of the time).

Most interesting and diagnostic were test patterns containing some irrelevant lines or which presented mirror images of the parent patterns. Suppose a pattern (Fig. 2.5) contains two lines from Category A and two irrelevant (new) lines (2A2I). As stated previously, if subjects are using a global strategy they should assign this pattern to the category to which it bears the closest overall similarity. Pilot work showed that these patterns were rated as equally similar to Categories A and B. Hence, subjects using a global strategy should assign such patterns about equally often to the two categories. In contrast, a dimensional strategy would assign the pattern to the category with which it shared the most lines, namely Category A. The perceptual group showed the response pattern predicted by the global strategy hypothesis, whereas the imaginal and verbal-numeric groups showed the pattern predicted by the dimensionalization strategy.

Similar analyses were afforded by the mirror-image test patterns. Mirror images were rated as perceptually more similar to the original parent pattern than to the other parent, leading us to predict that use of a global strategy would yield assignments of the mirror image of the Category A parent to Category A more often than to Category B. Conversely, because an analysis of the mirror image of Category A delivered one line from Category A, two from Category B, and one irrelevant line, the mirror-image test pattern of Category A should be assigned more often to Category B than to Category A. Again, the perceptual group's assignments corresponded to the global predictions, whereas the imaginal and verbal-numeric groups' assignments corresponded to the dimensionalization predictions!

To gain more information about the composition of the patterns associated with each category, at the end of the experiment subjects in the imaginal and verbal-numeric groups were asked to draw the lines (or to give the numbers) that "went with" each category. The perceptual subjects were not asked to draw the lines because the parent patterns were on continuous display during the test trials.

The results were variable. Some subjects were very discerning. They drew or recorded the lines (numbers) critical to the category and excluded all irrelevant components. Others included some irrelevant lines (numbers) in their representations. This variability suggested two analyses.

The first analysis tabulated how often subjects identified an exact replica of the parent patterns. In other words, subjects had to identify all of the four correct lines (numbers) for each parent and *no others*. All four lines had to be identified to receive credit in the second, more lenient analysis, but other, irrelevant lines also could be included.

The strict criterion showed that imagery subjects correctly identified 64 percent of the components in each category; the verbal-numeric group identified 23 percent. This ordering was reversed on the more lenient criterion, with the verbal-numeric group identifying more parents than the imaginal group. These results indicate that the imagery group constructed quite precise representations, which contained relatively few extraneous components. The verbal-numeric group was less precise, for they included extraneous components along with the correct ones. In brief, the verbal-numeric group had wider, less restrictive boundaries for their category structures than did the imagery group. These results are similar to those of Goldstone (1991), who also found that imagers drew more faithful representations than a group told to focus on distinguishing between the features of two categories (his "Discriminate" group).

These results prompt a parenthetical remark. I know of no classification or imagery model that would have predicted the superior precision of imaginal representations, but the finding has an obvious parallel to solving jigsaw puzzles. With such puzzles, we readily reject many candidates, saving only a few pieces for additional scrutiny. The same may be true of other types of visual detection or classification, and we may use images in more precise ways in our daily lives than is typically realized. These results, then, nicely bolster my initial contention that, in general, imagery may play an important role in classification.

These results argue forcefully that imaginal processes can be employed in classification. These subjects were immediately able to transfer their knowledge of the parent categories from the pairwise presentation of line numbers during training to the presentation of lines during the transfer trials. Their performance was as accurate as that of the other groups.

Furthermore, in the setting described above, the imaginal and verbal-numeric groups appeared to use a dimensional strategy to classify items; the perceptual group used a global similarity one. It is not surprising that the verbal-numeric group would rely on analytic dimensionalization, for such a strategy is cultivated by both presentation of numbers as distinct and individual components of each category and the analytic nature of numbers themselves. Nor is it surprising that the perceptual group followed a global strategy. After all, the pictures of the parent patterns served as guides during their test trials. More interesting is the question of the imaginal group. Is imagery inherently analytic and prone to individuation of patterns? Does the use of dimensionalization simply reflect the sequential nature of presentation of the components? Or is the kind of processing elicited by these conditions flexible and accommodative, such that it adapts to the demands of the situation?

Answers to these questions were sought in a second experiment. What if the experimental demands are reversed, so that the use of a global strategy is encouraged for the imaginal and verbal-numeric groups and the use of a dimensional strategy is encouraged for the perceptual group? Will the pattern of responding to the test patterns show a corresponding reversal?

For the second experiment, we tried to induce the use of a global strategy for the imaginal group by having these subjects sketch the lines they imagined during the training trials. The drawings were removed before the participants were transferred to the test trials. The use of a dimensional strategy was induced in the perceptual group by showing them four separate cards to define each category. Each card presented one of the four lines.

If the use of dimensional strategies by the imaginal group and the use of global strategies by the perceptual group are both invariant, the pattern of responses on the transfer test trials should replicate those of the previous experiment. Contrarily, a more malleable, dynamic model would predict that the strategies would reflect the changing demands of the situation. As already noted, the latter proved to be the case. In this experiment, the imaginal group's pattern of responding on the test trials corresponded to the global pattern of the perceptual group on the first experiment, whereas the perceptual group of this experiment adopted a dimensional strategy.

Taken together, the two experiments demonstrate, satisfyingly, that no single, static model will accommodate all of the results. Both types of classification strategy patterns appeared in both experiments, but the group employing the strategy depended on the characteristics of the situation. In other words, we cannot appeal to the use of a global strategy as the major system underlying classification any more than we can appeal to a dimensional strategy. The apparent use of different underlying processes is inimical to such a resolution. This conclusion acknowledges the differences that were found; but it ignores the similarities. In other words, the results of both experiments showed different patterns predicted by the two strategies on some patterns but not on all of them, and this outcome surfaced in both experiments. A comprehensive model should include both.

Hence, we considered another possibility, a dynamics systems model (e.g., Fogel & Thelen, 1987; Thelen, 1989). In contrast to standard associationist and connectionist models, which typically assume stimulus variation on a limited number of variables (vectors) or strategies, dynamic models allow for the effect of many, multifaceted stimuli, processes, and strategies that vary over time. This approach could embrace the notion that processing strategies adapt to experience with different situations and cues.

At this stage, I offer no formal dynamic model, but the following principles may apply. Let us suppose that our perceptual classification system responds to multiple diverse stimulus features, including those that represent overall configuration and orientation as well as individual features. This system may respond stably, unaffected by the use of global or dimensional analyses, because these processes yield the same output. The situation would hold for both external (perceived) and internal (imagined) stimuli.

Unexpected perturbations may induce a shift from the more Gestalt-like attention to stable patterns to more individuated attention to the components or features of a pattern. This demand for focused attention would divert the system into alternative paths, possibly ones that are specialized for processing specific kinds of features.

Applied to the results of the two experiments, the stable portion produces the highly similar responding to test patterns that represent previously learned or presently depicted features of the patterns, whereas the divergent responding occurred to test patterns that introduced novel, unlearned components or altered configurations.

This approach hypothesizes an interaction between stimulus features and task demands, not that perceptual classification invariably follows one path and imaginal classification another. The change in responding to the novel test patterns from the first to the second experiment is consistent with this interpretation. In summary, these results tell us that parent prototypes may be constructed mentally, that subsequent test patterns were classified in ways that correspond to principled strategies, and that the use of these strategies is flexible. Specifically, the characteristics of the task govern the strategy chosen. A global strategy may be induced by encouraging subjects to treat the pattern components holistically, whereas a dimensional strategy may be invoked by encouraging subjects to adopt a more analytic, decompositional approach.

The very flexibility of imagery is particularly noteworthy—and strengthens our knowledge-weighted view as well as other treatments of imagery that accord language a prominent role.

Creativity, Discovery, and Imagery

At the complex end of linguistic contributions to imagery are sentences that require mental reconstruction. We already have considered some relatively simple imaginal reconstructions. At this point, I would like to consider three other, more complicated ones.

The first involves construction of what is usually called a "mental map." Mental maps may be a form of mental models, such as Johnson-Laird (1983) has proposed. As Johnson-Laird notes, it is important to distinguish between propositional representations and models. Although this task is difficult, when pushed to the extreme, one possibility is to give subjects descriptions of the spatial layout(s) of objects and then ask them later for either the spatial layouts or verbatim recall of defining texts. The descriptions may describe one or more layouts. Presumably, if mental models underlie recall, the spatial layouts will be recalled more easily than will verbatim texts, which describe different layouts, whereas if propositional representations underpin performance, subjects will remember verbatim details better than the spatial layouts when the descriptions are consistent with more than one layout. These predictions were supported (Johnson-Laird, 1983), suggesting that subjects first construct propositional representations to comprehend situations and then use these representations to update their model. The resulting mental model may then be retained and the contributing propositions are needed to distinguish among models.

Second, sentences also may be used to guide mental construction, which may then divulge emergent or creative components. The first work to be described was done by Beverly Roskos-Ewoldsen, and the second has been conducted by Ron Finke. As described earlier, Roskos-Ewoldsen (1993) had her subjects learn two 3-line parts by mentally or actually drawing lines connecting dots of a 3-by-3 dot array. In this work, the subjects had to translate the verbal instructions into an appropriate image or drawing. Subsequently, subjects were shown one of three types of 3-line tests, old parts, emergent parts that included lines spanning the two original parts, and noncomponents, which included at least one line not in either of the two 3-line parts. Her subjects, unselected for imagery ability, were clearly able to detect the emergent parts. Their ability to do so was affected by goodness ratings of the parts and of the overall 6-line pattern, as described before. In general, detection of old parts was aided by goodness ratings of the parts, whereas detection of emergent parts was inhibited by goodness ratings of the overall 6-line pattern. The latter result presumably reflects the difficulty of dissembling a coherent pattern.

A third approach to the role of creativity, discovery, and imagery is exemplified by Finke's (Finke, 1990; Finke & Slayton, 1988) recent work with imaginal creativity and discovery. His basic paradigm is to give subjects, unselected for creativity, three simple components, such as a circle, a vertical line, and an alphanumeric character. These components were drawn from limited sets. The subject's task was to construct a practical object from the components, without distorting the components. Subjects drew and described their products. These reports then were judged for correspondence of the drawings to the names given by the subjects and for creativity.

Intriguingly, additional research showed facilitation from linguistic constraints. Finke found that subjects produce more objects rated as creative when they are restricted to categories, such as furniture, personal items, and appliances, and when they were asked to develop a kind of generic form from the components (what Finke called a "preinventive form") before being given the category than when they were unconstrained. Why should these constraints foster creativity? They provide cues that delimit the search in much the same way that giving category levels facilitates recall of category exemplars. Furthermore, in my laboratory (Intons-Peterson, 1993), we found that practice distributed over a 2-week interval increased the number of products rated as creative, suggesting that this kind of mental play and combination may benefit from distributed rehearsal. Finke (1990) and Helstrup and Anderson (1991) did not find a benefit from massed rehearsal, nor did we.

It might seem that the externalization of mental activity by allowing a group to draw or doodle while they were generating the objects would facilitate performance. Not so, Anderson and Helstrup (1993) tell us. Such externalization does not seem to be systematically or reliably beneficial. Anderson and Helstrup report another interesting finding, namely that subjects' own ratings of the creativity of their products differed from those of independent judges. This curious result does not fit into our framework, of course, but it raises obvious questions about our ability to assess our own work and the bases on which we, and others, make these judgments.

The results that constraints, distributed practice, and the goodness of parts all affect imaginative creativity and discovery are characteristics commonly associated with memory and with propositional, conceptual aspects of language. Their comparable effects with imagery emphasize both imagery's memorial properties and its linguistic affinities. Imagery is cognitively penetrable.

THE NEUROPSYCHOLOGY OF IMAGERY

Recent explorations of the neuropsychological substrates of imagery, particularly image generation, hold promise for unlocking mysteries of imagery, including its neurological activity, involvement of early and late sensory-perceptual pathways, its operation distinct from its sensory-perceptual relatives, its relationship to linguistic aspects, and so forth.

Tippett (1992) offers the most recent summary of the area. Data have been collected using three principal strategies: single-case histories of patients suffering known cerebral deficits, group studies of brain-damaged individuals, and measures of regional brain activity with normal, intact organisms (Sergent, 1990). Before presenting the evidence, it is important to identify advantages and disadvantages of each approach.

Cautions

As Ehrlichman and Barrett (1983), Farah (1989), Paivio and te Linde (1982) and others have noted, to answer the question of the contribution of sensory-perceptual systems to imagery, we have to be able to distinguish between patterns recruited by each (or even among multiple systems of a particular sensory system, such as coordinate and categorical visual or auditory pathways, and imaginal ones). In brief, if imagery parallels its sensory "relative," it should show deficits akin to sensory ones. If imagery is a separate system, its sensory links would be considerably weaker, even to the point where it could be dysfunctional when its sensory relative is intact.

Alternatively, imagery may be functionally intact when the related sensory system is deficient. Although this latter alternative is theoretically possible, from a practical perspective it is unlikely because individuals with such a sensory deficit as cortical blindness typically have many other serious deficits (Farah, 1989). These additional problems sabotage efforts to satisfactorily identify separate and causative linkages.

Another concern is the mixture of sensory-perceptual and linguistic input characteristic of most imagery paradigms. This mixture is obvious when linguistic units judged to be easy or hard to imagine, concrete or abstract, are used to manipulate the likelihood of inducing imagery, but it also occurs with more "spatial" approaches such as mental rotation of shapes. In virtually all cases with intact normals, the instructions are presented verbally, in either oral or written form. These situations clearly invite implicit naming or subvocalization. This mixture thus is likely to recruit participation of both hemispheres of the brain, thereby challenging efforts to localize imagery components in one or the other hemispheres. Because the use of linguistic material probably biases processing toward left hemisphere (LH) involvement, it is difficult to assess the now-popular perspective that imagery is mediated primarily by the left hemisphere. Indeed, as we shall see, some reviewers (e.g., Corballis, 1989; Kosslyn, Koenig, Barrett et al., 1989; Richardson, 1991; Sergent, 1990; Tippett, 1992) now conclude that both left- and right (RH) hemispheres mediate imagery.

In the single-case approach, such as those reviewed retrospectively by Farah (1984, 1989), the reviewer is restricted to the information provided by the original observer-investigator, whose selection of tasks also was guided by a particular interest or perspective not necessarily articulated or consonant with our focus. This retrospective view thus depends in part on the techniques used to study the abilities of the patient (which tend to reflect the interests of the researcher and the methodological sophistication at the time of inquiry) and to evaluate the neurological effects/defects. Even with today's relatively advanced diagnostic tools, it is difficult to ascertain the extent of a patient's injury to areas that might have a tangential effect upon performance. Still another problem is that little is usually known about the patient's premorbid condition or abilities. Moreover, even though these cases, including those involving split-brain patients, may point to interesting associations or dissociations, it is difficult—and scientifically risky—to generalize on the basis of single individuals with idiosyncratic histories of brain damage.

The obvious extension is to group together individuals with similar cerebral insults. If they show similar patterns of sensory-perceptual and imaginal abilities or deficits, this would lend credence to generalizations. Hence, a few researchers have attempted to use this strategy, only to be at least partially foiled by substantial individual differences in brain pathology or abilities. In brief, the disadvantages of single cases are compounded by the seemingly inevitable intersubject variations.

The preceding approaches use patients with brain trauma. Although these cases may disclose valuable clues to unraveling some of the mysteries, they do not necessarily correspond to performance of the intact, normally functioning human brain. For this reason, various attempts have been made to study intact individuals. These approaches use techniques such as event-related potentials and cerebral blood flow, and have applied limited spatial analyses as a tool to identify critical areas of activity. These cerebral components may then be integrated to map a functioning distributed system. These approaches offer the promise of temporally tracking the processing of imaginal and perceptual events. The use of normal, intact individuals offers more precise information about the representative and standard spatial nature and distribution of processing than similar types of evidence gathered from individuals who have suffered naturally occurring brain damage. These approaches also have the advantage of controlling the subjects' expectation and demand characteristics because most subjects do not have voluntary control over discrete cerebral activation (Farah, 1989). The techniques afford less control over biases of the experimenters, however, and these biases may affect the methodology employed (e.g., scalp placements for assessing evoked potential responses) and the kinds of analyses used to aggregate responses, as well as the interpretation of the data.

Sergent (1990) identified some other problems inherent in studies of cerebral metabolism. Already familiar to us is the problem of individual differences in brain morphology. Even with intact normals, we need to map the pattern of activation onto a picture of each subject's brain (e.g., Roland & Friberg, 1985). Current technological advances make this problem increasingly easy to solve.

Another problem is the common use of the subtraction method. With this method, the difference between patterns of activation elicited by two tasks is used to identify the cortical areas representing the task components that differentiate these tasks. This approach assumes that a specific cerebral area is uniquely specialized for a single operation and that the same level of activation of this area in two different tasks reveals the same operation, an assumption largely invalidated by the common observations of activity distributed over various portions of the brain (e.g., Richardson, 1991; Tippett, 1992).

A third consideration is the assumption that the two hemispheres have the same functional organization, a clearly fallacious assumption. A fourth difficulty is particularly interesting: Does a high level of activity always signify better or more engaged performance? It seems plausible that skilled activity would require *less* energy than unskilled activity (Sergent, 1990). Computational approaches to imagery (e.g., Farah, 1984; Kosslyn, Chabris, Marsolek, & Koenig, 1992) postulate distinct memory components, such as the encoding of information from long-term memory, generation, transformation, inspection, description, matching, copying. Some of these components can be further decomposed. For example, image generation may utilize "picture," "put," "find" functions (e.g., Kosslyn, 1980).

Neuropsychological Evidence

We return from the digression to the central hypotheses and issues. Perhaps the major and most historical view is that images are faint representations of their sensory ancestors. To the extent that this is true, images should share cerebral manifestations with these sensory-perceptual forbears. It is possible, as Finke (1980) maintained, that imagery partakes of more advanced levels of perceptual rather than the early sensory part of processing. If so, such distinctions also should display cortical manifestations.

Farah (1989) argues, further, that we must make a sensory versus nonsensory distinction:

> *Sensory* representations occur relatively earlier in perceptual processing than *nonsensory* representations, and represent stimuli in terms of relatively simple categories such as local intensity, contour, color, spatial frequency, and direction of motion. They are often topographically mapped, that is, they preserve the spatial relations of the scene or object represented. In contrast, nonsensory representations occur later in perceptual processing and represent stimuli in terms of relatively abstract categories such as object identity (e.g., "face") or absolute location (e.g., with respect to a world-centered reference frame). (p. 184)

Thus, imagery and perception could share neural representations by activating one or more of the same cerebral regions (probably the occipital lobe in vision and in the temporal lobes in language-driven imagery paradigms). Or some of the same representations are recruited in recognition and localization of afferent patterns of activation by sensory systems and generation of efferent patterns of activation during imagery.

A strong articulation of the cortical *identity* of sensory-perceptual and imaginal processing is invalidated by brain-damaged individuals who manifest imagining deficits with intact sensory processing or the reverse (see reviews by Farah, 1989; Kosslyn et al., 1989; Richardson, 1991; Sergent, 1990; Tippett, 1992). Studies of brain activity in normals offer some support for a weaker version of this view. In research that used the subtraction technique, Farah et al. (1990) had some subjects hear and generate images of the referents of the words, and other subjects heard the words, with no instructions to imagine the referents. They contended that differences between event-related potentials (ERPs) associated with the two conditions would represent electrophysiological activity associated with image generation.

Significant differences were obtained, with the effects of imagery being maximal over the occipital and occipitotemporal regions of the scalp. Differences were found bilaterally, although the activity was greater for the LH than for the RH. These and other results summarized in the reviews (Farah, 1989; Kosslyn et al., 1989; Richardson, 1991; Sergent, 1990; Tippett, 1992) have led to the increasingly accepted conclusion that visual imagery recruits occipital activity, which is somewhat greater in the LH than in the RH.

Kosslyn et al. (1989) required normals to make categorical judgments of whether a dot was on or off a figure (line) or of distance of the dot from the figure or line. Other types of categorical judgments were also tested (e.g., left/right, above/below). In general, judgments were faster when the stimuli were initially presented to the right visual field (LH) than to the left visual field (RH). Because stimuli were shown briefly (about 100 ms), we can assume that subjects responded on the basis of some memory (image?). No control conditions were tested, with the stimuli remaining in view until the subjects responded, although central presentation was used in some conditions. The upshot is that we cannot assess the relative activation of the hemispheres associated with imagery per se. This is a common problem.

Other evidence has not found a significant left-hemisphere advantage for imagery. For example, Sergent (1989) tested image generation, using Weber and Harnish's (1974) task of requiring subjects to decide whether a lowercase letter extended above or below the main body of a letter. The stimuli actually seen by the subjects were presented in uppercase (the imagery condition) or in lowercase (the perceptual condition). In the former condition, the assumption was that subjects had to imagine the lowercase counterpart of the letter to perform the task. In Sergent's adaptation, the original stimuli were clear or blurred or were small or large. Her normal subjects showed a RH advantage in the image-generation condition, but equal hemispheric performance in the perceptual condition. Sergent interpreted these results as evidence that the RH could participate in image generation of multipart images. In fact, her conclusion was that both hemispheres could contribute to such image generation, although the contributions of each might vary somewhat.

This conclusion was further bolstered by Sergent's (1991) exploration of the coordinate and categorical structures hypothesized by Kosslyn et al. (1989; see above). Sergeant was unable to replicate the cerebral asymmetry of an LH advantage for categorical processing and a slight RH advantage for coordinate (distance) judgments. Even when Sergent used the same types of stimulus patterns as those used by Kosslyn and colleagues, neither normals nor commissurotomized patients showed this asymmetry. However, when Sergent reduced stimulus luminance, normal subjects manifested an RH advantage for coordinate judgments. The two hemispheres were equally adept with categorical ones. Sergent (1991) concluded "that the 2 hemispheres can operate on both types of spatial relations, but their respective efficiency depends on the quality of the representations to be processed" (p. 762).

Currently, then, the most reasonable conclusion appears to be that image generation and image-based spatial judgments recruit activity in both hemispheres of the brain, but that the relative processing of the hemispheres varies somewhat. This conclusion certainly makes sense for the normal brain, given our current state of knowledge, but it leaves as indeterminate the respective contribution of linguistic and abstract conceptual processing to cortical processing of images.

Does imagery activate sensory and nonsensory perceptual representations? Data from brain-imaging techniques suggest that visual imagery affects cortical areas, most notably the occipital lobes. In this work, Farah and co-workers (1990) compared imaging and reading. They found that the patterns during the first 450 ms were identical. Both probably reflected "common visual and lexical processing stages." The patterns then diverged, with imagery showing highly localized positivity, particularly in occipital ERPs, relative to the reading-only condition. From this work, Farah et al. (1990) consider mental images to be abstract propositional memory representations related to perception. But, this will be true only if imaginal representations are like perceptual (sensory ones) and unlike verbal-lexical representations, which presumably activate abstract, propositional representations. It is possible that these results may speak against a single abstract propositional code.

The evidence discussed above focuses on the cortex. Other components of the brain are involved in cognition, of course, and various reviews, already cited, examine the evidence. At this point, I mention only that studies with brain-damaged individuals implicate the hippocampus in imagery (e.g., Jones-Gotman, 1979; Jones-Gotman & Milner, 1978).

The difficulty here is that virtually all imagery paradigms admit some linguistic influence. Hence, I think that, at least for the moment, we must concede this indeterminism.

Having said this, I now address the implications for my view. The relation between sensory-perceptual and imaginal patterns of cortical activation in normals seems sufficiently related to provide at least some support. Moreover, it is clear that cortical activity associated with imaginal tasks is anatomically (and therefore spatially) distributed within a single hemisphere. The likely recruitment of both hemispheres further strengthens the evidence. However, the evidence is not definitive; nonimaginal aspects of the tasks, such as processing the stimuli, task manipulation, and response generation, may initiate activity in either or both hemispheres of the brains of normal subjects.

Connectionist Models and Neuropsychology

Connectionist models have been applied to imaginal materials (e.g., Glasgow & Conklin, 1992; Kosslyn et al., 1992). The use of this approach has the obvious advantages of hypothesizing distributed representations in contradistinction to tightly localized and circumscribed neural organizations. Like most models, connectionistic ones can be used to evaluate the fit to data achieved when specific assumptions are tested.

Kosslyn and his colleagues (Kosslyn et al., 1992) used neural network simulations to model various predictions of their contention that vision, and imagery, are divided into relatively simple component systems. Recently, Kosslyn et al. (1992) suggested that

> the brain represents spatial relations in two ways. First, *coordinate* representations specify precise spatial locations in a way that is useful for guiding action. The units of these representations are not equivalence classes; rather, they delineate the finest possible division of space (subject to the resolution limitations of the visual system). These representations do not correspond to particular movements; rather, they specify spatial coordinates in a way that can be used to guide a variety of movements. . . . Second, *categorical* representations assign a range of positions to an equivalence class (such as connected/unconnected, above/below, left/right). For many objects, parts retain the same categorical spatial relations, no matter how the object contorts; thus, the specification of categorical spatial relations is a critical aspect of a robust representation of an object's shape [cf. Marr, 1982]. For example, even though its position in space varies widely, a cat's paw remains connected to (a categorical spatial relation) its foreleg regardless of whether the cat is curled up asleep, running, or batting an insect. (pp. 562–563)

Kosslyn (1987; Kosslyn et al., 1989) assumes, further, that the left hemisphere handles categorical coding somewhat more effectively than the right hemisphere and that the right hemisphere processes the coordinate system somewhat more efficiently than the left hemisphere.

Sergent (1991) criticized this approach on both theoretical and empirical grounds, noting that Kosslyn's definition of categorical coding inevitably involves assessments of relative position of objects, just as Kosslyn's definition of coordinate coding implies a frame of reference, with axes specifying not only the distance between objects and between an object and the coordinates but also the position (absolute and relative) of the objects in space. Therefore, a coordinate representation conveys information about the two types of spatial relations, and there ought to be no need to postulate two separate processing subsystems localized in different cerebral loci to represent these spatial relations. (p. 763)

Sergent (1991) used a number of tasks to assess evidence for differential types of spatial processing by the two hemispheres. Five tasks failed to deliver such evidence, although Sergent did find some support for superiority of the right hemisphere with coordinate representations when stimulus luminance was reduced.

In partial response to these findings, Kosslyn et al. (1992) used connectionist models to identify both promising and unpromising avenues for various kinds of exploration. Specifically, neural networks were used to simulate possible coordinate and categorical spatial representations in the brain. This approach may identify simulations most compatible with current knowledge and, hence, most promising avenues for experimental exploration. The outcome of actual experimentation is the final arbiter, of course, but simulations may be a facilitating means to the end. In this application, connectionist simulations are used to winnow possible avenues of further exploration, just as they may be used descriptively.

As mentioned previously, Glasgow and Conklin (1992) developed a computational model of mental imagery. The model has three interrelated representations: a long-term descriptive representation, and two working-memory representations, one for visual and the other for spatial components of mental imagery. The actual program for the model, written in a computer language called "Nial" (Jenkins, Glasgow, & McCrosky, 1986), has not been made widely available, as far as I know.

At this point, it is pertinent to identify some advantages and disadvantages of the application of connectionist modeling to imagery. In general, these situations mirror the advantages and disadvantages of connectionist modeling.

One clear advantage flows from some basic assumptions about connectionist architecture, namely that representations are distributed and parallel. It now is clearly the case that at least higher mental processes are not strictly localized; rather, they appear to be fairly widely distributed across the brain. Moreover, given this distribution, substantial processing must be done in parallel to achieve the response times characteristic of humans. These assumptions may be combined with those of localized representation and serial processing, as may be needed to accommodate early stages of processes and efferent responses. Connectionist models afford a description of the system and the kinds of architecture and weight changes required to produce the desired outcome.

Disadvantages also attend connectionist models. One of the most obvious and common is that connectionist models are too powerful. They can made to predict almost anything by manipulating levels of the networks, weight space, and so forth. In brief, these models are not falsifiable, the hallmark of an adequate model.

Another disadvantage is that, to date, these models often have not had much grounding in the reality of the nervous system and may, therefore, be quite divorced from reality. It has become commonplace to complain about this discontinuity, but, as we shall see, at least in the area of the neuropsychology of imagery, much remains unknown.

An additional disadvantage comes in the form of learning algorithms. As is often stated, there is little neuropsychological or cognitive evidence that learning occurs according to principles such as backpropagation or any other approach that operates on the systematic reduction of the difference between current and a target state.

Massaro (1988) argues that connectionist models based on assumptions of interactive activation predict interactions between levels of, say, letters and words, which do not occur (see Massaro, 1979), and continuous, rather than categorical perception of speech perception. He protests that connectionist models with hidden units are too powerful to be disconfirmable and that either the hidden units or the power may conceal processes that contribute to a task. In general, the processes subsumed by hidden units may be just that—hidden.

Massaro and others have concluded that connectionist and related models may be useful if the assumptions are carefully delineated and particularly if various connectionist models are compared. There have been relatively few applications of connectionist models to imagery; most have involved applications to what is more aptly called "cognitive neuropsychology," exemplified by the approach of Kosslyn described above.

CONCLUSIONS AND IMPLICATIONS

Evidence considered in the chapter suggests that imagery is a bona fide phenomenon, that it is something that has to be explained, not just explained away or ignored. Nevertheless, I think that imagery is basically a special phenomenon of memory.

Both confirmative and disconfirmative evidence supports these conclusions. The data speak to what imagery is and to what it is not. I begin with disconfirmations to bring confirmative conclusions into clear relief.

Imagery does not seem to be cognitively impenetrable. It is not the same as the processes initiated by presentation of concrete words or sentences or words or sentences judged to be easily imagined. Imagery is not equivalent to subvocalization, nor is it a simple, faint replication of sensory or perceptual initiators. Thus, imagery is not an exact parallel of perception. Imagery also is not a rapid process in the sense of developing within a few milliseconds.

Conversely, imagery appears to be the opposite of the features just named. These conclusions reflect the following evidence.

Pylyshyn (1981) maintained that unless imagery is shown to be cognitively impenetrable it is more parsimonious to explain it as propositional than as analogical. This view is challenged by much of the research cited in the chapter. Imagery is cognitively penetrable. It also has features difficult or awkward to capture propositionally. In the mental transport of balls described as having different weights, mental transport times varied with not only the hypothetical weight of the balls but also with whether the maps were physically present (the "perceptual" group) or were remembered (the "imagery" group). The increase in transport times as functions of weight and distance could be explained in terms of differential propositional instantiations of real-world knowledge, but the differences as functions of the presence or absence of the maps are more resistant and discommodious. The construction of composite images in the imaginal priming, classification, mental maps, and creativity work is guided by directional language or narratives, clearly documenting cognitive penetrability; the subsequent imaginal performance, some of which involved detection of novel or emergent parts, also resists facile codification into propositional calculus.

Simple presentation of concrete or easy-to-imagine words does not necessarily invoke imagery, as indicated by both behavioral (e.g., reviews by Marschark & Cornoldi, 1991; Marschark et al., 1987; Potter et al., 1986) and neuropsychological evidence (e.g., Farah et al., 1990; Goldenberg et al., 1987). There seems to be something important about the imaging process. Moreover, the behavioral concreteness and ease-of-imagining effects can be explained in terms of distinctiveness and relational processing (Marschark & Cornoldi, 1991; Marschark & Surian, 1992).

Appeals to subvocalization as the basis for imaginal performance falter, with imaginal comparisons requiring discriminations that defy verbal recounting of small differences. For example, Lyman and McDaniel (1990) tested imaginal and perceptual comparisons of odors; Crowder (1989), Pitt and Crowder (1992), and Surprenant (1993) used timbre or other subtle auditory features. Even though it would have been difficult to articulate the differences between pairs in these studies, subjects were able to distinguish reliably between them even when the referents of the pairs were imagined.

In contrast, when subvocalization supports supposedly imaginal performance, as with Reisberg et al.'s (1989) explorations of auditory ambiguous words, subjects detect the same auditory switches from one word to another that they heard when speaking the word repetitively. It seems likely that articulatory or other cues of the subvocalization may underlie these phenomena because subjects fail to detect the switches when subvocalization is suppressed by chewing or clamping the mouth shut.

Images, then, are not simple, faithful replications of percepts. If they were, reconstrual of classical ambiguous figures, such as Jastrow's duck-rabbit, would occur as consistently with imagined figures as with perceived figures. Although Hyman (1993; Hyman & Neisser, 1991) and M. A. Peterson (1993; Peterson et al., 1992) showed that some reconstruals could be obtained under certain conditions, they replicated Chambers and Reisberg's (1985) central finding that reconstruals of imagined ambiguous figures occurred rarely. Similarly, the failure of Reed's subjects (Reed, 1974; Reed & Johnsen, 1975) to detect embedded figures in imagined patterns that could be identified in perceived patterns attests to imaginal-perceptual differences, as does neuropsychological research (e.g., Farah et al., 1990; Goldenberg et al., 1987). The occasional differences between imaginal and perceptual performance contraindicate either functional or structural equivalence of the two.

This same conclusion is delivered by most of the research cited in the main section of this chapter. Nevertheless, imagery and perception often provide very similar performance (see reviews by Finke & Shepard, 1986; Intons-Peterson & McDaniel, 1991). Examinations of the conditions used to test imaginal-perceptual parallelism suggested that the similarity of imaginal-perceptual performance decreased with the familiarity of the task. That is, the more familiar the task, in general, the *less* likely imagery and perception were to yield similar performance, whereas the less familiar the task, the *more* likely the two were to show similar performance.

Although a precise test of these relations remains to be conducted, and thus constitutes a task for the future, the relation is not as counterintuitive as it might seem at first reading. The more familiar the task, the less vulnerable performance should be to idiosyncratic tacit demands and to inadvertent influence from experimenters' expectations. That is, the performance should reflect more typical perceptual and, perhaps, more typical imaginal performance than with unfamiliar tasks. With unfamiliar tasks, subjects rely on subtle cues from task demands and experimenters to try to ascertain what is expected of them. This will be true for both perceptual and imaginal tasks that are unfamiliar. Future research presumably will examine possible underlying mechanisms as well.

Images take time to develop. As Suprenant (1993) demonstrated, image generation does not seem to be fast enough to "model" the very rapid dynamical changes characteristic of onset times of consonants, for example. Her findings do not suggest that image generation is sluggish, of course, but rather that it requires somewhat more milliseconds than the very fast sensory processing of, say, audition.

Conversely, images have various characteristics that argue for their distinctiveness. They are cognitively penetrable, are influenced by tacit knowledge, have sensory and perceptual ties and spatial extent, are sensitive to steady states to a greater extent than rapid onsets, and so forth. These characteristics impressively instantiate implications of the definition of images as memories with sensory-perceptual and spatial components. They also integrate the linguistic influence and spatial-perceptual elements of the two traditional lines of imagery research.

In like vein, most of the evidence surveyed demonstrated the contributions of language to imagery. This influence occurs at various levels, from the phonological (e.g., Surprenant, 1993) to real-world knowledge invoked by descriptions of imaginary objects (e.g., mental transport of the balls in Intons-Peterson & Roskos-Ewoldsen, 1989). Thus, I interpret the combined evidence as compelling support for a knowledge-weighted model of imagery (e.g., Intons-Peterson & McDaniel, 1991). Less clear, however, is evidence for the distinction between canonical and ancillary components of images. The motivating force behind such a view is simply that the images generated by subjects include not only information specifically provided to them but also real-world knowledge presumably elicited by associations already in long-term memory. Mental transport and the tendency to require a visual image of some objects before an auditory image can be generated (e.g., *popcorn popping*) are examples. It is tempting to posit that ancillary cues determine the extent of image-percept parallelism, an open research question.

Perhaps the dichotomous canonical-ancillary distinction is inappropriate. Investigations of imaginal classification attest to imagery's flexibility, which may mean that imagery reflects gradations on such continua as typicality, family resemblance, and similar factors as occur with perceptually and conceptually based classification. If so, the canonical-ancillary distinction may need to be recast.

This research raises other issues. What are the exact conditions that trigger the use of different strategies, such as global or holistic ones, and more analytic, dimensional ones? How is it that imagery can be so flexible and adaptive? Is its ability to mimic perceptual and verbal-numeric strategies as appropriate for task demands an indication that imagery does not have distinct features of any kind? Do such perceptual effects as goodness (e.g., Roskos-Ewoldsen, 1993) affect canonical or ancillary features of imagery?

Other implications and research avenues spring from my framework of imagery and from the research surveyed in the chapter. Consider, for example, the evidence that physical primes are not incorporated into images, even though both presumably activate visual pathways. Is this an attentional distinction? A temporal one? If so, brain-imaging techniques should reflect differences in timing and in anatomical distribution. Similarly, differences in cerebral activity reported by Farah et al. (1990) and Goldenberg et al. (1987) to concrete words when subjects were or were not told to imagine also may reflect attentional differences. The use of designs that elicit imagery more implicitly should reduce differential attention demands.

Neuropsychological research may disclose other important evidence. It already suggests that imagery has both distributed and local properties, which partially reflect sensory origins. Even though external stimuli may be distinguishable from imaginally activated recruitment, the latter corresponds to its sensory parentage. Mechanisms underlying these relations clearly cry out for further specification. The underlying processes may explain why auditory images may depend on the preceding generation of a visual image, as with *popcorn popping*. This is an open, fertile field for research, particularly when normal, intact subjects are used. Its feasibility increases as cortical scanning techniques and procedures for mapping activity in various regions across time become more sophisticated.

Images permit identification of emergent features and creative combination. Why are there more creative constructions with limited categories? A likely but as yet unexplored answer is that category names cue possibilities; they offer associations, places to begin a search. Hence, they help in much the same way as retrieval cues aid any search.

Some images arise seemingly unbidden. Why? What is their source? Creative combinations provide numerous examples of the detection or production of emergent features in images, as do the generation of mental maps from narratives when the observers have not been told to construct the maps. These approaches offer opportunities for studying imagery's contributions to everyday life.

Is imagery a separate process? Probably not. It seems more likely to me that it is a memory with specific properties. Nevertheless, the very conjoining of these properties confers a uniqueness that may underlie the experiential aspects of imagery. Consequently, I remain open to the possibility that imagery is indeed a distinct and separate process.

REFERENCES

Anderson, J. R. (1976). *Language, memory, and thought.* Hillsdale, NJ: Erlbaum.

Anderson, J. R. (1978). Arguments concerning representations for mental imagery. *Psychological Review, 85,* 249–277.

Anderson, R. E., & Helstrup, T. (1993). Multiple perspectives on discovery and creativity. In B. Roskos-Ewoldsen, M. J. Intons-Peterson, & R. E. Anderson (Eds.), *Imagery, creativity, and discovery: A cognitive approach* (pp. 223–254). Amsterdam: Elsevier.

Attneave, F. (1955). Symmetry, information, and memory for patterns. *American Journal of Psychology, 68,* 209–222.

Baddeley, A. D. (1986). *Working memory.* Oxford: Clarendon Press.

Balota, D. A., & Lorch, R. (1986). Depth of automatic spreading activation: Mediated priming effects in pronunciation but not in lexical decision. *Journal of Experimental Psychology: Learning, Memory, and Cognition, 12,* 336–345.

Becker, C. A. (1980). Semantic context effects in visual word recognition: An analysis of semantic strategies. *Memory & Cognition, 8,* 493–512.

Brandimonte, M. A., Hitch, G. J., & Bishop, D. V. M. (1992a). Influence of short-term memory codes on visual image processing: Evidence from image transformation tasks. *Journal of Experimental Psychology: Learning, Memory, and Cognition, 18,* 157–165.

Brandimonte, M. A., Hitch, G. J., & Bishop, D. V. M. (1992b). Verbal recoding of visual stimuli impairs mental image transformation. *Memory & Cognition, 20,* 449–455.

Bugelski, B. R., Kidd, E., & Segmen, J. (1968). Image as a mediator in one-trial paired-associate learning. *Journal of Experimental Psychology, 76,* 69–73.

Carmichael, L., Hogan, H. P., & Walter, A. A. (1932). An experimental study of the effect of language on the reproduction of visually perceived form. *Journal of Experimental Psychology, 15,* 73–86.

Chambers, D. (1993). Images are both depictive and descriptive. In B. Roskos-Ewoldsen, M. J. Intons-Peterson, & R. E. Anderson (Eds.), *Imagery, creativity, and discovery: A cognitive approach* (pp. 77–98). Amsterdam: Elsevier.

Chambers, D., & Reisberg, D. (1985). Can mental images be ambiguous? *Journal of Experimental Psychology: Human Perception and Performance, 11,* 317–328.

Corballis, M. C. (1989). Laterality and human evolution. *Psychological Review, 96,* 492–505.

Cornoldi, C., & Paivio, A. (1982). Imagery value and its effects on verbal memory: A review. *Archivio di Psicologia, Neurologia e Psichiatria, 43,* 171–192.

Crowder, R. G. (1989). Imagery for musical timbre. *Journal of Experimental Psychology: Human Perception and Performance, 15,* 472–478.

De Beni, R., & Cornoldi, C. (1988). Imagery limitations in totally congenitally blind subjects. *Journal of Experimental Psychology: Learning, Memory, and Cognition, 14,* 650–655.

de Groot, A. M. B. (1984). A word's meaning affects the decision in lexical decision. *Quarterly Journal of Experimental Psychology, 36A,* 253–280.

de Groot, A. M. B. (1985). Word-context effects in word naming and lexical decision. *Quarterly Journal of Experimental Psychology, 37A,* 281–297.

Denis, M. (1991a). *Image and cognition* (M. Denis & C. Greenbaum, Trans.). Exeter, England: BPCC Wheatons Ltd. (Original work published 1989)

Denis, M. (1991b). Imagery and thinking. In C. Cornoldi & M. A. McDaniel (Eds.), *Imagery and cognition* (pp. 103–131). New York: Springer-Verlag.

Denis, M., & Cocude, M. (1992). Structural properties of visual images constructed from poorly or well-structured verbal descriptions. *Memory & Cognition, 20,* 497–506.

Dennett, D. C. (1969). *Content and consciousness.* New York: Humanities Press.

de Vega, M. (1991, June). *Characters and their perspectives in narratives describing spatial environments.* Paper presented at the Workshop on Mental Models, University of Paris.

Di Vesta, F. I., Ingersoll, G., & Sunshine, P. (1971). A factor analysis of imagery tests. *Journal of Verbal Learning and Verbal Behavior, 10,* 471–479.

Ehrlichman, H., & Barrett, J. (1983). Right hemispheric specialization for mental imagery: A review of the evidence. *Brain and Cognition, 2,* 55–76.

Einstein, G. O., & Hunt, R. R. (1980). Levels of processing and organization: Additive effects of individual item and relational processing. *Journal of Experimental Psychology: Human Learning and Memory, 6,* 588–598.

Engelkamp, J. (1986). Motor programs as part of the meaning of verbal items. In I. Kurcz, E. Shugar, & J. H. Danks (Eds.), *Knowledge and language* (pp. 115–138). Amsterdam: North-Holland.

Engelkamp, J. (1991). Imagery and enactment in paired-associate learning. In R. H. Logie & M. Denis (Eds.), *Mental images in human cognition* (pp. 119–128). Amsterdam: Elsevier.

Ernest, C. (1987). Imagery and memory in the blind: A review. In M. A. McDaniel & M. Pressley (Eds.), *Imagery and related mnemonic processes: Theories, individual differences, and applications* (pp. 218–238). New York: Springer-Verlag.

Farah, M. J. (1984). The neurological basis of mental imagery: A componential analysis. *Cognition, 18,* 245–272.

Farah, M. J. (1985). Psychophysical evidence for a shared representation medium for mental images and percepts. *Journal of Experimental Psychology: General, 114,* 91–103.

Farah, M. J. (1989). The neuropsychology of mental imagery. In J. W. Brown (Ed.), *Neuropsychology of visual perception* (pp. 183–201). Hillsdale, NJ: Erlbaum.

Farah, M. J., Weisberg, L. L., Monheit, M., & Peronnet, F. (1990). Brain activity underlying mental imagery: Event-related potentials during mental image generation. *Journal of Cognitive Neuroscience, 1,* 302–316.

Favreau, M., & Segalowitz, N. (1983). Automatic and controlled processes in the first- and second-language reading of fluent bilinguals. *Memory & Cognition, 11,* 565–574.

Finke, R. A. (1980). Levels of equivalence in imagery and perception. *Psychological Review, 87,* 113–132.

Finke, R. A. (1985). Theories relating mental imagery to perception. *Psychological Bulletin, 98,* 236–259.

Finke, R. A. (1990). *Creative imagery: Discoveries and inventions in visualization.* Hillsdale, NJ: Erlbaum.

Finke, R. A. (1993). Mental imagery and creative discovery. In B. Roskos-Ewoldsen, M. J. Intons-Peterson, & R. E. Anderson (Eds.), *Imagery, creativity, and discovery: A cognitive approach* (pp. 255–286). Amsterdam: Elsevier.

Finke, R. A., & Shepard, R. N. (1986). Visual functions of mental imagery. In K. R. Boff, L. Kaufman, & J. P. Thomas (Eds.), *Handbook of perception and human performance* (Vol. 2, Chapter 37, pp. 1–55). New York: Wiley-Interscience.

Finke, R. A., & Slayton, K. (1988). Explorations of creative visual synthesis in mental imagery. *Memory & Cognition, 16,* 252–257.

Fogel, A., & Thelen, E. (1987). Development of early expressive and communicative action: Reinterpreting the evidence from a dynamics systems perspective. *Developmental Psychology, 23,* 747–761.

Forster, K. I. (1979). Levels of processing and the structure of the language processor. In W. E. Cooper & E. C. T. Walker (Eds.), *Sentence processing: Psycholinguistic studies presented to Merrill Garrett* (pp. 27–85). Hillsdale, NJ: Erlbaum.

Forster, K. I. (1981). Priming and the effects of sentence and lexical contexts on naming time: Evidence for autonomous lexical processing. *Quarterly Journal of Experimental Psychology, 33A,* 465–495.

Franklin, N., & Tversky, B. (1990). Searching imagined environments. *Journal of Experimental Psychology: General, 119,* 63–76.

Garner, W. R., & Clement, D. E. (1963). Goodness of pattern and pattern uncertainty. *Journal of Verbal learning and Verbal Behavior, 2,* 446–452.

Georgopoulos, A., Lurito, J., Petrides, M., Schwartz, A., & Massey, J. (1989). Mental rotation of the neuronal population vector. *Science, 243,* 234–236.

Glasgow, J., & Conklin, D. (1992). Simulating theories of mental imagery. *Proceedings of the Fourteenth Annual Conference of the Cognitive Science Society* (pp. 112–117).

Goldenberg, G., Podreka, I., Steiner, M., & Willmes, K. (1987). Patterns of cerebral blood flow related to memorizing of high and low imagery words—an emission computer tomography study. *Neuropsychologia, 25,* 473–485.

Goldstone, R. L. (1991). Feature diagnosticity as a tool for investigating positively and negatively defined concepts. *Proceedings of the Thirteenth Annual Conference of the Cognitive Science Society* (pp. 263–268). Hillsdale, NJ: Lawrence Erlbaum.

Helstrup, T., & Anderson, R. E. (1991). Imagery in mental construction and decomposition tasks. In R. H. Logie & M. Denis (Eds.), *Mental images in human cognition* (pp. 229–240). Amsterdam: North-Holland.

Hochberg, J., & McAlister, E. (1953). A quantitative approach to figure "goodness." *Journal of Experimental Psychology, 46,* 361–364.

Holt, R. R. (1964). Imagery: Return of the ostracized. *American Psychologist, 19,* 254–264.

Humphreys, M. S. (1978). Item and relational information: A case for context independent retrieval. *Journal of Verbal Learning and Verbal Behavior, 17,* 175–188.

Hyman, I. E., Jr. (1993). Imagery, reconstructive memory, and discovery. In B. Roskos-Ewoldsen, M. J. Intons-Peterson, & R. E. Anderson (Eds.), *Imagery, creativity, and discovery: A cognitive approach* (pp. 99–122). Amsterdam: Elsevier.

Hyman, I. E., Jr., & Neisser, U. (1991). *Reconstructing mental images: Problems of method.* Emory Cognition Project Technical Report 19, Emory University, Atlanta, GA.

Intons-Peterson, M. J. (1980). The role of loudness in auditory memory. *Memory & Cognition, 8,* 385–393.

Intons-Peterson, M. J. (1983). Imagery paradigms: How vulnerable are they to experimenters' expectations? *Journal of Experimental Psychology: Human Perception and Performance, 9,* 394–412.

Intons-Peterson, M. J. (1993). Imaginal priming. *Journal of Experimental Psychology: Learning, Memory, and Cognition, 19,* 223–235.

Intons-Peterson, M. J. (1993). Imagery's role in creativity and discovery. In B. Roskos-Ewoldsen, M. J. Intons-Peterson, & R. E. Anderson (Eds.), *Imagery, creativity, and discovery: A cognitive approach* (pp. 1–38). Amsterdam: Elsevier.

Intons-Peterson, M. J., Hinshaw, A., Yarnall, H., Angotti, C., & Zhang, W. (1993). *The effects of naming on a visual manipulation task.* Manuscript submitted for publication.

Intons-Peterson, M. J., & McDaniel, M. A. (1991). Symmetries and asymmetries between imagery and perception. In C. Cornoldi & M. A. McDaniel (Eds.), *Imagery and cognition* (pp. 47–76). New York: Springer-Verlag.

Intons-Peterson, M. J., & Roskos-Ewoldsen, B. B. (1989). Sensory-perceptual qualities of images. *Journal of Experimental Psychology: Learning, Memory, and Cognition, 15,* 188–199.

Jastrow, J. (1900). *Fact and fable in psychology.* Boston and New York: Houghton Mifflin.

Jenkins, M. A., Glasgow, J. I., & McCrosky, C. (1986). Programming styles in Nial. *IEEE Software, 86,* 46–55.

Job, R., Rumiati, R., & Lotto, L. (1992). The picture superiority effect in categorization: Visual or semantic. *Journal of Experimental Psychology: Learning, Memory, and Cognition, 18,* 1019–1028.

Johnson-Laird, P. N. (1983). *Mental models: Towards a cognitive science of language, inference, and consciousness.* Cambridge: Cambridge University Press.

Jolicoeur, P. (1985). The time to name disoriented natural objects. *Memory & Cognition, 13,* 289–303.

Jolicoeur, P. (1988). Mental rotation and the identification of disoriented objects. *Canadian Journal of Psychology, 42,* 461–478.

Jones-Gotman, M. (1979). Incidental learning of image-mediated or pronounced words after right temporal lobectomy. *Cortex, 15,* 187–197.

Jones-Gotman, M., & Milner, B. (1978). Right temporal-lobe contribution to image-mediated verbal learning. *Neuropsychologia, 16,* 61–71.

Kaufmann, G., & Helstrup, T. (1993). Mental imagery: Fixed or multiple meanings? Nature and function of imagery in creative thinking. In B. Roskos-Ewoldsen, M. J. Intons-Peterson, & R. E. Anderson (Eds.), *Imagery, creativity, and discovery: A cognitive approach* (pp. 123–150). Amsterdam: Elsevier.

Kolinsky, R., Morais, J., Content, A., & Cary, L. (1987). Finding parts within figures: A developmental study. *Perception, 16,* 399–407.

Kosslyn, S. M. (1975). Information representation in visual images. *Cognitive Psychology, 7,* 341–370.

Kosslyn, S. M. (1980). *Image and mind.* Cambridge, MA: Harvard University Press.

Kosslyn, S. M. (1987). Seeing and imagining in the cerebral hemispheres: A computational approach. *Psychological Review, 94,* 148–175.

Kosslyn, S. M., Ball, T., & Reiser, B. J. (1978). Visual images preserve metric spatial information: Evidence from studies of image scanning. *Journal of Experimental Psychology: Human Perception and Performance, 4,* 47–60.

Kosslyn, S. M., Chabris, C. F., Marsolek, C. J., & Koenig, O. (1992). Categorical versus coordinate spatial relations: Computational analyses and computer simulations. *Journal of Experimental Psychology: Human Perception and Performance, 18,* 562–577.

Kosslyn, S. M., Koenig, O., Barrett, A., Cave, C. B., Tang, J., & Gabrieli, J. D. E. (1989). Evidence for two types of spatial representations: Hemispheric specialization for categorical and coordinate relations. *Journal of Experimental Psychology: Human Perception and Performance, 15,* 723–735.

Lorayne, H., & Lucas, J. (1974). *The memory book.* New York: Ballantine.

Lyman, B. J., & McDaniel, M. A. (1990). Memory for odors and odor names: Modalities of elaboration and imagery. *Journal of Experimental Psychology: Learning, Memory, and Cognition, 16,* 656–664.

Marmor, G. S., & Zaback, L. A. (1976). Mental rotation in the blind: Does mental rotation depend on visual imagery? *Journal of Experimental Psychology: Human Perception and Performance, 2,* 515–521.

Marr, D. (1982). *Vision.* New York: Freeman.

Marschark, M. (1985). Imagery and organization in the recall of prose. *Journal of Memory and Language, 24,* 734–745.

Marschark, M. (1988). Why does concreteness improve memory? The roles of imagery, distinctiveness, and relational processing. In C. Cornoldi (Ed.), *Imagery and Cognition: Proceedings of the Second European Workshop on Imagery and Cognition* (pp. 157–172), University of Padova, Italy.

Marschark, M., & Cornoldi, C. (1991). Imagery and verbal memory. In C. Cornoldi & M. A. McDaniel (Eds.), *Imagery and cognition* (pp. 133–182). New York: Springer-Verlag.

Marschark, M., & Paivio, A. (1977). Integrative processing of concrete and abstract sentences. *Journal of Verbal Learning and Verbal Behavior, 16,* 217–231.

Marschark, M., Richman, C. L., Yuille, J. C., & Hunt, R. R. (1987). The role of imagery in memory: On shared and distinctive information. *Psychological Bulletin, 102,* 28–41.

Marschark, M., & Surian, L. (1992). Concreteness effects in free recall: The roles of imaginal and relational processing. *Memory & Cognition, 20,* 612–620.

Massaro, D. W. (1979). Letter information and orthographic context in word perception. *Journal of Experimental Psychology: Human Perception and Performance, 5,* 595–609.

Massaro, D. W. (1988). Some criticisms of connectionist models of human performance. *Journal of Verbal Learning and Verbal Behavior, 27,* 213–234.

McKim, R. H. (1972). *Experiences in visual thinking.* Monterey, CA: Brooks/Cole.

Miller, A. I. (1984). *Imagery in scientific thought: Creating 20th-century physics.* Boston: Birkhäuser.

Mitchell, D. B., & Richman, C. L. (1980). Confirmed reservations: Mental travel. *Journal of Experimental Psychology: Human Perception and Performance, 6,* 58–66.

More, T. (1979). The nested rectangular array as a model of data. From proc. APL79, *APL Quote Quad, 9.*

Moyer, R. (1973). Comparing objects in memory: Evidence suggesting an internal psychophysics. *Perception & Psychophysics, 13,* 180–184.

Murphy, G. L. (1991). Parts in object concepts: Experiments with artificial categories. *Memory & Cognition, 19,* 423–438.

Neely, J. H. (1977). Semantic priming and retrieval from lexical memory: Roles of inhibitionless spreading activation and limited-capacity attention. *Journal of Experimental Psychology: General, 106,* 226–254.

Neely, J. H., Keefe, D. E., & Ross, K. L. (1989). Semantic priming in the lexical decision task. Roles of prospective prime-generated expectancies and retrospective semantic matching. *Journal of Experimental Psychology: Learning, Memory, and Cognition, 15,* 1003–1019.

Neisser, U. (1972). Changing conceptions of imagery. In P. W. Sheehan (Ed.), *The functions and nature of imagery* (pp. 233–251). New York: Academic Press.

Nelson, D. L., Brooks, D. H., & Borden, R. C. (1973). Sequential memory for pictures and the role of the verbal system. *Journal of Experimental Psychology, 101,* 242–245.

Nelson, D. L., Reed, V. S., & McEvoy, C. L. (1977). Learning to order pictures and words: A model of sensory and semantic encoding. *Journal of Experimental Psychology: Human Learning and Memory, 3,* 485–497.

Norris, D. (1986). Word recognition: Context effects without priming. *Cognition, 22,* 93–136.

Paivio, A. (1971). *Imagery and verbal processes.* New York: Holt, Rinehart and Winston.

Paivio, A. (1986). *Mental representations: A dual-coding approach.* New York: Oxford University Press.

Paivio, A., & Csapo, K. (1969). Concrete image and verbal memory codes. *Journal of Experimental Psychology, 80,* 279–285.

Paivio, A., & Okovita, H. W. (1971). Word imagery modalities and associative learning in blind and sighted subjects. *Journal of Verbal Learning and Verbal Behavior, 10,* 506–510.

Paivio, A., & te Linde, J. (1982). Imagery, memory, and the brain. *Canadian Journal of Psychology, 36,* 243–272.

Palmer, S. E. (1977). Hierarchical structure in perceptual representation. *Cognitive Psychology, 9,* 441–474.

Perrig, W. J. (1988). *Vorstellungen und gedachtnis.* Berlin: Springer-Verlag.

Petersen, R. C. (1974). Imagery and cued recall: Concreteness or context? *Journal of Experimental Psychology, 102,* 841–844.

Peterson, L. R., Rawlings, L., & Cohen, C. (1977). The internal construction of spatial patterns. In G. H. Bower (Ed.), *The psychology of learning and motivation* (pp. 245–276). New York: Academic Press.

Peterson, M. A. (1993). The ambiguity of mental images: Insights regarding the structure of shape memory and its function in creativity. In B. Roskos-Ewoldsen, M. J. Intons-

Peterson, & R. E. Anderson (Eds.), *Imagery, creativity, and discovery: A cognitive approach* (pp. 151–186). Amsterdam: Elsevier.

Peterson, M. A., Kihlstrom, J. F., Røse, P. M., & Glisky, M. L. (1992). Mental images can be ambiguous: Reconstruals and reference-frame reversals. *Memory & Cognition, 20,* 107–123.

Peterson, M. J., & Graham, S. E. (1974). Visual detection and visual imagery. *Journal of Experimental Psychology, 103,* 509–514.

Pitt, M. A., & Crowder, R. G. (1992). The role of spectral and dynamic cues in imagery for musical timbre. *Journal of Experimental Psychology: Human Perception and Performance, 18,* 728–738.

Posner, M. I., Boies, S. J., Eichelman, W. H., & Taylor, R. L. (1969). Retention of visual and name codes for single letters. *Journal of Experimental Psychology: Monographs, 74,* 392–409.

Posner, M. I., & Snyder, C. R. R. (1975). Attention and cognitive control. In R. L. Solso (Ed.), *Information processing and cognition: The Loyola symposium* (pp. 55–85). Hillsdale, NJ: Erlbaum.

Potter, M. C., & Faulconer, B. A. (1975). Time to understand pictures and words. *Nature, 253,* 437–438.

Potter, M. C., Kroll, J. F., Yachzel, B., Carpenter, E., & Sherman, J. (1986). Pictures in sentences: Understanding without words. *Journal of Experimental Psychology: General, 115,* 281–294.

Pylyshyn, Z. (1973). What the mind's eye tells the mind's brain: A critique of mental imagery. *Psychological Bulletin, 80,* 1–24.

Pylyshyn, Z. (1979). The rate of "mental rotation" of images: A test of a holistic analogue hypothesis. *Memory & Cognition, 7,* 19–28.

Pylyshyn, Z. (1980). Computation and cognition: Issues in the foundations of cognitive science. *Behavioral and Brain Sciences, 3,* 111–169.

Pylyshyn, Z. (1981). The imagery debate: Analogue media versus tacit knowledge. *Psychological Review, 88,* 16–46.

Pylyshyn, Z. W. (1984). *Computation and cognition.* Cambridge, MA: MIT Press.

Raaijmakers, J. G., & Shiffrin, R. M. (1981). Search of associative memory. *Psychological Review, 88,* 93–134.

Reed, S. K. (1974). Structural descriptions and the limitations of visual images. *Memory & Cognition, 7,* 205–213.

Reed, S. K., & Brown, J. L. (1979). Temporal organization of pattern structure. *Memory & Cognition, 7,* 205–213.

Reed, S. K., & Johnsen, J. A. (1975). Detection of parts in patterns and images. *Memory & Cognition, 3,* 569–575.

Reisberg, D., & Chambers, D. (1991). Neither pictures nor propositions: What can we learn from a mental image? *Canadian Journal of Psychology, 45,* 288–302.

Reisberg, D. & Logie, R. (1993). The ins and outs of working memory: Overcoming the limits of learning from memory. In B. Roskos-Ewoldsen, M. J. Intons-Peterson, &

R. E. Anderson (Eds.), *Imagery, creativity, and discovery: A cognitive approach* (pp. 39–76). Amsterdam: Elsevier.

Reisberg, D., Smith, J. D., Baxter, D. A., & Sonenshine, M. (1989). "Enacted" auditory images are ambiguous; "pure" auditory images are not. *Quarterly Journal of Experimental Psychology, 41A,* 619–641.

Richardson, J. T. E. (1991). Imagery and the brain. In C. Cornoldi & M. S. McDaniel (Eds.), *Imagery and cognition* (pp. 1–45). New York: Springer-Verlag.

Richman, C. L., Mitchell, D. B., & Reznick, J. S. (1979). Mental travel: Some reservations. *Journal of Experimental Psychology: Human Perception and Performance, 5,* 13–18.

Roland, P. E., & Friberg, L. (1985). Localization of cortical areas activated by thinking. *Journal of Neurophysiology, 53,* 1219–1243.

Roskos-Ewoldsen, B. (1993). Discovering emergent properties of images. In B. Roskos-Ewoldsen, M. J. Intons-Peterson, & R. E. Anderson (Eds.), *Imagery, creativity, and discovery: A cognitive approach* (pp. 187–222). Amsterdam: Elsevier.

Rubin, D. C. (1980). 51 properties of 125 words: A unit analysis of verbal behavior. *Journal of Verbal Learning and Verbal Behavior, 19,* 736–755.

Rumelhart, D. E., & Siple, P. (1974). Process of recognizing tachistoscopically presented words. *Psychological Review, 81,* 99–118.

Ryle, G. (1949). *The concept of mind.* London: Hutchinson.

Saltz, E., & Donnenwerth-Nolan, S. (1981). Does motoric imagery facilitate memory for sentences? A selective interference test. *Journal of Verbal Learning and Verbal Behavior, 20,* 322–332.

Segal, S. J., & Fusella, V. (1970). Influence of imaged pictures and sounds on detection of visual and auditory signals. *Journal of Experimental Psychology, 83,* 458–464.

Seidenberg, M. S., Waters, G., Sanders, M., & Langer, P. (1984). Pre- and post-lexical loci of contextual effects on word recognition. *Memory & Cognition, 12,* 315–328.

Sergent, J. (1989). Image generation and processing of generated images in the cerebral hemispheres. *Journal of Experimental Psychology: Human Perception and Performance, 15,* 170–178.

Sergent, J. (1990). The neuropsychology of visual image generation: Data, method, and theory. *Brain and Cognition, 13,* 98–129.

Sergent, J. (1991). Judgments of relative position and distance on representations of spatial relations. *Journal of Experimental Psychology: Human Perception and Performance, 91,* 762–780.

Shepard, R. N. (1975). Form, formation, and transformation of internal representations. In R. Solso (Ed.), *Information processing and cognition: The Loyola symposium* (pp. 87–122). Hillsdale, NJ: Erlbaum.

Shepard, R. N. (1978). Externalization of mental images and the act of creation. In B. S. Randhawa & W. E. Coffman (Eds.), *Visual learning, thinking, and communication* (pp. 133–189). New York: Academic Press.

Shepard, R. N., & Cooper, L. A. (1982). *Mental images and their transformations.* Cambridge, MA: MIT Press.

Shorter, J. M. (1952). Imagination. *Mind, 61,* 527–542.

Snodgrass, J. G., Burns, P. M., & Pirone, G. V. (1978). Pictures and words in space and time: In search of the elusive interaction. *Journal of Experimental Psychology: Human Learning and Memory, 107,* 206–230.

Snodgrass, J. G., & Vanderwart, M. (1980). A standardized set of 260 pictures: Norms for name agreement, image agreement, familiarity, and visual complexity. *Journal of Experimental Psychology: Human Learning and Memory, 6,* 174–215.

Surprenant, A. M. (1993). *Steady-state versus dynamic acoustic properties in memory for synthetic speech.* Manuscript submitted for publication.

Tarr, M., & Pinker, S. (1989). Mental rotation and orientation-dependence in shape recognition. *Cognitive Psychology, 21,* 233–282.

Thelen, E. (1989). Self-organization in developmental processes: Can systems approaches work? In M. Gunnar & E. Thelen (Eds.), *Systems and development: The Minnesota symposium on child psychology* (Vol. 22, pp. 77–117). Hillsdale, NJ: Erlbaum.

Thompson, A. L., & Klatzky, R. L. (1978). Studies of visual synthesis: Integration of fragments into forms. *Journal of Experimental Psychology: Human Perception and Performance, 4,* 244–263.

Tippett, L. J. (1992). The generation of visual images: A review of neuropsychological research and theory. *Psychological Bulletin, 112,* 415–432.

Tversky, B. (1973). Encoding processes in recognition and recall. *Cognitive Psychology, 5,* 275–287.

Tversky, B. (1989). Parts, partonomies, and objects. *Developmental Psychology, 25,* 983–995.

Tversky, B. (1991). Spatial mental models. In G. H. Bower (Ed.), *The Psychology of Learning and Motivation: Advances in Research and Theory,* Vol. 27 (pp. 109–145).

Tversky, B., & Hemenway, K. (1984). Objects, parts, and categories. *Journal of Experimental Psychology: General, 113,* 169–193.

Weber, R. J., & Brown, S. (1986). Musical imagery. *Music Perception, 3,* 411–426.

Weber, R. J., & Harnish, R. (1974). Visual imagery for words: The Hebb test. *Journal of Experimental Psychology, 102,* 409–414.

Zimler, J., & Keenan, J. M. (1983). Imagery in the congenitally blind: How visual are visual images? *Journal of Experimental Psychology: Learning, Memory, and Cognition, 9,* 269–282.

CHAPTER 3

Images, Models, and Propositional Representations

Philip N. Johnson-Laird

How many sorts of mental representation are there? One answer is: none. Mental representations according to this view are figments in the minds of cognitive psychologists. They do not really exist. Versions of this view—or at least of views suspiciously close to it—have been held by followers of Heidegger, by Behaviorists, by Gibsonians, by advocates of "situated action," and by a further chorus of philosophical skeptics. There are a priori arguments to the contrary— dreams, hallucinations, vivid images, and even figments in the minds of cognitive scientists all suggest that there *are* mental representations, and in some of these cases, ironically, representations that do not correspond to anything in the world.

On a different tack, any attempt to construct computer models of perception seems bound to postulate representations—e.g., the sequence from the gray-level array to three-dimensional models of the world proposed by the late David Marr (1982). These arguments fail to convince resolute defenders of the skeptical position. Like solipsists, they seem impervious to any case to the contrary, theoretical or empirical. This chapter has no more to say about the view that mental representations do not exist, other than to throw down a challenge to its adherents: Explain how people think!

Despite the wide divergence among existing theories of thinking, they all depend on mental representations of one sort or another. At the other end of the logical continuum from the skeptical position is the view that there are infinitely many different sorts of mental representation. Fodor (1975) states that

> there is an indefinite range of cases in between photographs and paragraphs. These intermediate cases are, in effect, images under descriptions; they convey some information discursively and some information pictorially, and they resemble their subjects only in respect of those properties that happen to be pictorial. (p. 190)

Some commentators appear to take this claim to imply an infinite variety of representations (Kaufmann, Wenevold, & Murdock, 1992). But how does one distinguish between one sort of mental representation and another? The difficulty is to draw a line between what is represented and how it is represented. Our concern is not with the *what,* but with the *how*—not with content, but with the format of mental representations. A distinct format implies a distinct form of processing, just as in computer programming a distinct sort of data-structure calls for a distinct sort of procedure. Indeed, as Anderson (1978) argued, a theory of mental representations needs to specify both the form of the representation and the nature of the procedures that construct and manipulate it. If there are infinitely many sorts of representation, then there are infinitely many modes of processing to construct and to manipulate them. The complexity of a device capable of this task seems to go beyond the capacity of any finite device, such as the human brain. If sorts of representation are distinguished by different modes of processing, then Fodor does not appear to be arguing for the existence of infinitely many sorts of representation, but merely for admixtures in varying proportions of pictorial and discursive representations. No one, as far as the author knows, has ever defended an infinite variety of representations; no phenomena support the hypothesis; and parsimony surely counts against it.

We are left with those hypotheses that postulate a finite number of different sorts of mental representation. We will consider three such hypotheses. The first is that only one sort of mental representation exists. By analogy with the machine code of digital computers in which all high-level constructs in a programmer's source code are compiled into strings of binary symbols, so too one can argue that all mental representations are ultimately compiled into the "machine code" of the brain—i.e., nerve impulses and synaptic events. This version of the hypothesis is perhaps irrefutable on the assumption that all mental phenomena finally depend on physical events in the brain.

A more controversial version of the hypothesis has been advanced by several theorists: The only representations are expressions in a mental language—i.e., syntactically structured sequences of symbols (see, e.g., Baylor, 1971; Palmer, 1975; Pylyshyn, 1973, 1984). Images, whether generated by perception or the mind's eye, are thus epiphenomenal, and what underlies them are representations written in the language of the mind. Hence, from a causal or functional level of analysis—higher than the mere machine code of the brain—the mind has according to this hypothesis a unitary system of representations into which all information impinging on the organism is translated.

The second hypothesis is that there are two sorts of mental representations: propositional representations and images. The principal architect of this "dual code" hypothesis is Allan Paivio (1971, 1986), although it can be traced back to earlier authors—for example, Störring (1908). Paivio postulates two separate cognitive systems: one for language and one for nonverbal objects and events. The two systems are functionally independent, but they are partly interconnected. Intons-Peterson (this volume) describes the background to Paivio's pioneering studies. She characterizes research on imagery as deriving from either a linguistic tradition or a spatial tradition. The linguistic tradition is based on the experimental paradigm in which subjects imagine situations that are described verbally (as in Paivio's research). The spatial tradition is based on the paradigm in which subjects manipulate images (as in Shepard & Metzler's, 1971, study of mental rotations). It is important to realize, as we shall see, that the mental-rotation experiments demonstrate the need for more than a dual code.

The third hypothesis is that there is a small finite number of different sorts of representation, including propositional representations, images, and mental models (Johnson-Laird, 1983). The aim of the present chapter is to reexamine this idea in the light of a decade's research. According to the initial account in 1983, visual images are a special case of mental models; they now seem to be distinct sorts of representation calling for distinct sorts of processes, although images often function like models, and the two sorts of representation are more closely related to one another than either is related to propositional representations. Thus, this "triple-code" hypothesis adds mental models to the two sorts of representation postulated by Paivio.

To establish the case for a triple code, the chapter will proceed as follows. It begins with the case for *propositional representations*. It shows that the psychological evidence from studies of deductive reasoning—studies for the most part carried out by the author and his colleagues—refutes theories based solely on propositional representations and formal rules of inference. A better account of the phenomena is given by the theory of *mental models*, although the argument in this part of the chapter does not distinguish between models and images. The model theory does not abandon propositional representations but rather postulates that they are constructed from linguistic expressions and then used to build mental models. They also play a crucial role in testing the validity of deductions.

The next part of the chapter takes up the notion of a mental model, and shows that the theory yields testable predictions about the causes of difficulty in reasoning. It reviews the experimental evidence that corroborates that deductions calling for the construction of more than one model are difficult, that erroneous conclusions arise from a failure to consider all possible models, and that individuals' beliefs can influence the process of reasoning.

The third part of the chapter turns to *visual images,* and the contrast between them and models. Images are representations of the perceptible aspects of a situation from an observer's point of view. Models, as the experimental evidence bears out, are distinct from images. Models contain abstract elements that cannot be visualized, and they correspond, not to a single situation, but to a class of situations or, in some cases, to a set of such classes. Both models and images can be used to reason in certain circumstances, and a study contrasting diagrams with verbal premises suggests that images can lead to more efficient reasoning.

Finally, the chapter draws some theoretical distinctions among images, models, and propositional representations. The result is a justification for the triple-code hypothesis. The three sorts of representation are distinct; they are all used in thinking, and none is epiphenomenal.

PROPOSITIONAL REPRESENTATIONS

In practice, we can establish the existence of two distinct sorts of representation by showing a dissociation between them. That is, we demonstrate empirically that two aspects of performance can be independently manipulated. For example, in one case the representation of the verbatim details of a description is good whereas the representation of the situation described is poor, and in another case the representation of the situation is good whereas the representation of verbatim details is poor. Such a result, which will be reported next, implies the existence of two separate representational systems—one for verbatim detail, and the other for situations. Before we consider this result, however, let us examine the theory of propositional representations.

If the mind has a unitary system of mental representations based on a language of thought, then the following description

The spoon is to the left of the knife

The plate is to the right of the knife

will be encoded in a propositional representation. Individuals presented with the description and asked what follows from it readily infer the following conclusion:

The spoon is on the left of the plate.

The propositional theory explains this ability in terms of a mental logic containing formal rules of inference. Thus, the two premises are encoded in propositional representations of, say, the following predicate-argument form (see, e.g., Fodor, 1975; Kintsch, 1974):

1. (left-of spoon knife)

2. (right-of plate knife)

Indeed, for the rest of this chapter, "propositional representation" will refer to a mental representation that has some sort of predicate-argument structure of an unknown syntax and lexicon, and that captures the explicit information conveyed by verbal assertions and other illocutions. It can also contain quantifiers and variables, and so the logical properties of the spatial terms are captured in meaning postulates, such as:

3. $(\forall x)\ (\forall y)\ ((\text{right-of } x\ y) \leftrightarrow (\text{left-of } y\ x))$

4. $(\forall x)(\forall y)(\forall z)(((\text{left-of } x\ y) \land (\text{left-of } y\ z)) \rightarrow (\text{left-of } x\ z))$

where $\forall$ denotes the universal quantifier "any," $\leftrightarrow$ denotes material equivalence ("if, and only if _ then _"), $\rightarrow$ denotes material implication ("if _ then _"), and $\land$ denotes conjunction ("and"). Again, the important point is not the nature of the mental syntax or lexicon, which are obviously unknown, but the content of these postulates. Thus, (3) asserts:

for any x and y, if, and only if, x is on the right of y then y is on the left of x

and (4) asserts:

for any x, y, and z, if x is on the left of y, and y is on the left of z, then x is on the left of z.

If the inferential system is equipped with these two postulates and formal rules of inference, the conclusion can be derived from the premises. The proof calls for the appropriate instantiations of the two postulates (3) and (4), i.e., we replace the variables by the names of particular objects:

5,6. $((\text{right-of plate knife}) \leftrightarrow (\text{left-of knife plate}))$

7,8,9 $(((\text{left-of spoon knife}) \land (\text{left-of knife plate})) \rightarrow (\text{left-of spoon plate}))$

The next steps use formal rules of inference, including a rule known as *modus ponens* and a rule for conjunctions, to derive the required conclusion. *Modus ponens* stipulates that given premises of the form:

$$p \rightarrow q$$
$$p$$

one can derive the conclusion:

$$q$$

The rest of the derivation proceeds as follows:

10. (left-of knife plate) [*modus ponens* from lines 2 and 6]

11. ((left-of spoon knife) ∧ (left-of knife plate))
[conjunction of lines 1 and 10]

12. (left-of spoon plate) [*modus ponens* from lines 9 and 11]

This expression in the language of thought can be translated back into English:

The spoon is on the left of the plate.

Theories based on propositional representations and formal rules of inference have been defended both in specific accounts of spatial inference (Hagert, 1984; Ohlsson, 1984) and in accounts of deduction more generally (e.g., Braine, 1978; Macnamara, 1986; Rips, 1983; Smith, Langston, & Nisbett, 1992).

Experimental evidence supports the existence of propositional representations but together with another sort of representation. In a series of experiments carried out in collaboration with Kannan Mani, we examined our subjects' ability to recognize spatial descriptions that they had encountered earlier (Mani & Johnson-Laird, 1982). We presented them with the following determinate description, for example:

The spoon is to the left of the knife.

The plate is to the right of the knife.

The fork is in front of the spoon.

The cup is in front of knife.

After they had listened to this description, they had to decide whether it was true or false of a particular diagram, such as:

spoon   knife   plate
fork   cup

that depicted the relevant objects on a tabletop. Thus, the description is true of this particular layout. Half the descriptions were determinate (as this one was), and half were indeterminate in that they were consistent with more than one layout. An indeterminate description can be created by changing one word in the second premise, and leaving the other premises unchanged:

The plate is to the right of the spoon.

This description is consistent with two distinct layouts:

spoon   knife   plate
fork   cup

and:

spoon   plate   knife
fork   cup

The overall set of descriptions was presented to the subjects in different random orders. On half the trials the description was true of the layout in the diagram, and on half the trials it was false of the layout in the diagram. After the subjects had finished classifying the descriptions as true or false of the diagrams, they were given an unexpected recognition task. For each description that they had encountered, they had to rank-order four versions of the description in terms of their resemblance to the actual description. The four versions were:

i. The actual description itself, i.e., the original four sentences.

ii. A version that described the same layout but that had a different meaning. That is, the sentence describing the relation between the spoon and the knife in the original example above was: The spoon is to the left of the knife. It was replaced by a sentence describing instead the relation between the fork and the cup: The fork is to the left of the cup. The resulting description is of the same layout, but the two descriptions are not synonymous.

iii. A foil describing a slightly different spatial layout among the five objects.

iv. Another foil describing another slightly different layout.

Subjects were told to rank-order these descriptions in terms of their resemblance to the actual description, and they carried out the task for all 16 of the original trials in the same order as their original presentation.

We analyzed two independent aspects of the results. The first measure was the percentage of trials on which the actual description and the description consistent with the layout were ranked higher than the two foils. This percentage was reliably higher for the determinate descriptions (88% of trials) than for the indeterminate descriptions (58% of trials). The second measure was the percentage of trials on which the actual description was ranked higher than the one consistent with the layout. In contrast to the previous result, this percentage was reliably higher for the indeterminate descriptions (88% of trials) than for the determinate descriptions (68% of trials).

A plausible interpretation of these results is that subjects attempted to envisage the layout corresponding to a determinate description—they constructed an image or a more abstract model of the situation—whereas they abandoned this attempt with indeterminate descriptions, which are consistent with more than one layout, and instead tried to hold on to a propositional representation of the description. Images or models lead to a relatively good memory for the layout but to a memory for verbatim details that is barely above chance: One cannot reconstruct the original description merely from a knowledge of the layout. Propositional representations lead to a poor memory for the layout but to a memory of sufficient verbatim details for subjects to rank the original descriptions above the descriptions merely consistent with the layout. The cross-over in the results on the two measures is difficult to explain in terms of a single sort of mental representation. It strongly suggests a dissociation between *two* sorts of representation—i.e., a preference for models or images for spatially determinate descriptions, and a preference for propositional representations for spatially indeterminate descriptions.

Denis (1991) reports some results on differences in individuals' ability to form images that corroborate the present account. Subjects in an experiment read spatial descriptions of the various topographical features of an island (see Denis & Denhière, 1990). When the descriptions leaped from one part of the island to another almost haphazardly, the subjects who were better at forming images were much less disrupted in their reading, as shown by their reading times for individual sentences, than were the subjects who were poorer at forming images. A good image presumably allows readers to incorporate the information from each new sentence even if it does not follow a coherent topographical order. De Vega (1991) has obtained comparable results from a study in which readers had to adopt different spatial points of view.

The existence of two sorts of mental representation is also supported by Sag and Hankamer's (1980) analysis of the phenomena of linguistic anaphora. On the one hand, as these authors points out, "surface" anaphora such as the verb-phrase ellipsis in the second sentence in the following example depend on access to a propositional representation:

The psychologists were being teased by the linguists. The biologists were too.

The ellipsed element in this case corresponds to "being teased by the linguists." The need for a record of verbatim details is borne out by the contrasting example:

The linguists were teasing the psychologists. The biologists were too.

In this case, the ellipsed element corresponds to "teasing the psychologists." The elliptical sentence is identical in both examples; the preceding sentences are synonymous, differing only in voice (active versus passive), and yet the elliptical sentences differ in meaning. Evidently the ellipsis is sensitive to the difference between active and passive verb phrases, a relatively superficial syntactic feature. On the other hand, "deep" anaphora such as the pronoun "it" in

I hate it

depend on access to a mental representation of the situation under discussion, which will provide the entity to which the pronoun refers. This argument comes from Sag and Hankamer (1980), but psycholinguistic studies by Garnham and his colleagues have shown that the distinction between surface and deep anaphora is more complicated than envisaged in the linguistic theory (Garnham & Oakhill, 1989). Nevertheless, the moral is clear. There are at least two sorts of mental representation: propositional representations and images-cum-models.

Spatial and Temporal Reasoning

If there are at least two sorts of mental representations, then which of them is used in order to reason? Proponents of propositional representations are bound to suppose that reasoning consists in the manipulation of such representations using formal rules of inference. Once we admit the existence of image- or model-like representations, however, then another possibility is evident. Reasoning could consist in the construction of such representations, the formulation of a conclusion based on them, and the search for other such representations of the premises to test the validity of the conclusion. This idea is at the heart of the model theory of reasoning (Johnson-Laird, 1983; Johnson-Laird & Byrne, 1991). This theory will be described in greater detail in the Mental Models section later in the chapter, when we began to tease apart images and models. For the time being, however, we will contrast theories of reasoning based on propositional representations and formal rules of inference with an alternative theory based on image- or model-like representations.

Ruth Byrne and the author have corroborated the predictions of such an alternative theory in many domains of deduction (Johnson-Laird & Byrne, 1991). One of our initial studies examined spatial reasoning using materials similar to those in the study above of memory for descriptions. Subjects carried out three sorts of spatial inference. The first sort were one-model problems, such as:

The knife is on the right of the plate.

The spoon is on the left of the plate.

The fork is in front of the spoon.

The cup is in front of the knife.

What's the relation between the fork and cup?

Individuals tend to construct symmetric arrangements of the following sort:

spoon   plate   knife
fork   cup

and so they respond:

The fork is on the left of the cup.

There is no model of the premises that refutes this conclusion, and so it follows validly from one model of the premises. In contrast, if individuals reach this conclusion on the basis of a formal derivation, they must first derive the relation between the spoon and the knife in the way that was illustrated in the previous section, and then use two-dimensional postulates to derive the relation between the fork and the cup (see Hagert, 1984; and Ohlsson, 1984; for such formal rule systems for spatial inference).

The second sort of problems yield multiple models because of a spatial indeterminacy, but they nevertheless support a valid response. They were constructed by changing one word in the second premise:

The knife is on the right of the plate.
The spoon is on the left of the knife.
The fork is in front of the spoon.
The cup is in front of the knife.
What's the relation between the fork and cup?

The description is consistent with two distinct layouts:

spoon   plate   knife
fork   cup

and:

plate   spoon   knife
          fork   cup

But both layouts support the conclusion:

The fork is on the left of the cup.

The model theory predicts that this problem should be harder than the previous one, because reasoners have to construct more than one model. In contrast, theories based on formal rules and propositional representations predict that this problem should be easier than the previous one, because there is no need to infer the relation between the spoon and the knife—it is directly asserted by the second premise.

The third sort of problem was similar, but it did not yield any valid relation between the two items in the question: e.g.,

The knife is on the right of the plate.

The spoon is on the left of the knife.

The fork is in front of the spoon.

The cup is in front of the plate.

What's the relation between the fork and cup?

Subjects in the experiment acted as their own controls and carried out the task with problems of all three sorts presented in a random order. They drew reliably more correct conclusions to the one-model problems (70%) than to the multiple-model problems with valid answers (46%). Their correct conclusions were also reliably faster to the one-model problems (a mean of 3.1 seconds) than to the multiple-model problems with valid answers (3.6 seconds). It might be argued that the multiple-model problems are harder because they contain an irrelevant premise that plays no part in the inference, but, as a control, the one-model problems also contained cases in which there was an irrelevant premise; e.g.,

The knife is on the right of the plate.

The spoon is on the left of the plate.

The fork is in front of the spoon.

The cup is in front of the plate.

What's the relation between the fork and cup?

This description yields the following sort of model:

spoon   plate   knife

fork   cup

and the first premise is irrelevant to the deduction. Such problems, however, are just as easy as the one-model problems described earlier.

The model theory and the rule theories make opposite predictions about these spatial inferences; the results corroborate the model theory and run counter to the rule theories. Critics argue, however, that human reasoners may rely on visual images only because the content of the problems concerns easily visualizable objects in spatial relations. Recently, Walter Schaeken and the author have obtained entirely similar results in an unpublished series of experiments on temporal reasoning. In one of our studies, for example, subjects were given problems concerning the times of various cartoons on television. The problems were made up of such assertions as:

> The cartoon "The Strong Mouse" is shown before the cartoon "The Wicked Witch."
>
> The cartoon "The Wicked Witch" is shown while the cartoon "The Spider Woman" is showing.

We constructed one-model problems corresponding to the following temporal relations:

A   B   C
D   E

where the horizontal relations correspond to "before" and "after," and the vertical relations correspond to "while." The subjects' task was to state the relation between D and E, and so the task was isomorphic to the previous spatial task. Another sort of one-model problem had the structure:

A   B   C
D   E

The subjects also received multiple-model problems with valid answers, and, as a control, multiple-model problems with no valid answers. The results showed that one-model problems (95% correct responses) were reliably easier than the multiple-model problems (78% correct responses). Other experiments using simple everyday materials, such as "John takes a shower before he drinks his coffee," produced similar results. Hence, the model theory extends to reasoning about temporal relations. It is possible that the subjects represent these premises using a spatial image; it is also possible that they represent them directly in time—i.e., to represent "A before B" they imagine event A and *then* they imagine event B. They are thus using time to represent time (see Johnson-Laird, 1983, p. 10). This idea is corroborated by Andre Vierdendonck, who reports that in an unpublished study subjects were faster to respond to the first sort of one-model problem, where the two relevant events are closer together in time, than to respond to the second sort of one-model problem where the two events are further apart in time. Walter Schaeken and the author, however, have failed so far to replicate this result when they measured subjects latencies, although they did confirm that subjects make correct responses faster to one-model problems than to multiple-model problems.

MENTAL MODELS

The first part of the chapter established that logically untrained individuals appear to reason by manipulating models or images rather than by applying formal rules of inference to propositional representations. The goal of this part of the chapter is to outline the theory of mental models and to show that models can be used to make deductions. Once both their nature and their status have been clarified, the way is clear to establish the distinction between models and images.

The structure of models differs in principle from the structure of propositional representations, which as we have seen have a syntactic structure based on the relation between a predicate and its arguments. Hence, the structure of a propositional representation of an assertion, such as

The knife is on the right of the plate

is quite remote from that of a situation in which there is a knife on the right of the plate. In contrast, a mental model represents individuals by mental tokens; it represents the properties of individuals by the properties of these tokens, and it represents the relations among individuals by the relations among these tokens. The simplest sort of model has an analogical structure that corresponds to the structure of the situation that it represents. Like a diagram, the parts of the model correspond to the parts of what it represents. And like diagrams, these simple models are isomorphic, or at least homomorphic, to what they represent (Johnson-Laird, 1983). Images, too, have these properties, but, as we shall see, models and images differ from one another, and the difference is most marked in the case of more complex models.

The model theory of deduction postulates that reasoners construct a model, or set of models, based on the meaning of premises or the perception of the world and any relevant general knowledge. They formulate a conclusion by describing a relation in the models that was not explicitly asserted by any single premise. Finally, they attempt to check that there are no alternative models that are true to their premises but that refute their conclusion. If there are none, then their conclusion is valid.

Deductions that depend on connectives, such as "if," "or," and "and," call for the construction of sets of models in which each model represents a different possibility (see Johnson-Laird & Byrne, 1991). Deductions that depend on quantifiers, such as "all," "some," and "none," call for the construction of models containing sets of tokens in which each token represents an individual (see Johnson-Laird, 1983). In both cases, however, the theory makes three principal predictions.

The first prediction is that the greater the number of models that have to be constructed to make a deduction, the harder the task should be. More models mean more work, and so the deduction should take longer and be more prone to error.

The second prediction is that erroneous conclusions should be consistent with the premises rather than inconsistent with them. The prediction reflects the following consideration. Valid conclusions are those that are necessarily true given the truth of the premises and so they hold in all possible models of the premises. Reasoners may overlook some of the models of the premises with the result that they draw a conclusion that holds in only some of the models of the premises. Such conclusions will be possibly true given the premises, that is, they will be consistent with the premises rather than following validly from them. Unlike the first prediction, this one does not require a detailed theory of the particular models of a set of premises—it can be checked merely by examining the premises and the conclusion, and determining whether they are consistent or inconsistent with one another.

The third prediction is that general knowledge can influence the mental process of deduction. When reasoners reach a conclusion that conforms to their knowledge, they will tend to abandon their search for alternative models; but, when they reach a conclusion that conflicts with their knowledge, they will tend to search assiduously for alternative models that might refute the conclusion. Thus, the model theory accounts for "inferential satisficing," i.e., the tendency to overlook the existence of models refuting plausible conclusions.

None of the three predictions can be made by existing theories based on propositional representations and formal rules of inference. Such theories have no elements corresponding to models, and no machinery for predicting the form of errors. Rules of inference do not allow errors to be derived, and so rule theories can postulate only that they will occur on a random basis as a result of the misapplication of rules. Once the logical form of a premise has been established, the process of inference is purely formal and so beliefs and knowledge can have no effect upon it.

Ruth Byrne and the author have corroborated the three predictions in the main domains of deduction (Johnson-Laird & Byrne, 1991). The next section describes some typical results with sentential connectives, which presage a study of the effects of diagrams on reasoning, and the subsequent section outlines the results with quantifiers, which prepare the way for the studies that drive a wedge between models and images.

Deduction with Connectives: A Study of "Double Disjunctions"

To test the predictions about number of models and errors, we carried out an experiment based on so-called double disjunctions (Johnson-Laird, Byrne, &

Schaeken, 1992). The subjects had to state what, if anything, follows from two disjunctive premises, such as

Julia is in Atlanta or Raphael is in Tacoma, but not both.

Julia is in Atlanta or Paul is in Philadelphia, but not both.

Each of these exclusive disjunctions calls for two models, but when the possibilities are multiplied out, they yield only two models:

[a]

[t]   [p]

where each line represents a separate model, a denotes Julia in Atlanta, t denotes Raphael in Tacoma, and p denotes Paul in Philadelphia. It follows that:

Julia is in Atlanta, or Raphael is in Tacoma and Paul is in Philadelphia.

The task should be harder when the disjunctions are inclusive:

Julia is in Atlanta or Raphael is in Tacoma, or both.

Julia is in Atlanta or Paul is in Philadelphia, or both.

Each premise now calls for three models, and the resulting combinations yield five models:

[a]   [t]   [p]
[a]   [t]
[a]   [p]
[a]
      [t]   [p]

These models yield the conclusion:

Julia is in Atlanta, or Raphael is in Tacoma and Paul is in Philadelphia.

We also manipulated whether the proposition about the same individual in the two premises located that individual in the same place (as above) or in different places; for example:

Julia is in Atlanta or Raphael is in Tacoma, or both.

Julia is in Seattle or Paul is in Philadelphia, or both.

An additional step is needed to determine that one possibility rules out another, and so these "negative" problems should be harder than the "affirmative" problems. In the case of the exclusive disjunctions, there are also three resulting models with a "negative" problem; in the case of the inclusive disjunctions, there remain five models of the premises. Results of the experiment confirmed the predictions. The percentages of valid conclusions to the four sorts of deduction were as follows:

Exclusive affirmative: 21%

Exclusive negative: 8%

Inclusive affirmative: 6%

Inclusive negative: 2%

The most striking result, however, was that the modal errors for all four sorts of problem were conclusions consistent with just one model of the premises. There were few errors inconsistent with the premises, and none whatsoever for the inclusive disjunctions.

Syllogistic Reasoning

Syllogisms are deductions based on two premises that each contain a single quantifier; for example:

Some of the athletes are boxers.

All the boxers are chefs.

∴   Some of the athletes are chefs.

If we ignore the content of the premises, there are 64 logically distinct varieties of syllogistic premises, because each premise can be in one of four so-called moods:

All X are Y

Some X are Y

No X are Y

Some X are not Y

and the terms in the premises can be arranged in one of four so-called figures:

A–B   B–A   A–B   B–A

B–C   C–B   C–B   B–C

Hence, the example above is in the first of these figures, where A = athletes, B = boxers, and C = chefs. The reader will note that in our experiments we tend to use syllogistic premises with the definite article—e.g., "all the athletes are boxers" rather than "all athletes are boxers"—in order to insulate the content from everyday beliefs and to ensure, along with our instructions, that there is no doubt about the existence of members of each set in the domain of discourse.

Syllogisms differ strikingly in their difficulty. Some are so easy that even 7-year-olds can draw their own correct conclusions to them reliably better than chance (see Bara, Bucciarelli, & Johnson-Laird, 1995). Piaget and his colleagues argued that deduction is beyond the competence of children until they attain the stage of "formal operations" (see, e.g., Inhelder and Piaget, 1958). The Bara et al. cross-sectional study observed a steady growth in syllogistic ability with age. There was no striking breakthrough at any age, and some syllogisms are so difficult that hardly any logically untrained adults can perform at a better than chance level with them (see Johnson-Laird & Bara, 1984). If the mental model theory is correct, then obviously there is no such thing as the stage of "formal operations" and the Piagetian account of the development of reasoning collapses.

One cause of difficulty in syllogistic reasoning is indeed number of models. According to the model theory, the premises above have one model:

athlete   [boxer]   chef

athlete   [boxer]   chef

            [boxer]   chef

athlete

            . . .

Each line in this diagram represents a separate individual—the number of individuals is arbitrary, though small. Hence, the first line represents an individual who is an athlete, a boxer, and a chef. The three dots allow for other sorts of individuals, who initially are not represented with any explicit properties. The square brackets indicate that the set of boxers has been exhaustively represented, and so, if the implicit individuals are rendered explicit, boxers cannot be included among them. (Strictly speaking, exhaustion is a relative notion: Boxers are exhaustively represented in relation to chefs.) The model yields the following conclusion:

Some of the athletes are chefs

and no alternative model of the premises can refute this conclusion, which is accordingly valid.

In contrast, the following premises yield a difficult problem:

None of the authors is a baker.

All the bakers are clowns.

According to the theory, these premises yield the initial model:

[author]	¬baker	
[author]	¬baker	
	[baker]	clown
	[baker]	clown

. . .

where "¬" represents negation—i.e., the first individual in the model is an author but *not* a baker. This model supports the conclusion:

None of the authors is a clown

or its converse:

None of the clowns is an author.

Individuals often draw these conclusions, although they are incorrect: Johnson-Laird and Bara report that about 90 percent of their subjects drew these conclusions. The conclusions can be refuted by constructing an alternative model of the premises:

[author]	¬baker	clown
[author]	¬baker	clown
	[baker]	clown
	[baker]	clown

. . .

Subjects who considered the first of the two conclusions above are now likely to conclude in the light of this second model:

There is no valid conclusion (5%)

because in this second model all the authors are clowns, whereas none of them was a clown in the first model. If any subjects considered the second of the two conclusions above, they should now conclude:

Some of the clowns are not authors.

In fact, not a single subject reached this valid conclusion in the experiment.

The example illustrates another factor affecting difficulty, the so-called figural effect, which was first discovered in syllogistic reasoning experiments when subjects were allowed to draw their own conclusions in their own words (Johnson-

Laird, 1975). In general, subjects prefer to draw conclusions in which the two end terms occur in the same order as they are used in constructing models. Hence, the present problem, which is in the figure

A–B

B–C

predisposes subjects toward conclusions of the form

A–C

The correct conclusion, however, requires the end terms to be stated in the opposite order, and this bias contributes to the difficulty of the syllogism. The cause of the figural effect is a matter of controversy. The phenomena associated with figure, which include more than just the response bias described here, probably arise from the order in which information enters working memory. Wetherick and Gilhooly (1990), however, have argued that it is a pragmatic or rhetorical phenomenon: Reasoners prefer to maintain an end term occurring as the subject of a premise as the subject of the conclusion. One finding that counts in favor of the working-memory hypothesis and against a grammatical account is that, as Victoria Shaw and the author have shown in an unpublished study, the following types of premises—

All the authors and all the bakers are in the same place

All the bakers and all the clowns are in the same place

—still create a figural bias toward conclusions of the form

All the authors and all the clowns are in the same place

or:

All the authors are in the same place as all the clowns.

Because both end terms occur in the subject of a premise, the grammatical theory makes no prediction about a response bias. But, because they occur in the order author–clown, the working-memory hypothesis predicts the observed bias.

In general, one-model syllogisms are reliably easier than multiple-model syllogisms, and erroneous conclusions are typically those supported by one model of a multiple-model syllogism. These errors also happen to be in the same mood as one of the premises—a fact that probably renders the "atmosphere hypothesis" superfluous. According to this long-standing hypothesis, logically untrained individuals do not reason properly but tend to generate a conclusion that matches the mood of a premise (see, e.g., Woodworth & Sells, 1935). As we will see later, there is evidence against the hypothesis, and its apparent effects are explained by the failure to consider all the models of premises.

Syllogisms also provided a test of the model theory's prediction that beliefs can bias the process of reasoning. Oakhill, Johnson-Laird, and Garnham (e.g., 1989) carried out several experiments to examine this prediction. One phenomenon that they observed can be described by contrasting two illustrative examples. Subjects were asked to state in their own words what follows from the premises:

All the Frenchmen are gourmets.

Some of the gourmets are wine drinkers.

The majority of subjects (72%) drew the conclusion:

Some of the Frenchmen are wine drinkers

which is invalid, but highly believable as shown by the ratings of an independent panel of judges. However, given the premises

All the Frenchmen are gourmets

Some of the gourmets are Italians

only a small minority of subjects (8%) draw the equivalent conclusion:

All the Frenchmen are Italians

which is invalid, but highly unbelievable, as the judges' ratings showed. Polk and Newell (1992) have proposed an alternative model-based theory of syllogistic reasoning, but they downplay the role of searching for alternative models. The present results suggest that reasoners do search for alternative models, and that they are particularly motivated to do so if their initial model of the premises yields an unbelievable conclusion.

Model-Based Reasoning Requires
Propositional Representations

The evidence reviewed in this part of the chapter has corroborated the theory of mental models. The theory postulates that propositional representations are constructed on the basis of a compositional semantics called into play as sentences are parsed—that is, the meanings of sentences are composed from the meanings of their parts according to the syntactic relations among them. These representations are then the input to a process that constructs models from them. The formulation of conclusions is based on the models, and their validity is tested by searching for alternative models of the premises that refute the conclusions (see Johnson-Laird & Byrne, 1991, Chap. 9, for a description of computer programs implementing the compositional semantics and the model-building procedures). Human reasoners are often none too successful in searching for alternative models, as is shown by their erroneous conclusions. These errors are almost always based on just some of the possible models of the premises—typically just a single model. For this reason, most erroneous conclusions are consistent with the premises rather than inconsistent with them; they are *possibly* true given the premises rather than *necessarily* true.

The search for alternative models depends on access to the propositional representations of the premises. The point is crucial to the theory, because models do not enable the premises from which they derive to be uniquely reconstructed. As an illustrative example, consider the spatial model:

|○|Δ|*|

where the verticals separate different places. The model supports the putative conclusion:

The triangle is on the left of the star.

To test the validity of the conclusion, it is necessary to show that no other model of the premises refutes it. The following model refutes the conclusion:

|○|*|Δ|

but is it a model of the premises? There is no way of telling from the model alone. If the premises were

The circle is on the left of the triangle

The star is on the right of the circle

then the new model is indeed a model of the premises, and it falsifies the conclusion. But if the premises were

The circle is on the left of the triangle

The star is on the right of the triangle

then the new model is not a model of the premises, and it is irrelevant to the test of the conclusion. Because premises cannot be uniquely reconstructed from models, it follows that deductions need an independent record of the premises, and such a record is provided by their propositional representations. This requirement is a further argument in favor of both propositional representations and mental models. The next task is to drive a wedge between images and models.

IMAGES

Some subjects carrying out syllogistic reasoning report that they rely on images, but many do not—a finding that goes back to one of the earliest psychological studies of syllogisms (Störring, 1908). If reasoners do rely on images, then the easier it is to visualize the situation described by the premises, the better their reasoning should be. We turn now to an experimental test of this prediction.

Imageability and Multiply-Quantified Reasoning

Various theorists have suggested that syllogistic reasoning depends on mental representations akin either to Euler circles (Erickson, 1974; Guyote & Sternberg, 1981; Stenning & Oberlander, 1992) or else to Venn diagrams (Newell, 1980). Figure 3.1 shows the two Euler circle diagrams required in order to represent a premise of the form: All A are B. Figure 3.2 shows the single Venn diagram

Figure 3.1. The two Euler circle diagrams required to represent an assertion of the form: All A are B. The diagram on the left depicts the case where A is properly included in B—i.e., there are B's that are not A's, and the diagram on the right depicts the case where the two sets are co-extensive—that is, All B are A, too.

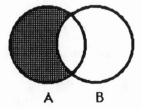

Figure 3.2. The Venn diagram representing an assertion of the form: All A are B. The circle on the left depicts the set A and the circle on the right depicts the set B. The region that is shaded out contains no members—i.e., there are no A that are not B.

required to represent this premise. One reason to doubt whether logically un-trained individuals spontaneously represent premises in the form of Euler circles or Venn diagrams is that they do not report using such diagrams. Another reason is that these diagrammatic systems do not generalize to deductions based on multiply-quantified relations; for example:

Some of the Bury letters are in the same place as every Avon letter.

We might try to represent this assertion by a circle, *A*, denoting the Avon letters that is properly inscribed within a circle, *B*, denoting the Bury letters (see the left-hand side of Figure 3.1). Does each point within the *A* circle represent a different member of the set of Avon letters, and does each point within the *B* circle represent a different member of the set of Bury letters? If so, it appears that the diagram represents the case where each Avon letter is in the same place as exactly one Bury letter, but this interpretation restricts "some of the Bury letters" to exactly one Bury letter. Now consider an alternative example:

Every Avon letter is in the same place as some Bury letters.

To represent this assertion, circle *A* for Avon letters must be properly included within circle *B* for Bury letters, but we have already used this diagram to represent the previous assertion. Hence, it is impossible to use traditional Euler circles to distinguish between the two examples. In contrast, they are easily distinguished by mental models in which individual tokens stand for individuals. The first assertion is represented by the following sort of model:

| bury bury [avon] [avon] [avon] |

in which the vertical lines demarcate a separate place, and the Avon letters are exhaustively represented to show that they comprise the entire set in the situation. The second assertion is represented by the following sort of model:

| [avon] bury bury | [avon] [avon] bury bury |

A series of experiments carried out in collaboration with Ruth Byrne and Patrizia Tabossi have shown that one-model problems based on multiply-quantified premises were reliably easier than multiply-model problems with valid conclusions (Johnson-Laird, Byrne, & Tabossi, 1989). For example, the following premises:

None of the Avon letters is in the same place as any of the Bury letters.

All of the Bury letters are in the same place as all of the Caton letters.

yield the model:

| [avon] [avon] [avon] | [bury] [bury] [caton] [caton] |

This model supports the conclusion:

None of the Avon letters is in the same place as any of the Caton letters

which was drawn by 67 percent of our subjects. No model of the premises refutes this conclusion, and so it is valid. When the second premise is changed to
include an existential quantifier:

None of the Avon letters is in the same place as any of the Bury letters.

All of the Bury letters are in the same place as some of the Caton letters.

the premises yield the following model:

| [avon] [avon] [avon] | [bury] [bury] caton caton |

This model supports the conclusion:

None of the Avon letters is in the same place as any of the Caton letters

which was drawn by 22 percent of our subjects. The conclusion is invalid, however, because it is refuted by the following model:

| [avon] [avon] [avon] caton | [bury] [bury] caton caton |

The additional token representing a Caton letter can be added to the model because Caton letters are not exhaustively represented. Some subjects (13%) appear
to construct only this model, or to forget the first model, because they draw the
otherwise inexplicable conclusion:

Some of the Caton letters are in the same place as all the Avon letters.

Among these subjects, some sensibly qualify their conclusion to make clear that
it is only a possibility:

Some of the Caton letters *may* be in the same place as all the Avon letters.

As the model theory predicts, such modal conclusions occur significantly more
often with multiple-model problems (20%) than with one-model problems (2%).
The correct valid conclusion that holds for both of the models above is:

None of the Avon letters is in the same place as *some* of the Caton letters.

or equivalently:

Some of the Caton letters are not in the same place as any of the Avon letters.

Such conclusions were drawn by only 19 percent of subjects.

If subjects are reasoning by constructing visual images of the situations described by the premises, then their performance should be affected by the ease of visualizing these situations. We therefore carried out a further experiment in which we manipulated the imageability of the situations described by the premises. We contrasted three different relations, which an independent panel of judges rated for imageability:

equal in height to

in the same place as

related to (in the sense of kinship)

The ratings showed a reliable decline in the imageability of the premises over these three relations. The experiment confirmed the predictions of the model theory, but imageability had no discernible effect on performance. This failure, coupled with similar reports in the literature (Newstead, Manktelow, & Evans, 1982; Richardson, 1987), suggests that reasoning is perfectly feasible without having to construct images. And this conclusion is hardly surprising given that so many concepts in daily life transcend what is perceptible—e.g., ownership, justice, truth (see Miller & Johnson-Laird, 1976, for the impossibility of reducing all concepts to perceptible predicates). Yet null results are hardly decisive, and so the next section considers a different line of research that helps to distinguish between models and images.

The Case for Abstract Elements in Mental Models

Inder (1987) has argued that individuals reason on the basis of models, but that these models correspond to the physical and perceptible aspects of situations. If he is right, then all reasoning could be based on images, and there would be no need to postulate models as a distinct sort of mental representation. The results reported in the previous section suggest that reasoning does not depend on images, but to examine the issue further Ruth Byrne and the author carried out a series of experiments on the quantifier "only" (Johnson-Laird & Byrne, 1989). The experiments showed that models can represent negation, which is an abstract relation, and they hinged on the contrast between "all" and "only." The assertion

All the guests are ticketholders

is affirmative, whereas the assertion

Only the ticketholders are guests

has a negative component (see also Keenan's, 1971, linguistic analysis): There are ticketholders who are guests but those who are not ticketholders are not guests. The model theory accordingly postulates the following initial model for the assertion based on "all":

[g]   t

[g]   t

. . .

where "g" denotes a guest and "t" denotes a ticketholder. In contrast, the assertion based on "only" calls for a more complicated initial model containing both affirmative and negative elements:

  t   [g]

  t   [g]

[¬t]   ¬g

[¬t]   ¬g

. . .

Assertions of the form "All the A are B" and "Only the B are A" have the same truth conditions, but logically untrained individuals are unlikely to realize this fact—certainly our subjects did not recognize the identity—because of the difference between the initial models of the two sorts of assertion. We can demonstrate the identity by considering how the initial model of the "all" assertion can be fleshed out. Because guests are exhaustively represented in the initial model, any individual who is not a ticketholder cannot be a guest:

[g]   t

[g]   t

¬g   [¬t]

¬g   [¬t]

. . .

The only difference between this model and the initial model of the "only" assertion is the order of the terms.

The initial model for "all" assertions is simpler than the initial model for "only" assertions, and so the model theory predicts that in general it should be easier to reason with "all" than with "only." Our first experiment corroborated this prediction. Syllogisms with two "all" premises yielded more correct conclusions (46%) than did logically equivalent syllogisms with "only" premises (26%); and correct responses to the "all" premises (6.5 seconds) were also reliably faster than those to "only" premises (8.0 seconds).

Our second experiment examined all 64 possible syllogistic premises, substituting "only" for "all," and confirmed that one-model problems (55% correct) were reliably easier than multiple-model problems with valid conclusions (15% correct). This experiment also revealed a phenomenon that is devastating to the long-standing "atmosphere" hypothesis. According to this hypothesis, which we described in the section on syllogisms, reasoners are biased toward conclusions that match the mood of a premise—i.e., that have the same quantifier and affirmative (or negative) predicate. The hypothesis was originally proposed as an explanation of error (Begg & Denny, 1969; M. Levine, personal communication; Wetherick & Gilhooly, 1990; Woodworth & Sells, 1935). It has also been proposed as a mechanism for "reasoning" (Revlis, 1975), and as a procedure for generating initial conclusions, which are validated by model-based procedures (Madruga, 1984; Polk & Newell, 1988). What counts against all variants of the atmosphere hypothesis is the singular reluctance of subjects to draw conclusions containing "only." When both premises contained the quantifier, only 16 percent of conclusions were based on it, whereas 45 percent of conclusions contained "all." When only one premise contained "only," a mere 2 percent of conclusions contained it. Although we did not predict this phenomenon, the reason for it is obvious in the light of our analysis—"only" has a more complex semantics than "all."

The theory postulates that models contain elements representing negation. Negation, however, is an abstract notion that cannot be visualized. Individuals might have an image, say, of a large cross superimposed on the image of the relevant situation, but, as Wittgenstein (1953) pointed out, the image itself does not do the work of negation. It depends on the procedures for interpreting the image—that is, for mapping a negative sentence into the image, and for mapping the image back into a negative sentence. Most people, however, do not report using such images as a regular basis for understanding negative sentences. We carried out an experiment to test whether abstract elements for negation occur in mental models. The experiment contrasted two sorts of deduction, *modus ponens* and *modus tollens,* and two sorts of premises, "all" premises and "only" premises. *Modus ponens* with an "all" premise should be easy:

All the guests are ticketholders.

Lisa is a guest.

What follows?

The first premise yields the initial model:

[g]   t
[g]   t
. . .

where "g" denotes a guest, and "t" denotes a ticketholder. The second premise adds the information:

L   [g]   t
     [g]   t
. . .

where "L" denotes Lisa. The conclusion follows at once:

Lisa is a ticketholder.

Modus tollens with the following premises should be more difficult:

All the guests are ticketholders.
Lisa is not a ticketholder.

The first premise yields the same model as before, but the result of adding the information from the second premise is

[g]   t
[g]   t
       ¬t   L
. . .

and nothing seems to follow. In fact, a conclusion can be deduced, but it is necessary first to flesh out the initial model of the "all" premise more explicitly. Because guests are exhaustively represented in the initial model, the model can be fleshed out only by adding individuals who are *not* guests:

   g   t
   g   t
  ¬g   t
  ¬g   ¬t

Now, when the information from the second premise is added to the model, an informative conclusion can be drawn:

   g   t
   g   t

$\neg$g   t

$\neg$g $\neg$t   L

The model supports the conclusion:

Lisa is not a guest.

In summary, *modus ponens* should be easier than *modus tollens* when both are based on an "all" premise. The difference should disappear, however, when both inferences are based on "only" premises. An "only" premise, such as

Only the ticketholders are guests

has the following initial model (see above):

   t   [g]

   t   [g]

[$\neg$t] $\neg$g

[$\neg$t] $\neg$g

 .   .   .

A conclusion can be drawn at once from the *modus ponens* premise

  ∴   Lisa is a guest.

Similarly, a conclusion can be drawn at once from the *modus tollens* premise

  ∴   Lisa is not a ticketholder

without the need to flesh out the initial model. Hence, the model theory predicts an interaction: The difference between *modus ponens* and *modus tollens* should be greater for "all" premises than for "only" premises.

Our experiment examined all four sorts of deduction. We presented the problems in a random order and asked our subjects what, if anything, followed from the premises. The percentages of correct conclusions were as follows:

"All" premises.   *Modus ponens:*   96% correct.

                     Modus tollens: 73% correct.

"Only" premises.   *Modus ponens:*   90% correct.

                     Modus tollens: 86% correct.

The interaction was reliable, and there was a significant difference between *modus ponens* and *modus tollens* with "all" premises, but no such difference between them with "only" premises. The results support the model theory and lend credence to its assumption that the representations used in deduction can contain elements encoding negation.

Earlier we encountered the idea that a simple model, like an image, is isomorphic or homomorphic to what it represents. A model containing a negation, however, represents an infinite class of possible situations (see Barwise, 1993; Inder, 1987). The advantage of such models is that only a finite number need to be explored to validate deductions. Models of quantified assertions are still more abstract. Thus, the premises

Some of the athletes are boxers

All the boxers are chefs

have the initial model:

athlete	[boxer]	chef
athlete	[boxer]	chef
	[boxer]	chef
athlete		

. . .

where boxers are exhaustively represented in relation to chefs. This model is consistent with 32 distinct classes of situation. They all contain individuals with the three properties:

athlete   boxer   chef

When the model is fleshed out explicitly, it may or may not contain each of five other sorts of individual ($2^5 = 32$):

athlete   ¬boxer   chef

and:

athlete   ¬boxer   ¬chef

and:

¬athlete   boxer   chef

and:

¬athlete   ¬boxer   chef

and:

¬athlete   ¬boxer   ¬chef

The initial model represents these possibilities implicitly. They emerge only as options in fleshing out the model. If the possibilities were not condensed into a single initial model as the theory postulates, then the theory's predictions would not have been corroborated by the experimental data: The syllogism is the easiest one of all. The most general theoretical formulation is accordingly: *A mental model represents a finite set of alternative classes of situation, where each class has a potentially infinite number of members.* Such representations cannot be visualized; they cannot be images. It does not follow that individuals never use images in reasoning, and indeed their performance might improve if they were able to visualize the alternative situations described by the premises. This possibility is one that we will explore next.

Diagrams as an Aid to Reasoning

Reasoning becomes difficult when the number of alternative possibilities increases disjunctively. A suggestion that is often made is that if individuals are reasoning by constructing models, then an external model or diagram ought to improve performance. Malcolm Bauer and the author investigated this prediction by comparing deductions based on verbal premises with deductions based on diagrams. Larkin and Simon (1987) have argued that diagrams can improve the ability to find information and to recognize it, but they are doubtful about the effect of diagrams on reasoning—a doubt that arises from their conception of reasoning as the triggering of relevant rules in a production system. Barwise and Etchemendy (1992) suggest that diagrams are excellent for presenting conjunctive information, but a poor way for presenting disjunctive alternatives. Their pedagogical program for logic, *Hyperproof,* reflects these principles: Conjunctions are represented by diagrams, whereas disjunctions are represented by sentences. If the model theory is correct, however, then logically naive individuals should have difficulty in keeping track of disjunctive alternatives. Hence, diagrams that help them to do so should be a useful aid to reasoning.

We carried out two experiments to test this prediction (Bauer & Johnson-Laird, 1993). Our first experiment used diagrams in which disjunctions were represented by combining their constituents using an arbitrary sign: Squares stood for inclusive disjunctions, and squares containing crosses stood for exclusive disjunctions. These diagrams did not help subjects to reason. Our second experiment used diagrams designed by analogy with circuits of electrical switches. Figure 3.3 shows the diagram corresponding to the following verbal premises:

Julia is in Atlanta or Raphael is in Tacoma, or both.

Julia is in Seattle or Paul is in Philadelphia, or both.

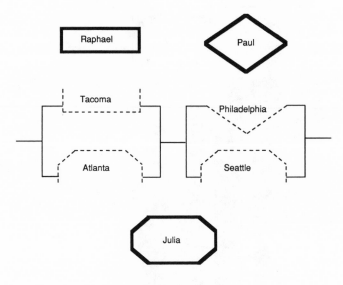

The event is occurring.
What follows?

Figure 3.3.   The diagram representing a double disjunctive problem (negative inclusive) about people and places.

Subjects were told how to interpret the diagrams, which were presented without any verbal premises. They were instructed that for a certain event to occur a path from one side of the diagram to the other had to be completed by moving appropriate pieces (corresponding to people) into places (corresponding to cities). We tested four independent groups of subjects: a pair of verbal groups and a pair of diagram groups, and in each pair, one group had problems based on people and places and the other group had problems based on electrical switches. All the groups carried out four disjunctive problems based on the combination of exclusive or inclusive disjunctions with "affirmative" or "negative" premises (as in the study reported earlier).

The percentages of correct conclusions are shown in Figure 3.4, where we have collapsed the data for the two sorts of content—people-and-places and electrical circuits—because this variable had no reliable effect on performance. As Figure 3.4 shows, there was a large and robust effect of the format of the problems. Overall, 78 percent of the conclusions in the diagram groups were correct in comparison to only 46 percent correct conclusions in the verbal groups. The results also corroborated the model theory's other predictions: Exclusive disjunctions were easier than inclusive disjunctions, and affirmative problems were easier than negative problems. The latencies of the subjects' conclusions also reli-

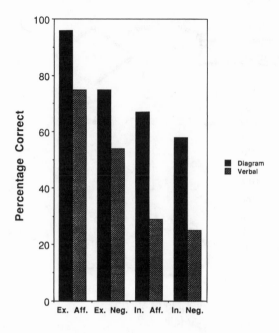

Form of Disjunction

Figure 3.4. The percentages of correct conclusions in the second diagram experiment. *Ex* denotes exclusive disjunction, *In* denotes inclusive disjunction, *Aff* denotes an affirmative problem, and *Neg* denotes a negative problem.

ably corroborated these predictions, and bore out the effect of format: Conclusions in the diagram groups had a mean latency of 99 seconds, whereas the conclusions in the verbal groups had a mean latency of 135 seconds. The most frequent errors were conclusions consistent with the premises rather than inconsistent with them.

These results show that certain sorts of diagrams can help individuals to reason. They improve both the speed and the accuracy of deductive performance. Subjects evidently attempt to construct models of all the different situations compatible with the disjunctive premises. In the case of verbal premises, this task calls for the recovery of propositional representations that are used to construct models of the premises. The process is taxing on the capacity of working memory, and it is all too easy to lose track of which particular situations have been represented by models.

In the case of the diagrammatic problems, the subjects form a visual representation of the diagram, and in their mind's eye they can imagine moving the pieces representing individuals into, or out of, the differently shaped slots representing cities. These mental operations are visual transformations of images, but the images have a symbolic function: Each position corresponds to propositions about people in places.

The diagrams of electrical switches, however, are isomorphic to actual switch configurations. Bypassing the construction of propositional representations appears to reduce the load on working memory, and the presence of the diagram throughout a trial may reduce the load still further. As a result, the subjects are much less likely to overlook possible configurations, and so they tend to draw more accurate conclusions. Imagery is in no way epiphenomenal in this experiment (*pace* Pylyshyn, 1973): Subjects manipulate their images of the diagrams in order to reach their conclusions. If the diagrams were translated into an underlying propositional representation, there would be no way to explain the improved performance with them—the verbal premises would presumably be translated into similar, or even simpler, propositional representations.

CONCLUSIONS

This chapter has argued for the existence of three sorts of mental representation. It first distinguished propositional representations, which encode the verbatim information in verbal discourse. It then showed that human reasoning depends on mental models, which are constructed from these propositional representations. Reasoners formulate conclusions based on models, and search—often inadequately—for alternative models of the propositional representations to refute the conclusions. The model theory was vindicated by the success of its predictions: More models mean more work; erroneous conclusions are consistent rather than inconsistent with premises; and general knowledge can influence the search process, leading subjects to search more, or less, assiduously for counterexamples.

The subsequent evidence drove a wedge between models and images. Subjects appear to reason primarily on the basis of models of verbal premises. They are unaffected by the relative "imageability" of the premises; their representations readily accommodate elements that cannot be visualized; and, as the results with "only" bore out, their representations can contain abstract elements corresponding to negation. Because a model can contain such abstract elements, it can represent a set of alternative classes of situation, and so it cannot be visualized.

In contrast, a visual image represents how a particular situation looks from a particular point of view, and it may well take the form of a "two-and-a-half" dimensional sketch (Marr, 1982). Lying behind such images is a different sort of representation: a three-dimensional model of the world, from which the image is projected. The evidence for this claim is that the mental rotations of objects in depth produced the same pattern of results as did mental rotations in the picture plane (see Metzler & Shepard, 1982, p. 45). Hence, as these authors point out, individuals must be rotating a three-dimensional model of the object rather than rotating its image. Operations on images per se correspond to visual rearrangements. They can lead to the construction of new configurations out of existing elements or shapes (see, e.g., Finke & Slayton, 1988). They can also, as we saw, play a symbolic role when diagrams are used to represent situations. By manipulating a visual image, reasoners can construct the alternative possibilities more readily than they can do so from verbal premises. It follows that diagrams are not merely encoded in propositional representations equivalent to those constructed from verbal premises.

We have now completed the case for a triple code of propositional representations, models, and images. Propositional representations have a predicate-argument structure closely related to linguistic structure, and they can contain quantifiers and variables. Their precise syntactic structure is unknown, and various theories are to be found in the literature, ranging from semantic networks to representations akin to the predicate calculus. Models can be three-dimensional, kinematic, and dynamic. But everyday thinking depends on many concepts that cannot be visualized; models can embody these abstract predicates, and they can capture classes of situations in a parsimonious way. Hence, they can represent any situation, and operations on them can be purely conceptual. Finally, images represent how something looks from a particular point of view, and operations on images are visual or spatial rearrangements. These operations, however, can serve a symbolic function. As the diagram study showed, individuals can imagine moving a shape from one position to another, and in this way visualize a proposition with quite a different content.

REFERENCES

Anderson, J. R. (1978). Arguments concerning representations for mental imagery. *Psychological Review, 85* 249–277.

Bara, B., Bucciarelli, M., & Johnson-Laird, P. N. (1995). The development of syllogistic reasoning. *American Journal of Psychology,* (in press).

Barwise, J. (1993). Everyday reasoning and logical inference. *Behavioral and Brain Sciences, 16,* 337–338.

Barwise, J., & Etchemendy, J. (1992). Hyperproof: Logical reasoning with diagrams. In N. H. Narayanan (Ed.), *AAAI Symposium on Reasoning with Diagrammatic Representations* (pp. 8–40). Stanford, CA:

Bauer, M. I., & Johnson-Laird, P. N. (1993). How diagrams can improve reasoning. *Psychological Science, 4,* 372–378.

Baylor, G. W. (1971). Programs and protocol analysis on a mental imagery task. *First*

International Joint Conference on Artificial Intelligence, n.p.

Begg, I., & Denny, J. (1969). Empirical reconciliation of atmosphere and conversion interpretations of syllogistic reasoning. *Journal of Experimental Psychology, 81,* 351–354.

Braine, M. D. S. (1978). On the relation between the natural logic of reasoning and standard logic. *Psychological Review, 85,* 1–21.

Denis, M. (1991). *Image and cognition.* New York: Harvester Wheatsheaf.

Denis, M., & Denhière, G. (1990). Comprehension and recall of spatial descriptions. *European Bulletin of Cognitive Psychology, 10,* 115–143.

de Vega, M. (1991). Change of character and change of perspective in narratives describing spatial environments. Communication au Colloque Européen sur les Modèles Mentaux, Paris, France.

Erickson, J. R. (1974). A set analysis theory of behaviour in formal syllogistic reasoning tasks. In R. Solso (Ed.), *Loyola symposium on cognition* (Vol. 2). Hillsdale, NJ: Erlbaum.

Finke, R. A., & Slayton, K. (1988). Explorations of creative visual synthesis in mental imagery. *Memory & Cognition, 16,* 252–257.

Fodor, J. A. (1975). *The language of thought.* New York: Crowell.

Garnham, A., & Oakhill, J. V. (1989). The everyday use of anaphoric expressions: Implications for the "mental models" theory of text comprehension. In N. E. Sharkey (Ed.), *Modelling cognition: An annual review of cognitive science* (Vol. 2). Norwood, NJ: Ablex.

Guyote, M. J., & Sternberg, R. J. (1981). A transitive-chain theory of syllogistic reasoning. *Cognitive Psychology, 13,* 461–525.

Hagert, G. (1984). Modeling mental models: Experiments in cognitive modeling of spatial reasoning. In T. O'Shea (Ed.), *Advances in artificial intelligence.* Amsterdam: North-Holland.

Inder, R. (1987). *Computer simulation of syllogism solving using restricted mental models.* Unpublished doctoral dissertation, Cognitive Studies, Edinburgh University, Edinburgh, Scotland.

Inhelder, B. & Piaget, J. (1958). *The growth of logical thinking from childhood to adolescence.* London: Routledge.

Johnson-Laird, P. N. (1975). Models of deduction. In R. J. Falmagne (Ed.), *Reasoning: Representation and process in children and adults.* Hillsdale, NJ: Erlbaum.

Johnson-Laird, P. N. (1983). *Mental models: Towards a cognitive science of language, inference and consciousness.* Cambridge: Cambridge University Press.

Johnson-Laird, P. N., & Bara, B. (1984). Syllogistic inference. *Cognition, 16,* 1–61.

Johnson-Laird, P. N., & Byrne, R. M. J. (1989). *Only* reasoning. *Journal of Memory and Language, 28,* 313–330.

Johnson-Laird, P. N., & Byrne, R. M. J. (1991). *Deduction.* Hillsdale, NJ: Erlbaum.

Johnson-Laird, P. N., Byrne, R. M. J., & Schaeken, W. (1992). Propositional reasoning by model. *Psychological Review, 99,* 418–439.

Johnson Laird, P. N., Byrne, R. M. J., & Tabossi, P. (1989). Reasoning by model: The case of multiple quantification. *Psychological Review, 96,* 658–673.

Kaufmann, G., Wenevold, E., & Murdock, M. C. (1992, December). *Reconstrual of images.* Paper presented at the Fourth European Workshop on Imagery and Cognition, Puerto de la Cruz, Tenerife, Canary Islands.

Keenan, E. L. (1971). Quantifier structures in English. *Foundations of Language, 7,* 255–284.

Kintsch, W. (1974). *The representation of meaning in memory.* Hillsdale, NJ: Erlbaum.

Larkin, J., & Simon, H. (1987). Why a diagram is (sometimes) worth 10,000 words. *Cognitive Science, 11,* 65–99.

Macnamara, J. (1986). *A border dispute: The place of logic in psychology.* Cambridge, MA: MIT Press, Bradford Book.

Madruga, J. A. G. (1984). Procesos de error en el razonamiento silogistico: Doble procesamiento y estrategia de verificacion por. In M. Carretero & J. A. G. Madruga (Eds.), *Lecturas de psicologia del pensamiento.* Madrid: Alianza.

Mani, K., & Johnson-Laird, P. N. (1982). The mental representation of spatial descriptions. *Memory & Cognition, 10,* 181–187.

Marr, D. (1982). *Vision: A computational investigation into the human representation and processing of visual information.* San Francisco: W. H. Freeman.

Metzler, J., & Shepard, R. N. (1982). Transformational studies of the internal representations of three-dimensional objects. In R. N. Shepard & L. A. Cooper (Eds.), *Mental images and their transformations* (pp. 25–71). Cambridge, MA: MIT Press. Originally published in R. L. Solso (Ed.), *Theories in cognitive psychology: The Loyola symposium.* Hillsdale, NJ: Erlbaum.

Miller, G. A., & Johnson-Laird, P. N. (1976). *Language and perception.* Cambridge, MA: Harvard University Press.

Newell, A. (1980). Reasoning, problem solving and decision processes: The problem space as a fundamental category. In R. Nickerson (Ed.), *Attention and performance* (Vol. VIII). Hillsdale, NJ: Erlbaum.

Newstead, S. E., Manktelow, K. I., & Evans, J. St. B. T. (1982). The role of imagery in the representation of linear orderings. *Current Psychological Research, 2,* 21–32.

Oakhill, J. V., Johnson-Laird, P. N., & Garnham, A. (1989). Believability and syllogistic reasoning. *Cognition, 31,* 117–140.

Ohlsson, S. (1984). Induced strategy shifts in spatial reasoning. *Acta Psychologica, 57,* 46–67.

Paivio, A. (1971). *Imagery and verbal processes.* New York: Holt, Rinehart and Winston.

Paivio, A. (1986). *Mental representations: A dual-coding approach.* Oxford: Clarendon Press.

Palmer, S. E. (1975). Visual perception and world knowledge: Notes on a model of sensory-cognitive interaction. In D. A. Norman, D. E. Rumelhart, & the LNR Research Group (Eds.), *Explorations in cognition.* San Francisco: W. H. Freeman.

Polk, T. A., & Newell, A. (1988). Modeling human syllogistic reasoning in Soar. In *Tenth Annual Conference of the Cognitive Science Society* (pp. 181–187). Hillsdale, NJ: Erlbaum.

Polk, T. A., & Newell, A. (1992). A verbal reasoning theory for categorical syllogisms. Mimeo, Department of Computer Science, Carnegie Mellon University, Pittsburgh, PA.

Pylyshyn, Z. (1973). What the mind's eye tells the mind's brain: A critique of mental imagery. *Psychological Bulletin, 80*, 1–24.

Pylyshyn, Z. (1984). *Computation and cognition: Toward a foundation for cognitive science.* Cambridge, MA: MIT Press, Bradford Book.

Revlis, R. (1975). Two models of syllogistic reasoning: Feature selection and conversion. *Journal of Verbal Learning and Verbal Behavior, 14*, 180–195.

Richardson, J. T. E. (1987). The role of mental imagery in models of transitive inference. *British Journal of Psychology, 78*, 189–203.

Rips, L. J. (1983). Cognitive processes in propositional reasoning. *Psychological Review, 90*, 38–71.

Sag, I. A., & Hankamer, J. (1980). Toward a theory of anaphoric processing. In J. Barwise & I. A. Sag (Eds.), *Stanford working papers in semantics* (Vol. 1). Stanford University: Cognitive Science Group.

Shepard, R. N., & Metzler, J. (1971). Mental rotation of three-dimensional objects. *Science, 171*, 701–703.

Smith, E. E., Langston, C., & Nisbett, R. E. (1992). The case for rules in reasoning. *Cognitive Science, 16*, 1–40.

Stenning, K., & Oberlander, J. (1992). A cognitive theory of graphical and linguistic reasoning: Logic and implementation. Research Paper 20, Human Communication Research Centre, University of Edinburgh, Edinburgh, Scotland.

Störring, G. (1908). Experimentelle Untersuchungen über einfache Schlussprozesse. *Archiv für die gesamte Psychologie, 11*, 1–27.

Wetherick, N., & Gilhooly, K. (1990). Syllogistic reasoning: The effects of premise order. In K. Gilhooly, M. T. G. Keane, R. Logie, & G. Erdos (Eds.), *Lines of thinking: Reflections on the psychology of thinking* (Vol. 1). London: John Wiley.

Wittgenstein, L. (1953). *Philosophical investigations.* New York: Macmillan.

Woodworth, R. S., & Sells, S. B. (1935). An atmosphere effect in formal syllogistic reasoning. *Journal of Experimental Psychology, 18*, 451–460.

CHAPTER 4

Imagery and the Description of Spatial Configurations

Michel Denis

Imagery and language are two basic components of the human cognitive system. This chapter focuses on their interactions in communicative situations where people produce verbal messages with the intention of having their addressees construct the mental representation of spatial configurations. How can imagistic and linguistic representations cooperate when a cognitive system has to interact with another one with the purpose of conveying information about spatial entities?

In recent years, cognitive research has become more and more concerned with situations in which people process information in order to act on objects placed at a distance and not available to their immediate perception. These situations provide special significance to the mechanisms involved when people construct a *representation* of the object or situation being processed. The issue is especially important in interactive situations, where two people have to communicate on shared representations of absent objects. These situations raise the issue of the test of both internal coherence and external validity of these representations, in particular when speakers try to have their addressees build the representation of a perceptually nonavailable object, and then the addressees have to perform cognitive computations on their representations of the object. Such situations illustrate quite general theoretical issues, including that of the nature, structure, and construction of cognitive representations as these are approached by multimodal conceptions of the human mind (e.g., Baddeley, 1986; Engelkamp & Denis, 1990; Johnson-Laird, 1989; Paivio, 1991; Rumelhart & Norman, 1988).

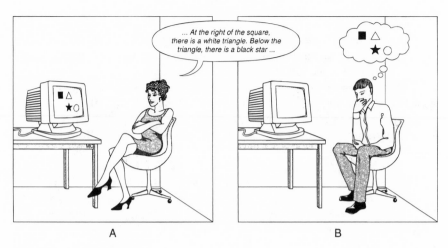

Figure 4.1. The task situation.

The research program in which most of the experiments reported below have been undertaken can be described by the situation shown in Figure 4.1. This situation involves two people. The first one (A) is in the presence of an object or a visual scene. The second one (B) is at some distance, in some other location (say, another room, or maybe in another city), without any perceptual contact with object.[1] Subject A's task is to describe the object to Subject B with the only means of discourse, with the intention to have him build a representation as similar as possible to the representation he would have built from direct perception of the object or configuration. By "similar," I mean "which carries the same information" and, more importantly, "which can support the same kinds of cognitive operations." For instance, if Subject A has described a territory, Subject B may be required to draw the map of this territory, or use his mental representation in order to compare distances among landmarks, or plan an appropriate route when he will be on the spot.

This paradigm has at least a twofold value. First, it is representative of many natural situations where people have to communicate about space (description of scenes, description of itineraries in unfamiliar environments). Second, it should help us to understand better the underlying mechanisms of the image and language interface, an important issue if we consider that these two basic components of cognitive architecture have radically different properties but nevertheless are permanently required to cooperate. There is, in fact, a growing number of attempts to explore how the construction of a mental representation from a text is facilitated by accompanying pictorial illustrations. Experiments by Bower and Morrow (1990; Morrow, Bower, & Greenspan, 1989; Morrow, Greenspan, & Bower, 1987) attest to the possibility of articulating the processing of a narrative with previously memorized map information. The accessibility of information attached to different parts of this map is shown to depend on the location of the main character of the narrative in the described environment. Furthermore, it is well established that the spatial structure of illustrations has a significant impact on comprehension and memorization of texts describing complex processes (cf. Glenberg & Langston, 1992). Finally, abundant evidence is available that when subjects learn a text reporting facts associated with geographical features, learning is significantly enhanced for subjects who previously studied the map of the described environment (e.g., Kulhavy, Lee, & Caterino, 1985; Kulhavy, Stock, Verdi, Rittschof, & Savenye, 1993).

One preliminary question, however, may be raised at the outset of this chapter: When people have to communicate their spatial knowledge to others, why do they *speak* or *write* about space when it seems so easy and natural to *draw* pictures or maps? Several answers may be considered. First, language permits us to circumvent some of the inconveniences resulting from the fact that pictures are committed to specification, and that the act of drawing implies the permanent risk of introducing some erroneous information. For instance, although the statement that "you will find the bookshop after crossing a few streets" is acceptable, even a rough sketch cannot express this indeterminate quantifier, or it has to show a definite number of streets. Although indeterminate descriptions sometimes create cognitive difficulties for comprehenders (cf. Mani & Johnson-Laird, 1982), language can take on some amount of indeterminacy in the description of space without this being detrimental to comprehension. If you are told that "along the street, you will find a garage," it may not be necessary to know whether the garage will be on your right or on your left. Note also that there exist many constrained situations where discourse is the only available vehicle for communicating information to your addressee, which justifies researchers' concern about language-based spatial cognition. Finally, a good reason for producing verbal descriptions of space might rely in one of their potential advantages, that is, the linearity of language can mimic the linearity of perceptual experience in routes.

THE LISTENER SIDE

Imagery research provides some hints that most people are able to process the linguistic description of an object or configuration they have never seen before and elaborate a mental representation of this object, with reasonable accuracy in comparison with the model (e.g., Finke, Pinker, & Farah, 1989; Foos, 1980). However, we are still largely ignorant of the characteristics of those mental representations constructed in the absence of direct perceptual cues. Do these representations possess the same properties as images derived from perceptual experi-

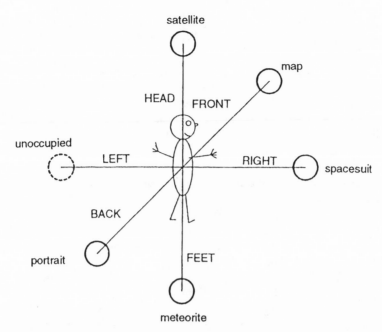

Figure 4.2.   The task situation investigated by Bryant, Tversky, and Franklin (1992).

ence? Do they entertain a relationship of structural isomorphism with described objects? Will computations performed on these representations be as valid in both cases? The importance of these questions is evident when we consider the situations where an individual, who has just processed a description, will have to make a decision on the basis of his evaluation of distances or relative positions of objects or landmarks.

There is ample evidence of people's capacities to compute the relative positions of objects and their successive changes, in particular from studies by Nancy Franklin and Barbara Tversky (1990; Bryant, Tversky, & Franklin, 1992). In these experiments, subjects were asked to read texts describing a character oriented toward one object and surrounded by other objects beyond the character's head, feet, back, left, and right (Fig. 4.2). The texts then described the character facing each object in turn, and subjects were asked to determine which object was in each direction from the character. Experiments showed that readers are able to perform this task, presumably adopting the point of view of the character and using a spatial mental model (or "spatial framework"; see Franklin & Tversky, 1990; Tversky, 1991) in order to keep track of the objects as the character's orientation changes.

When subjects have to retrieve each object's location, all spatial dimensions are not equally accessible. The head-feet dimension is most accessible, presumably because it is a strongly asymmetric axis of the perceptual world. As a consequence, subjects retrieve very quickly information about objects located either above or below the described character. The front-back dimension is also an asymmetric one, with important behavioral consequences, but its cognitive salience is somewhat lower than that of head-feet. Response times to identify object locations are longer on this dimension than on the head-feet dimension. The left-right dimension has no salient asymmetries. Decisions regarding the positions of objects on this axis are the most difficult to make, and response times are the longest in this case.

Further experiments using the same paradigm investigated whether subjects are capable of switching perspectives in spatial mental models constructed from descriptions. Can subjects adopt different points of view on the described scene? Data collected by Franklin, Tversky, and Coon (1992) indicated that readers did not adopt the points of view of two characters, but rather that they used more general, comprehensive mental models, including both characters. In short, readers appear to take neutral perspectives rather than those of each character in turn.

On the other hand, de Vega (1994) collected evidence suggesting that when subjects have memorized the description of a scene involving two characters surrounded by several objects (see Fig. 4.3a), their responses reflect their capacity to adopt several points of view, but also the cost of switching perspectives. For instance, after reading introductory sentences that place the focus on the priest, subjects are faster at verifying the sentence "The priest has the kiosk on his left" than the sentence "The postman has the kiosk on his right." Furthermore, when the original description has introduced two characters with the same point of view on the scene (see Fig. 4.3b), verification responses are faster than if the description mentioned that the two characters had different points of view

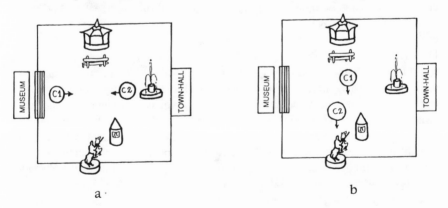

a   b

Figure 4.3. Scenes used by de Vega (1994). C1 and C2 represent "the priest" and "the postman," respectively.

on the scene. Finally, in line with Franklin and Tversky's (1990) results, verification responses are faster on the front-back than on the left-right dimension.

Imagery and Spatial Mental Models

Which cognitive processes are responsible for the construction of mental representations of spatial configurations? Beyond the parsing mechanisms involved in the processing of linguistic inputs, which mechanisms are involved in the construction of spatial mental models from verbal descriptions? This chapter focuses on visual imagery for its potential contribution to the construction of spatial models. Visual imagery is an obvious candidate for such a role, although it should be emphasized at the same time that it is not the only representational process suitable to mental modeling. Alternate forms of representation can be recruited as well to implement spatial mental models.

Consider, for instance, the distinction made by Perrig and Kintsch (1985) between models that rely on the coding of *procedures* and those that involve *visuospatial representations.* These two forms of representation were contrasted in an experiment where, for a group of subjects, the description of a town was based on the moves of an automobile driver, whereas for another group of subjects, the town was described from a bird's-eye view. After memorization of one or the other descriptions, subjects were capable of drawing spatial inferences from their available knowledge, but these inferences were closely dependent on the type of model they had been biased to construct during reading—that is, either procedural or visuospatial. The merit of Perrig and Kintsch's approach was to integrate the concept of visuospatial image as one form in which a mental model can be embodied, and it suggested that in a hierarchy of representations, the concept of mental model is probably more general or abstract than the concept of visual image proper.

The relationships between images and models have been discussed with an effort to identify their common properties as forms of mental representation (cf. Denis & de Vega, 1993; Johnson-Laird, 1983). One essential property that images share with mental models is that both are representations, wherein information is not inscribed according to arbitrary syntactical structures. Rather, images and mental models belong to the class of *analog representations*—that is, representations essentially based on a semantics of resemblance. However, analogy is not an all-or-none property of analog representations. In particular, analogy can be achieved at various degrees in a mental model. There probably exists a basic (minimal) analogical property inherent in any mental model, but analogy can be increased through the implementation of processes that *specify* the model and that *instantiate* it. If the model is intended to represent the spatial relations among a few items, a purely *topological model* can be sufficient for this purpose. However, in some circumstances, it may be desirable to incorporate the *metric*

(Euclidean) structure of the represented world. Starting from a gross topological model, it is then necessary to proceed further—that is, to represent distances accurately and to preserve the whole set of inter-object spatial relations. Visual imagery is especially useful in such a case. Indeed, visual imagery is a process that usually constructs representations with a very high degree of analogy (with an exact metric of distances and accurate expression of relative positions). In this context, although imagery should not be purely equated to mental modeling, it should be recognized as a mode of specification (or instantiation) of mental models under specific points of view.

Taylor and Tversky (1992a) provided arguments to substantiate the view that, in some contexts, it is helpful for a mental model to be relatively schematic and abstract. Taylor and Tversky compared pairs of texts describing the same spatial environment. One version described the environment by giving readers the perspective of a person following a specific route. The other version was a survey description—that is, the territory was described from a bird's-eye perspective. The question was whether the representation constructed from each of these perspectives would preserve the specific perspective or, on the contrary, would be perspective-free. The task following text learning consisted in verifying statements about spatial relations that had not been explicitly stated in the text, but could be inferred from it. Results showed that subjects were equally fast and accurate in their inference judgments regardless of the perspective used in the text or the perspective taken in asserting the relation to be judged. Thus, if subjects based their judgments upon consulting a mental model, this model did not seem to be biased by the specific perspective taken during reading. Hence, the model should be considered as general and abstract enough to capture the spatial relations between landmarks either from survey or route descriptions.

These data contradict any assumption that mental models are always highly saturated in visual imagery. According to Tversky (1991), spatial mental models would be like three-dimensional models used in architecture, which can be visualized from different points of view, but not from all points of view together. Models would be like "structural descriptions," that is, abstract representations specifying the relations between parts of a complex object. These representations should be differentiated from the representations typically investigated by imagery researchers, namely quasi-perceptual representations tightly associated with specific perspectives. While the possibility remains that visual imagery might be used to instantiate a model by adopting a specific "view" on it (cf. Denis & de Vega, 1993; Johnson-Laird, 1983), mental modeling cannot be viewed as being uniquely associated with a mode of representation like imagery, which mandatorily generates perspective-bound mental representations.

This being stated, it is important in the context of this chapter to look carefully at the situations where people who have to process verbal materials describing spatial configurations implement their visual imagery in this process. In the next section, I will consider situations requiring that subjects construct fine-grained visual images of the patterns described because they expect to have to make fine decisions on these images, like those decisions required in comparing distances or judging subtle angular differences. In such cases where the model must be detailed enough to preserve the Euclidean properties of physical space, it is useful to rely on visual imagery. Experiments investigating the processes by which subjects create images from verbal descriptions and manipulate them will be reported.

A later section will be devoted to cases where the construction of a model from a verbal description is not expected to incorporate a very accurate metric since the type of task to be performed later does not require it urgently. In this case, only gross topological relations have to be inscribed in the model. Does this mean that imagery is totally irrelevant in such contexts? I will report data suggesting that imagery may be implied in a constructive way even in cases where no urgent need in accurateness weighs on the situation.

Mental Operations on Fine-Grained Visuospatial Representations Constructed from Discourse

In this section, I report results from experiments designed to test the similarity of visual images of spatial configurations either derived from perception or constructed from verbal descriptions. Marguerite Cocude and I first tried to test such similarity by using the mental scanning paradigm originally developed by Kosslyn (1980; Kosslyn, Ball, & Reiser, 1978).

Mental Scanning

Two learning conditions were compared in the original study of this series of experiments (Denis & Cocude, 1989): learning from a map, and learning from a verbal description of this map (Fig. 4.4). In the first condition, subjects had to memorize the map of a fictitious island that had six geographical features located on the periphery. They then were required to perform mental scanning on the visual image of the map. Scanning was executed according to the following instructions: Subjects were to focus mentally on a feature that was orally mentioned to them. They then had mentally to scan across the map to another mentioned feature. Subjects were required to indicate the moment when scanning had been completed by depressing a button that stopped a timer triggered by the onset of the second feature named. (In some cases, the feature named did not belong to the map, and subjects then had to depress another button.) Analysis of response times confirmed Kosslyn's finding that the longer the distance separating two features, the longer the time to scan the corresponding distance (Fig. 4.5). The positive correlation between scanning times and distances is seen as

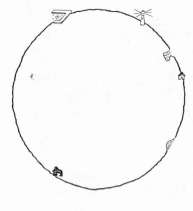

"The island is circular in shape. Six features are situated at its periphery. At 11 o'clock there is a harbor. At 1, there is a lighthouse. At 2, there is a creek. Equidistant from 2 and 3, there is a hut. At 4, there is a beach. At 7, there is a cave."

MAP   DESCRIPTION

Figure 4.4. Map and text used in the mental-scanning study of Denis and Cocude (1989).

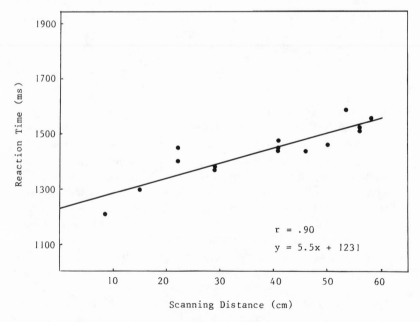

Figure 4.5. Reaction time as a function of scanning distance: Map condition.

indicating that mental images accurately preserve information on distances and that the structure of images reflects the structure of previously perceived objects in an analog fashion. This result, however, is only true for the case where temporal conditions of learning have allowed subjects to construct an accurate image, where each detail is represented at its exact location.

In the second condition, subjects were not presented with the map at any time of the experiment, but they were presented with a description of the island. Location of geographical features was based on the hour coding system used in aerial navigation. Subjects listened to the description three times in one group, six times in another group. In the mental scanning test, results showed a correlation between response times and distances, as in the previous condition (Fig. 4.6). However, for the group of subjects who were exposed to six learning trials (Fig. 4.7), the correlation was higher than for the group involved in three learning trials, and the correlation coefficient reached a value similar to that of the correlation produced by the group involved in perceptual learning. Furthermore, although after three learning trials, absolute scanning times were longer than after perceptual learning, these times reached the same order of magnitude after six trials as after three trials of perceptual learning.

These findings indicate that the mental representations constructed from ver-

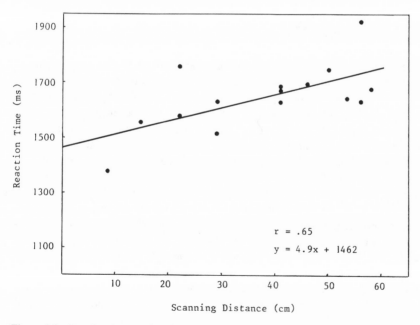

Figure 4.6.   Reaction time as a function of scanning distance: Text condition (after 3 learning trials).

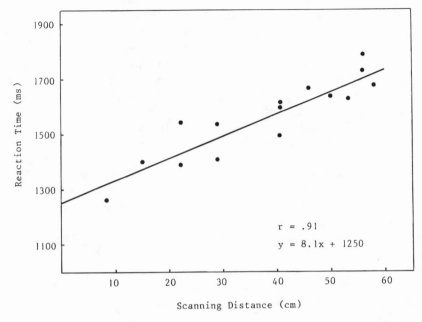

Figure 4.7.   Reaction time as a function of scanning distance: Text condition (after 6 learning trials).

bal descriptions—that is, without any perceptual contact of the subject with the configurations themselves—do contain information structured in a way similar to perceptual representations. Subjects can use these text-derived representations in a way comparable to perceptually derived ones, namely by short-circuiting corresponding perceptual experience. Obviously, this procedure has a cost for the cognitive system in terms of time and the capacity utilized. Constructing a detailed visual image usually requires a substantial amount of cognitive resources (cf. Kosslyn, 1980; Kosslyn, Reiser, Farah, & Fliegel, 1983). Once image construction is completed, however, the information available is basically the same as after perceptual learning, and it can be used in a similar fashion. It is important, in addition, to emphasize that the newly constructed representation contains more information than the text from which it has been elaborated. In particular, the text only mentions the positions of landmarks, without stating anything about their relative distances. The mental scanning task reveals that the representation not only contains landmarks, but also the relative distances among them. In short, the assumption of structural isomorphism of visual images to objects holds true also for images constructed from verbal descriptions without visual input (cf. Denis, 1991, 1993).

    In a further series of experiments (Denis & Cocude, 1992), two versions of the description were compared. One version was identical to that used in the previous experiments, where the six landmarks were mentioned in clockwise order. In the other version, landmarks were introduced in the description in random order. Subjects were presented with one of the two versions. They listened to the description three times, then they received a mental scanning test. They were presented again with the description three times, then had a second mental scanning test. Results at the first test of the Clockwise condition (Fig. 4.8) showed a positive correlation between scanning times and distances ($r = .73$), which reflected a high degree of structuring of their images. After additional learning, the correlation coefficient increased substantially ($r = .87$), and scanning times overall decreased (by 185 ms), a phenomenon confirming our previous findings.

The picture was quite different for subjects in the Random condition (Fig. 4.9). After three learning trials of the random description, the first scanning test did not reveal any sign of internal structuring of the visual image. Response times were very long (221 ms more than in the Clockwise condition, on the average), and no significant correlation between scanning times and distances emerged from the data ($r = .33$). After three additional learning trials, however, the pattern changed considerably: Scanning times decreased by 299 ms and, more importantly, we found a positive correlation between times and distances ($r = .76$). Apparently it was only after this extra period of learning that subjects had built a representation whose internal consistency and resolution were comparable to those attained after three trials by subjects who learned the well-structured (clockwise) version.

Two control experiments allowed for clarification of these results. First, the distance effect observed on the second mental scanning test seems to be due to the cognitive activity developed during the processing of the description, and not to training resulting from practice during the first scanning test. This conclusion was confirmed in a condition where subjects were involved in six successive learning trials and performed only one scanning test after the last trial. Second, performance in verbal recall of the description and graphic recall of the map after three and then six learning trials revealed that the text itself was memorized very rapidly and that even when memory for the text was perfect, the spatial structure of their image, as reflected by graphic responses, was enhanced by this overlearning.

The primary finding of this research was the demonstration that the structure of a verbal description can affect the intrinsic properties, and in particular the metric properties, of the image constructed from it. When text structure is essentially random or at least shows low coherence or systematicity, subjects are able to recall the verbal description very rapidly, but the correlation typical of mental scanning is attained rather late. Conversely, a well-structured description (or at least a description whose structure closely corresponds to listeners' expectations)

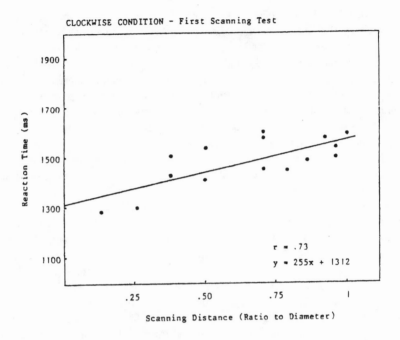

CLOCKWISE CONDITION - First Scanning Test

r = .73
y = 255x + 1312

Scanning Distance (Ratio to Diameter)

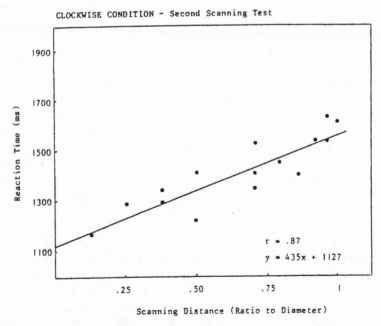

CLOCKWISE CONDITION - Second Scanning Test

r = .87
y = 435x + 1127

Scanning Distance (Ratio to Diameter)

Figure 4.8. Reaction time as a function of scanning distance: Clockwise condition. Distances are expressed as their ratios to the diameter of the island.

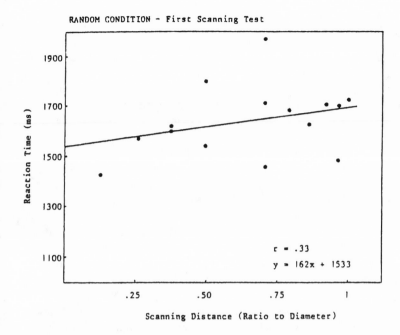

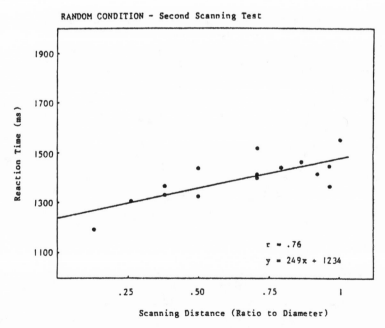

Figure 4.9. Reaction time as a function of scanning distance: Random condition. Distances are expressed as their ratios to the diameter of the island.

allows listeners to construct rather rapidly a "veridical" representation of the described situation. This type of description makes useless those additional learning trials required for constructing a coherent and cognitively useful representation from a poorly structured description. Thus, the referential validity of an image—that is, its capacity to reflect in an accurate manner the object it refers to—is not an all-or-none property, but results from a gradual construction. This process even seems to continue after memorization of the text itself has been completed.

It should be noted here that in the previous experiments we did not investigate the possible effects of semantic content of the geographical landmarks on the map. For instance, "harbor," "lighthouse," and so on were used as instantiations of points for which only topological and metric properties were considered. However, in memory for real-world spatial configurations, it is well known that the structure of mental representations depends to some extent on knowledge, experience, and value attached by the subjects to the landmarks. For example, subjects required to estimate distances in natural environments tend to underestimate distances that separate them from a landmark which is famous or with which they have had repeated interactions, whereas they tend to overestimate the distances to less frequently attended landmarks. This phenomenon is probably at work in the experiments showing that distances are underestimated in the center of cities and overestimated in peripheral zones (cf. R. W. Byrne, 1979; Moar & Bower, 1983).

The sensitivity of our paradigm to descriptions in which some of the landmarks underwent special cognitive processing likely to confer them particular cognitive salience also was examined. We wanted to show whether a specific manipulation of the description would be responsible for systematic biases in the

Description of Lighthouse as Secondary Landmark

> "This granit lighthouse, built fifty years ago, raises its lofty grey silhouette at the edge of the coast. From the top, twenty-five meters up, its powerful beam guides boats through the night. When fog sets in, its halo in the mist is extremely useful to ships who have lost their way."

Description of Lighthouse as Important Landmark

> "This strange lighthouse is painted red and white. It has been famous ever since the storm when a luxury liner ran into the cliffs nearby, with more than two hundred casualties. Since this catastrophy, jewelry and precious objects lie sunken at the foot of the lighthouse."

Figure 4.10. Alternative descriptions of the lighthouse.

representation constructed from it as in the case of real-world configurations. Our expectation was that such biases would be revealed through scanning times different from those recorded before.

The first of the three experiments devoted to this issue ensured that three of the six landmarks on the periphery of the island would be processed in a particular way. For this purpose, the text not only stated information regarding the location of the landmark, but it also provided a short narration containing many concrete details to increase salience of this landmark. By contrast, the other three landmarks were described in a rather neutral way. Figure 4.10 shows examples of how the lighthouse was described in one or the other versions. After learning of the description, subjects were required to perform the typical mental scanning task. The relevant aspect of the data here was the comparison between times of scanning toward either an important landmark or a secondary one. Results showed that these times were not different from each other (Fig. 4.11). Furthermore, time-distance correlation coefficients were virtually identical, whatever the type of scanning from which they were computed. This suggests that the time-distance correlation in the mental scanning paradigm is relatively robust, since the additional semantic content in this experiment did not affect the phenomenon. Several subjects reported that, although they had noticed differences in importance among the landmarks, they had developed special efforts in order to ignore this aspect and primarily concentrated themselves on the geometric (nonsemantic) properties of the configuration.

In the second experiment, variations in importance among landmarks were manipulated by additional descriptions referring to imaginary actions of the subjects themselves in the landmarks (the subjects had to imagine their own activity in three landmarks, whereas the other three landmarks were described in a neutral way and did not imply any associated activity). This manipulation did not produce any differential effect on scanning times, nor on correlations. Time-distance correlation coefficients were $r = .90$ when scanning was directed toward a location with an associated activity, and $r = .92$ when it was directed toward a neutral location.

In the last experiment, the manipulation consisted of enriching three of the six landmarks by a detailed picture expected to confer these landmarks stronger cognitive salience. The results still did not reveal any significant effect from differential treatment of the two sets of landmarks. The time-distance correlation reached $r = .92$ when scanning was directed toward an illustrated landmark, and $r = .77$ in the other case, this difference remaining below significance. On the whole, at least for materials newly learned by subjects from a verbal description (that is, materials not belonging to their previous experience), experimental attempts to modify the salience of landmarks did not result in representational biases similar to those that have been demonstrated in cognitive maps of natural spatial environments.

SCANNING TO SECONDARY LANDMARK

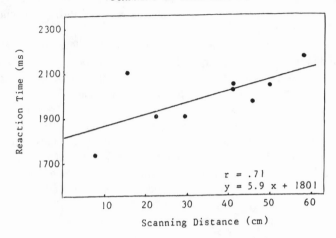

SCANNING TO IMPORTANT LANDMARK

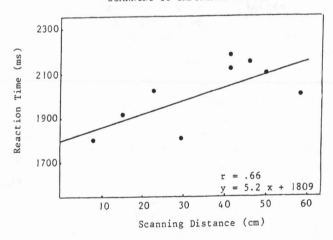

Figure 4.11. Reaction time as a function of scanning distance: Secondary versus Important landmark.

Finally, an attempt was made to test the sensitivity of mental scanning to subjects' individual characteristics. Until now, mental scanning has been studied without any serious concern about individual difference variability and its possible relationships with subjects' imagery capacities (see, however, Kosslyn, Brunn, Cave, & Wallach, 1984). The original concern of the present research was an attempt to unearth the effects of individual imagery capacities on mental

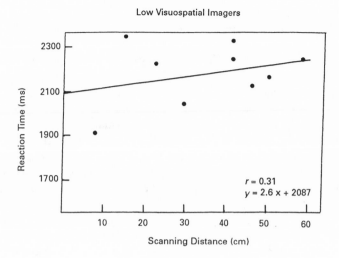

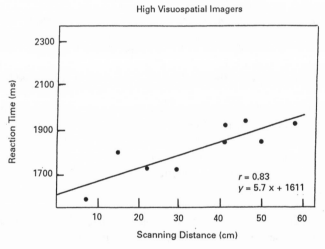

Figure 4.12. Reaction time as a function of scanning distance: Low versus High visuospatial imagers.

scanning of images constructed from a verbal description. After having been involved in a mental scanning test, subjects were asked to complete the Minnesota Paper Form Board (MPFB; Likert & Quasha, 1941), a visuospatial test widely used in imagery research (e.g., Paivio, 1986). Subjects were split into two groups—those who scored above and those who scored below the median of scores. Thus, we compared a group of subjects who were supposed to be relatively apt at generating and manipulating visual images and a group of subjects less prone to imaging.

On the basis of this distinction, two contrasting patterns of results emerged as regards mental scanning (Fig. 4.12): Subjects with higher visuospatial capacities were indeed those who produced the pattern typical of mental scanning (relatively short scanning times and a significant time-distance correlation coefficient). Conversely, subjects with poorer visuospatial capacities produced responses whose chronometric characteristics did not reflect that their images possessed any stable, consistent structural properties. Their scanning times were considerably long (476 ms longer than the other subjects), and no consistent relationship was seen between scanning times and distances. This pattern suggested that these subjects probably had particular difficulty in controlling the generation and exploration of their images. Their images likely contained a large amount of noise, which probably resulted from the difficulty experienced by these subjects in maintaining their mental representations at a sufficiently high level of activation.

Mental Comparison of Distances

Mental scanning is the paradigm most favored in imagery research as a support for the hypothesis of structural isomorphism of images to perceptual experiences from which images are constructed. This task, however, was criticized on several grounds, in particular because of the risks for mental scanning to reflect subjects' knowledge of the relationships among time, speed, and distance in the physical world, rather than an intrinsic property of images (e.g., Intons-Peterson & Roskos-Ewoldsen, 1989; Pylyshyn, 1981). Further data, however, minimized the value of this argument, showing in particular that the great majority of subjects were unable to predict the chronometric regularities of mental scanning (cf. Denis & Carfantan, 1985, 1990).

Two other problems regarding mental scanning should be emphasized here: First is the difficulty experienced by some subjects in understanding mental scanning instructions; second, the fact that subjects' responses essentially rely on their subjective evaluation of their own mental performance, without any available objective counterpart. These reasons led us to look for another sort of cognitive task that would be easier to describe to subjects and would make it possible to confront subjects' responses with an objective criterion. We thus turned to mental comparison of distances between landmarks of the configuration.

In this new series of experiments, the study phase consisted in asking one group of subjects to learn the perceptually presented map and another group to learn the verbal description, in the same conditions as those in previously reported experiments (with three learning trials). After learning, both groups were required to compare pairs of distances presented through audiotape. This task was performed for all pairs of distances having one location in common (for instance, the subjects had to indicate which of the two distances, lighthouse-harbor and lighthouse-beach, was the longest).

Items were grouped in three sets (D1, D2, D3) as a function of the magnitude of the difference between the two distances to be compared (D1 corresponds to pairs for which differences were the smallest, and D3 to pairs for which differences were the largest). Overall, responses of subjects who memorized the map were slightly more correct than those of subjects who memorized the description (95% vs. 91%, respectively), but the difference was not significant. On the other hand, there was a significant effect for the magnitude of the difference between compared distances. The overall rate of correct responses was 87 percent for D1, 94 percent for D2, and 98 percent for D3. This result reflects the existence of a *symbolic distance effect*—that is, the larger the difference between two items to be compared, the easier the comparison (whichever the indicator used, either the rate of correct responses or the time necessary for producing them). The symbolic distance effect is a well-established phenomenon in research on mental comparisons (cf. Marschark, 1983; Moyer, 1973; Paivio, 1975).

The very high level of performance achieved after memorization of either the map or the description confirms that learning of visuospatial information can effectively occur in a purely verbal situation. This is true, at least, for moderately complex materials likely to be reported in nonambiguous descriptions. Furthermore, the symbolic distance effect obtained in the two learning conditions supports the hypothesis that the representation constructed from the description contains metric information likely to be processed in the same way as after perceptual learning.

In a further experiment (partially reported by Denis & Zimmer, 1992), we looked for symbolic distance effects as reflected by response times. The experiment was restricted to the verbal learning condition, with sentence-by-sentence written presentation, which allowed for recording of study times for individual sentences. Mean study times per sentence decreased as learning proceeded (first reading: 12.72 seconds; second reading: 7.16 seconds; third reading: 5.48 seconds). Furthermore, poor visuospatial imagers showed overall longer study times than did high imagers. This result is compatible with the hypothesis of more difficult implementation of cognitive resources specialized for converting verbal information into visuospatial representations.

At the end of the learning phase, subjects had to perform mental comparison of all pairs of distances (with the restriction that the material only comprised pairs of distances with one location in common, namely the first-mentioned location). Figure 4.13 shows the mean number of correct responses for the three sets of items. Performance steadily increased from D1 through D3 items. Figure 4.14 shows the same information, separately, for the highest and the poorest visuospa-

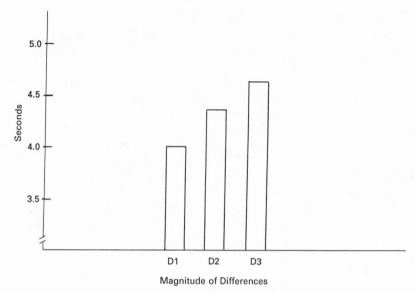

Figure 4.13. Mean number of correct responses in mental comparisons of distances.

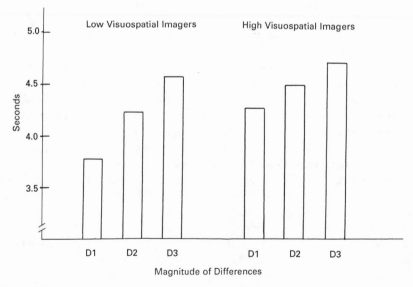

Figure 4.14. Mean number of correct responses in mental comparisons of distances: Low versus High visuospatial imagers.

tial imagers, respectively. High imagers produced a larger number of correct responses than did low imagers. This superiority, however, was the most clearcut for D1 items—that is, those items for which the comparison was the most difficult and presumably implied fine visual examination of the distances to be compared.

The most interesting findings were obtained from the analysis of subjects' response times. As Figure 4.15 shows, responses were consistently faster as the difference between two distances was larger. This result is typical of symbolic distance effect, which is obtained here in a situation where the representation on which computations are executed has been constructed from exclusively verbal information. Figure 4.16 shows response times for high and low imagers separately. High imagers' response times are overall faster that those of low imagers. This finding supports the hypothesis that visual images genuinely subtend the comparison process. It is important to note that a symbolic distance effect is evidenced in both groups of subjects. This is an important fact, for it suggests that low imagers effectively make efforts to perform comparisons from an imaginal representation, but that their available resources for generating and manipulating images are lower than those of high imagers.

Finally, as was the case for the rate of correct responses, the magnitude of the difference between high and low imagers is the largest for the most difficult (D1) items, then lower for D2 items, and the lowest for D3 items.

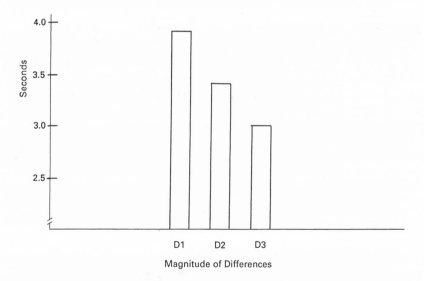

Figure 4.15.   Mean response times (in seconds) in mental comparisons of distances.

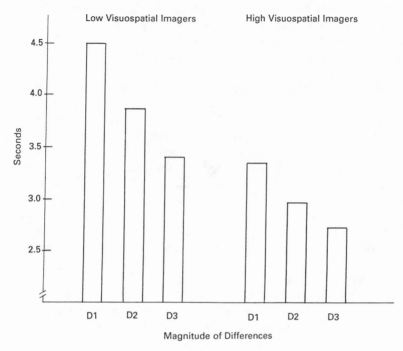

Figure 4.16.   Mean response times (in seconds) in mental comparisons of distances: Low versus High visuospatial imagers.

These findings, taken altogether with those obtained in mental scanning studies, confirm that subjects are capable of constructing mental representations of spatial configurations from verbal descriptions. Further, the high level of performance attests to the fact that subjects can process the metric properties of these configurations rather accurately. Finally, symbolic distance effects, along with time-distance correlations in mental scanning, support the assumption that representations constructed by subjects are endowed with structural properties that are isomorphic to those of real spatial configurations.

Visuospatial Abilities in the Construction and Manipulation of Spatial Mental Models

This section concentrates on situations where a lesser amount of constraint bears on the expression of metric qualities of the mental representation of a spatial configuration. In the studies reported here, the descriptions typically refer to topological relations rendered by prepositional expressions like "in front of," "behind," "on the left of," "on the right of," and so forth. Whereas visual imagery is obviously relevant for expressing such topological relations, there is probably no need for *fine-grained* imagery to be recruited in these contexts. Although topological mental models show less resolution than do highly detailed visual images considered in the previous section, they nevertheless provide subjects with potentially useful cognitive (nonlinguistic) equivalents of the real world. Information in these representations is structured in a nonarbitrary way, which reflects the structure of the objects represented.

Consequently, cognitive operations on these representations make possible decisions (for instance, inference judgments) whose mechanisms are similar to those of decisions made when the objects themselves are available (cf. Johnson-Laird, 1983, 1989). If mental models cannot be strictly equated with mental images (Johnson-Laird, this volume), however, the fact that the materials to be memorized are organized spatially makes it relevant for researchers to consider the potential impact of readers' or listeners' visuospatial capacities on the construction and manipulation of such models.

Furthermore, the issue of the *structure* of descriptions must be considered here in relation with the cognitive capacities of subjects who process these descriptions. As will be reported in more detail in the second part of this chapter, descriptions vary largely as regards their internal structure. It is an important objective of text research to identify whether certain types of structure create favorable (or, on the contrary, detrimental) conditions of processing. In particular, when a text is presented in a written form, reading times will reveal the amount of cognitive difficulty in the processing of the different parts of the text (sentences, for instance). To be less restrictive, rather than "reading times," we should speak of "processing times," since each recorded time will reflect more than reading proper, including the construction of sentence meaning and the integration of the new piece of information into the model under construction. A relevant question here is whether certain cognitive capacities, and in particular visual imagery, will compensate for the poor structure of a text.

Several studies have shown that processing times of descriptions are highly sensitive to the type of structure of the text. An especially important characteristic of texts is their *referential continuity.* A description is said to be *continuous* if every time a new element is introduced, this element is located relative to a recently mentioned element (ideally, an element mentioned in the immediately previous sentence).

The following example is that of a description conforming to the principle of * referential continuity: "(1) At the center of the island, there is a village. (2) To the east of the village, there is an airport. (3) To the north of the airport, there is a mountain. (4) To the east of the mountain, there is a plantation." Suppose that in a variant of this text, sentences 3 and 4 are inverted. This variant essentially provides the same pieces of information as the original version. However, when after sentence 2 a reader is presented with sentence 4, there is no possibility of integrating the information extracted from sentence 4 in the representation being constructed. It is only when sentence 3 has been processed that the relative positions of the four elements mentioned will be revealed. Thus, it is easier for the reader to integrate information from sentence $n + 1$ to information from sentence n when $n + 1$ locates the newly introduced item relative to the item mentioned in n. If a sentence occurs in a text without referring to any previously mentioned element, and if for this reason its content cannot be integrated in the representation under construction, the reader has to store the sentence as an isolated piece of information until the text refers to one of the elements of this sentence.

The effects of such structural factors were explored in a series of experiments on the construction of spatial mental models or cognitive maps from information presented in the form of sentences. Foos (1980) asked subjects to draw a map of a town after hearing sentences specifying the pairwise relationship between adjacent locations. For instance, after hearing "The church is north of the school" and "The park is east of the school," subjects should draw a map showing a west-to-east (i.e., left-to-right on the data sheet) school/park ordering with a north-to-south (i.e., top-to-bottom) church/school ordering. In line with previous research on the processing of three-term series problems and linear orderings (cf. Foos, Smith, Sabol, & Mynatt, 1976; Potts & Scholz, 1975), these experiments showed that successful construction of an integrated representation of four locations is a function of the order in which the relationships are presented. In particular, orders in which sentences (after the first) present one new and one previously presented item (*match* orders; e.g., AB, BC, CD) produce higher performance than do orders in which the second sentence presents two new items (*nonmatch* orders; e.g., AB, CD, BC).

Another interesting result in this series of experiments pertains to congruence of item locations with the spatial terms used in the description. For instance, the sentence "The church is north of the school" makes it more difficult to construct an ordering in which the school is the most southern item than the sentence "The school is south of the church." However, an examination of the strategies that subjects reported using showed that incongruent presentation was not detrimental to a specific group of subjects: those who reported using imagery to represent spatial information.

In experiments using sentence-by-sentence presentation of descriptions with recording of processing times, a typical result is that these times are overall longer in the case of discontinuous than in continuous descriptions. For instance, Ehrlich and Johnson-Laird (1982) presented subjects with short texts describing the spatial layout of a set of four objects. An example of a continuous description read as follows: "The knife is in front of the pot. The pot is on the left of the glass. The glass is behind the dish." The discontinuous variant of this description was constructed by simply inverting the second and third sentences of the continuous description.

In one experiment, subjects listened to sentences read one at a time, and they indicated when they were ready to hear the next sentence. In another experiment, subjects read the descriptions on a computer screen at their own pace. In both experiments, the results showed that subjects' processing times were consistently shorter for continuous than for discontinuous descriptions, and subjects' reconstructions of the layout by drawing were more correct after continuous than after discontinuous descriptions. The interpretation was that continuous descriptions mostly favor the construction of a mental model, since each new sentence can be immediately integrated to the existing representation. Discontinuities force subjects to store sentences independently in a propositional format before integrating them in a unified representation.

Further experiments by R. M. J. Byrne and Johnson-Laird (1989) tested a theory of spatial inference based on mental models. In particular, they showed that descriptions requiring only one model of the spatial layout to be constructed during reading were easier to process than those requiring several models to be constructed (see also Johnson-Laird & Byrne, 1991).

(1) The pepper is in front of the cucumber.
(2) Left to the cucumber is the potato.
(3) In front of the potato is the onion.
(4) The tomato is in front of the onion.

(a)

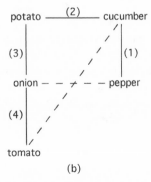

(b)

Figure 4.17. Description and configuration from Wagener and Wender (1985). Numbers in parentheses refer to corresponding sentences; dashed lines indicate Euclidean distances between objects in close and distant pairs.

In an extension of the Ehrlich and Johnson-Laird (1982) paradigm, Wagener and Wender (1985) asked subjects to learn short texts describing spatial configurations of five common objects (Fig. 4.17a). In a priming task, subjects were to decide whether or not pairs of objects belonged to the same configuration. The spatial relationship between the two objects of each of these pairs was not explicitly stated in the text, but could be inferred by the reader. In Figure 4.17b, onion and pepper are members of a "close pair," whereas cucumber and tomato are members of a "distant pair." The predictions were that if subjects construct a spatial representation from the verbal description, the priming effect should depend on the spatial distance between prime and target within each pair. As a result, decision times were overall shorter for the close than for the distant pairs. Under the assumption that descriptions are encoded propositionally, decision times should not have been different for close and distant pairs. The results thus speak in favor of the analog character of mental models constructed from spatial descriptions (cf. also Wagener-Wender & Wender, 1990).

Similar priming effects were reported from experiments on cognitive maps constructed from verbal descriptions (Denis & Zimmer, 1992). In these experiments, subjects were required to learn the configuration of a set of elements on an imaginary island either from a map or from a descriptive text. Afterwards, they performed a recognition task, with test items being presented one after the other on a computer screen. Recognition was more accurate in the Map than in the Text condition. However, both conditions showed a spatial priming effect. Primes located near the target produced a stronger priming effect than did those located far from it, and this was true even if this relationship had not been explicitly stated in the text. The assumption that a spatial mental model was constructed from the text was supported by the absence of any significant interaction between encoding conditions (map or text) and the type of prime target relation.

To return to the issue of text structure, this was a crucial variable in a series of experiments by Denis and Denhière (1990), in which subjects were first presented with a blank map of an island showing the locations of six geographical features. They then read a sentence-by-sentence description that specified which feature was at which location. One version (Text 1) adhered to the order of description used most frequently by subjects in a pilot experiment (iterated horizontal linear scanning) (Fig. 4.18a). In the other version (Text 2), the order of description completely deviated from linearity and violated the principle of continuity. Although it provided readers with essentially the same information as Text 1, the sequence followed by Text 2 did not fit the expectations of the majority of readers (Fig. 4.18b).

The major finding of these experiments was that reading times were longer for Text 2 than for Text 1, but a closer look at the data revealed that the increase of reading times was essentially true for sentences that occurred *after* the first

(a)

Version 1

1. In the extreme north-west part, there is a mountain.
2. To the east of the mountain, there is a forest.
3. To the east of the forest, there is a lake.
4. In the extreme south-west part, there is a meadow.
5. To the east of the meadow, there is a cave.
6. To the east of the cave, there is a desert.

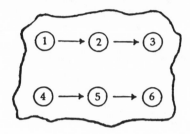

(b)

Version 2

1. In the extreme north-west part, there is a mountain.
2. To the east of the mountain, there is a forest.
3. To the south of the mountain, there is a meadow.
4. In the extreme south-east part, there is a desert.
5. To the west of the desert, there is a cave.
6. To the north of the desert, there is a lake.

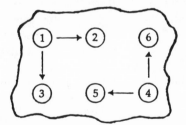

Figure 4.18. Alternative versions of description used by Denis and Denhière (1990).

break of linearity, namely sentences 3 through 6 (Fig. 4.19). This finding reflected the cognitive load resulting from processing conditions that require readers to adapt themselves to a poorly structured description that introduces new locations at unexpected times and alternatively calls for horizontal and vertical scanning. An expected consequence was that the construction of a mental model of the island would be more difficult, and thus less efficient, with Text 2 than

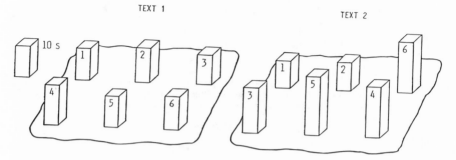

Figure 4.19. Mean reading times per sentence in Texts 1 and 2. Numbers refer to sentence position in each text.

with Text 1. These difficulties, indeed, were reflected by lower recall performance after Text 2 than after Text 1 when subjects were required to recall landmarks at their respective locations on a blank map.

The findings supported the assumption that the processing of descriptive texts calls for cognitive processes that serve to *integrate* newly received information into the ongoing representation and that poorly structured texts impair such integration. However, no direct indication of what sorts of processes contribute to the formation of this integrated representation was provided. Examination of postexperimental reports revealed that a good proportion of subjects claimed that visual imagery was involved in their processing of the texts. Subjects' comments stressed that visual images were useful as representations that helped them to integrate informational units, especially when information was presented in a totally unexpected sequence. To collect information about the potential contribution of visual imagery, the experiment was replicated, with the additional feature that subjects were given explicit imagery instructions.

The findings clearly replicated those from the original experiment. Reading-time *patterns* for each text were extremely similar in the two experiments, but the most striking finding was that, beyond this similarity of patterns, the *absolute values* of reading times were virtually identical to those in the first experiment, where subjects were not explicitly instructed to image while reading. Even though it is usually difficult to interpret the absence of a difference, a tempting hypothesis was that imaginal processing required from readers in the experiment with imagery instructions had in fact been developed spontaneously by subjects in the first experiment. In addition, the recall data did not show any significant effect for imagery instructions.

Given the repeated evidence for positive effects of imagery instructions in many learning contexts (cf. Paivio, 1986), the lack of any measurable effect in this experiment was considered as consistent with the hypothesis stated above.

Even in the absence of explicit instructions, the learning context created in the original experiment strongly encouraged subjects to elaborate a representation equipped to incorporate spatial information in a format similar to perceptual experience. Because visual imagery is the most readily available representational process for encoding spatial information, it is more than likely that it was called into play once subjects recognized that this form of encoding was the most efficient way of processing the spatial relations in the text. This hypothesis is consonant with the definition of visual images as "functional sites" specialized in the encoding of unfamiliar spatial information (cf. Dean & Enemoh, 1983; Dean & Kulhavy, 1981; Schwartz & Kulhavy, 1981).

However, we still wanted to examine the assumption that subjects required to read Text 2 were in a cognitive situation where mental imagery is especially useful for encoding pieces of information delivered according to an incoherent sequence. Imagery is a mode of representation that favors integration of units of information in a coherent structure and makes their spatial relations explicit. The visual image of a configuration is a framework in which is it cognitively advantageous to inscribe new information as it is processed so as to provide for maximal integration despite the discontinuities of the description. If reading of spatial descriptions calls upon visual imagery, this strategy should be especially useful when descriptions are poorly structured. In addition, if the generation of visual images, overall, requires additional processing times, increases of processing times in Text 2 as compared to Text 1 should be especially evident for people who have the lowest visuospatial abilities.

An experiment reported in Denis and de Vega (1993) involved contrasting subjects with the highest or the lowest visuospatial abilities, using both MPFB

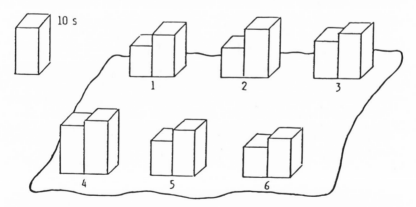

Figure 4.20. Mean reading times per sentence in Text 1 for high visuospatial imagers (left bar) and low visuospatial imagers (right bar). Numbers refer to sentence position in each text.

and the Mental Rotations Test (MRT; Vandenberg & Kuse, 1978). Results showed that in the case of Text 1, sentence-processing times were shorter for subjects with the highest visuospatial abilities (see Fig. 4.20). Short times probably reflect the special capacities of these subjects in transforming linguistic inputs into visual representations. Low visuospatial imagers are certainly able to perform such transformations, but these operations apparently require additional resources.

A similar pattern was evidenced for Text 2, but in a still more clear-cut way. Low imagers seemed to be much more disadvantaged here than high imagers, in the case of a poorly structured text which calls upon visuospatial imagery (see Fig. 4.21). Taking another perspective on the data, it should be stressed that differences between reading times for Texts 1 and 2 were moderate for high imagers, whereas they were more pronounced for low imagers. This phenomenon was reflected in a significant interaction between the type of text structure and subjects' visuospatial capacities. Apparently, the spontaneous inclination of some subjects to elaborate visuospatial representations placed them in better cognitive conditions when they had to read a poorly structured text.

Conversely, low imagers were relatively more handicapped than the others in a situation where visual imagery was an appropriate strategy. As concerns recall, high imagers performed better than did low imagers, but the overall effect was not significant. This finding means that for achieving similar recall performance, the "cost" of cognitive processing is greater for subjects who are not spontaneously inclined to construct vivid visual models of described configurations.

Quite similar results emerged from the previously reported experiment dem-

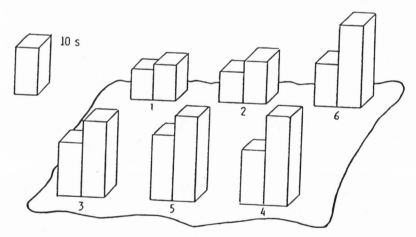

Figure 4.21.   Mean reading times per sentence in Text 2 for high visuospatial imagers (left bar) and low visuospatial imagers (right bar). Numbers refer to sentence position in each text.

onstrating readers' capacities to adopt different points of view on a spatial environment that was described verbally to them (de Vega, 1994). For the entire sample of subjects, verifying sentences describing the location of objects relatively to characters took more time when the points of view of several characters had been reported in the text. Furthermore, when subjects were distinguished in terms of their visuospatial abilities, it appeared that high visuospatial imagers made fewer errors and responded more rapidly than did the other subjects in the verification task. It is worth recalling that in this experiment and those reported above, subjects were presented with exclusively verbal material, both during learning and during verification. The fact that subjects contrasted in terms of their visuospatial capacities also differ from each other when they have to verify *verbal* statements strongly suggests that the representation on which they rely during the verification task possesses properties that actually reflect the spatial properties of the described scenes.

To summarize this section, the first point to stress is that even when mental modeling does not require the construction of highly detailed, fine-grained visuospatial representations, imagery capacities can be valuably implemented to provide more concreteness and integrative power to the ongoing representation. Such implementation depends on the amount of resources available to the reader or listener. In particular, high visuospatial imagers are clearly favored in situations calling for visualization. This facilitation is even more evident in situations where information is delivered according to a poorly organized sequence.

Second, this section reported evidence that the internal structure of spatial descriptions has significant impact on their processing. Some descriptions have internal organization that allows readers or listeners to process information according to a sequence well adjusted to their cognitive expectations. On the other hand, some descriptions may have an internal structure that does not follow any identifiable systematic sequencing, and are therefore more difficult to process. This difficulty is reflected in additional processing times and lower recall performance. It is thus especially important to develop research on structural characteristics which will guarantee maximal processing efficiency (and, in addition, proficient construction of visuospatial mental representations). This indicates the need to investigate the nature of speakers' or writers' *descriptive strategies* and to specify the procedures by which describers plan discourse or text production, while controlling for their coherence.

THE DESCRIBER SIDE

In the second part of this chapter, I consider the cognitive situation of a person who is required to produce a description. In her perceptual field, the speaker has a two- or three-dimensional spatial entity available. The objective is to have an addressee construct a mental representation that reflects the spatial information available in this configuration. The major cognitive problem for the speaker is that the device for communication available to her, namely language, generates outputs that by nature are linear and unidirectional. Translating a multidimensional entity in the form of a linear linguistic output thus requires constructing a sequential structure, which itself requires a series of cognitive decisions.

In this respect, description is a very particular type of discourse, because of the low constraints that usually weigh on the order in which the different parts of the scene have to be entered. This situation contrasts with the strong constraints that bear on the sequencing of discourse that describes entities having an explicit temporal structure. For instance, in the absence of any literary effects, reporting the events that compose a narrative episode in general requires writers to introduce events in the order of their natural succession. In this case, discourse linearization results from direct mapping of one structure (the sequence of events) onto another structure (the sequence of verbal outputs) (see Fig. 4.22a). Discourse linearity then totally adheres to the linearity of the described situation. This, obviously, is not the case in most forms of descriptive discourse (unless some temporal sequence is implicitly superimposed onto the object to describe). Figure 4.22b illustrates the case where a multidimensional object has to be linearized verbally. In comparison with a narrative sequence, many more degrees of freedom are available for ordering the components of descriptions.

The issue of discourse linearization has been given special consideration in Levelt's (1989) theory of discourse. The processes involved in the generation of messages are assumed to be subordinated to *planning* activities. The preparation of a message involves two steps. The first one is *macroplanning*. It consists in the elaboration of a communicative intention as a sequence of subgoals, and the selection of information to be expressed in order to realize these goals. When selecting information instrumental to these communicative goals, the speaker must sequence information to express it, and she must also continuously keep track in her working memory of what has been said previously. Therefore, a speaker's monitoring of her own production requires constant attention.

The conceptual activity involved during this initial step results in a preverbal message. In most cases, the speaker has to solve what Levelt calls the *linearization problem,* that is, she has to decide what will be said first, what will be said afterwards, and so on. An "expert" speaker is supposed to give special attention to the ways in which she will order or arrange information before transmitting it. Inappropriate structural organization (even simply inverting two propositions) can have dramatic effects on the addressee's interpretation (cf. Denis & Denhiere, 1990; Ehrlich & Johnson-Laird, 1982; Foos, 1980).

Some description orders are tightly constrained by the "natural" order of the content to be expressed. In event structures, for instance, the natural order corresponds to chronological order. Other domains also have natural ordering, such as spatial linear structures (e.g., describing an adequate route from a starting point

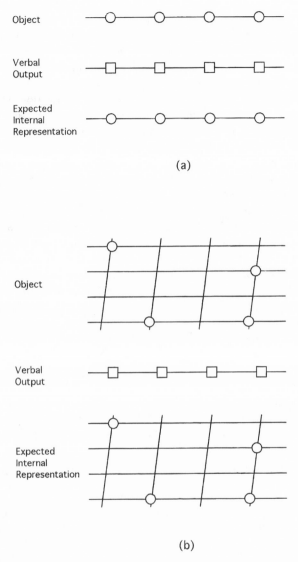

Figure 4.22. Structure of objects, discourse (verbal output), and internal representations.

to a goal place in a town; cf. Riesbeck, 1980; Wunderlich & Reinelt, 1982). The principle of natural order is only efficient because there is an implicit agreement of both the speaker and the addressee (partly based on culture-bound schemas, like scripts for temporally structured information). But if there is no natural order, then the speaker has to solve the linearization problem for herself.

The core of this problem is that linear expression of multidimensional objects in general can be achieved with a great many number of possible orders. What limits the number of actual choices, however, is that the speaker must keep in memory what has been said before and what remains to be said. The speaker thus will organize her discourse in a way that preserves maximal coherence between newly introduced and previously mentioned information. One important principle at work is that of *connectivity*—that is, wherever possible, the speaker should choose as the next piece of information to be described one that has direct connection to the currently described piece of information. Another critical principle consists of organizing discourse in such a way that this organization minimizes the cognitive load of the addressee as he constructs a supposedly integrated representation of the situation from successive pieces of information.

Once the first step of preparation of the message is completed, the second step is that of *microplanning*, which mainly consists of assigning a propositional format to information that is to be communicated. This step represents a transition from the preverbal message to a formulation, which consists in expressing a *conceptual* structure into a *linguistic* structure. Microplanning implies access to a mental lexicon and grammatical encoding in order to determine the surface structure of discourse, and phonological encoding in order to build an articulatory program.

Discourse planning thus consists to a large extent in monitoring a linearization process, which is mainly oriented toward the addressee so as to place him in conditions of most efficient processing. Planning requires successive steps (conceptualization, propositionalization, articulation), although in contrast with a purely serial model, incremental aspects of discourse production are assumed—that is, the generation of outputs is sometimes initiated before complete planning of the message to be expressed (cf. Schriefers & Pechmann, 1988).

Descriptive Discourse and the Issue of Its Internal Structure

Description is a type of discourse for which planning seems to be especially critical because of the variety of acceptable linguistic structures that can be produced when a speaker (or a writer) describes even very simple two-dimensional objects (see Jarvella & Deutsch, 1987). This state of affairs makes it relevant to consider the following question: What is the underlying structure of descriptive discourse? In fact, if we assume the existence of strategies in the production of any type of discourse, the question arises as to the structure (or structures) that these strategies produce.

At this point, however, a preliminary issue to be considered is whether there is *any structure* underlying descriptions. Should descriptions be thought of as though they possessed structural properties that can be described in terms of *descriptive superstructures,* comparable to the macrostructure of narratives (e.g., van Dijk & Kintsch, 1983; Kintsch, 1974)? To this question, two contrasting answers can be found in the existing literature. From one point of view, description is a type of discourse which simply lacks any structure, in comparison to highly structured materials like narratives. This view, which has been illustrated mainly in psycholinguistic studies of language comprehension and memory, has been recently challenged by proponents of theories in text linguistics, who argue for description as a type of discourse involving very specific (macro)structures.

To illustrate the first approach, Kintsch and Young (1984) pointed to the conventional organization of some types of texts, like narratives, which are organized in such a way that the macrostructures that readers form are highly predictable and serve as efficient retrieval cues for the texts. On the contrary, descriptive texts are assumed to have no consistent schematic structure underlying them and to provide less efficient cues to their proper organization. The fact that recall of descriptions is lower than recall of narratives was interpreted by Kintsch and Young as reflecting that readers of descriptions do not implement any preexisting schemata (which otherwise are used by readers of narratives to integrate incoming information).

Similar views were developed by Mark McDaniel and Gilles Einstein in two series of experiments on memory for narratives versus passages describing geographical information (Einstein, McDaniel, Owen, & Cot, 1990; McDaniel, Einstein, Dunay, & Cobb, 1986). Different text structures are thought to invite different processing modes. Narratives are expected to mainly favor relational processing (through the implementation of preexisting schemata), whereas no available schemata correspond to descriptive texts. Descriptions thus do not elicit relational processing, but rather the processing of individual items. Recall data from these experiments are in fact compatible with the predictions based on these premises.

However, the view that descriptions are simply *unstructured materials,* devoid of any internal organization, seems highly questionable. Various linguistic and psycholinguistic methods have been developed to identify the features characterizing descriptive discourse. Although there is obviously no unique feature of descriptions (nor of any other type of text), some relevant markers of description may be found in particular in verb tenses (at least in some languages, like French), as well as in the semantic content of verbs used (e.g., stative vs. action verbs). Probably the most relevant aspects to be considered here are *structural* aspects. Not only must the structure of the *texts* be considered, but also the structure of the *objects* or entities described in the texts. Descriptive discourse or texts all share the feature that they create an impression of *simultaneity* of the components of the entity they are telling about, whereas narratives generate the impression of their *succession.* Discourse or text is always structured in a sequential manner, but what is relevant here is the intrinsic structure of the object, situation, or episode that is told about. The structure of this entity places constraints on the structure of the verbal output that is produced to create a representation of this entity in the addressee's mind.

If we consider spatial configurations as composite patterns of more elementary parts, these configurations offer many possible entry points and are likely to elicit many plausible descriptive sequences. The low number of constraints that apparently bear on the sequencing of descriptions is probably responsible for the (wrong) assumption that these texts have a low degree of structure (contrary to narratives, which are characterized both by strong constraints and strong structure). A description *reviews* the aspects or properties of an object, but despite this function, which corresponds to some sort of *inventory*, describing is always much more than simply *enumerating* or *listing* these aspects or properties (just like a narrative is more than a simple chronology of events or actions).

Adam (1986; Adam & Petitjean, 1989) proposed the view that the mode of functioning of a descriptive system consists in articulating a name (name of an entity to be described) and an expansion (the enumeration of properties of the entity). Adam points to the analogy of this system with the mode of organization of lexicographic definitions (denomination + definition). A descriptive system thus establishes a relation between the denomination of an entity and a definition attached to this denomination in the form of a nomenclature with predicates. The nomenclature can be an enumeration—for example, parts of the human body (head, torso, arms, etc.) or parts of a visual scene (church, fountain, bus stop, etc.). The predicates assign properties (for instance, qualities) to elements of the nomenclature (the predicate for "church" may be "gothic," for instance). Furthermore, the relations among the enumerated parts of the described object or scene (mainly, their spatial relations) are asserted.

The inherent problem with nomenclatures is that they are, in most cases, unlimited. The describer has to *close* her description at some time, which implies that she makes a choice of which elements will be entered in her discourse and which will be left off. Selecting relevant information may be quite a difficult process, which assumes that a criterion for relevance is available. In many cases, relevance is defined relatively to the addressee's expectations, the kind of task he will have to perform, and so on. Thereafter, the problem will be that of *ordering* the elements judged to be relevant for the reader or listener.

Adam postulates that some *macro-operations* are specific of descriptive discourse or texts and affect their structure. One of them is *aspectualization,* namely the act of providing the addressee with information on the *properties* or *qualities* of an object (color, size, shape, etc.) and its *component parts.* This is the most evident operation required for description—that is, introducing the various *aspects* of an object (and taking into account a hierarchy of these aspects). Another important macro-operation consists in *establishing relations* between the described object and other objects. *Assimilation,* for instance, consists in establishing the parallel between the aspects of two objects. This operation implies comparison, metaphor, and negation, the latter of which allows the speaker to describe an object by specifying what this object is not. Description thus consists in generating "descriptive propositions" by anchoring to the name of an object a number of predicates resulting from implementation of macro-operations.

The issue of descriptive structures is a very difficult one, indeed, if only because of the *variety of discourse structures* likely to apply to any object (e.g., Paris & McKeown, 1987). There is no single structure that will always be perceived as a "good" description. There are many different ways of describing accurately a given object. Furthermore, the *variety of object structures* makes the problem still more difficult to approach. It doesn't seem reasonable to expect that the same descriptive rules will be applicable to descriptions of a city, a living person, or a technical object. Or these rules must be very general, and the risk, then, is that they lose their power and usefulness.

These considerations, however, should not discourage researchers to proceed further in exploring the structural characteristics of descriptions. The few studies available, in fact, reveal the existence of some *dominant* structures regulating the description of spatial objects. The high probability of occurrence of some descriptive sequences should not be interpreted as meaning that these are *canonical* structures, but at least that they reflect consistent modes of propositionalization of people's internal representations.

In particular, Linde and Labov (1975) defined the set of discourse rules governing the description of apartments. In most cases, the spatial representation is transformed by speakers into a temporal sequence, a pseudo-narrative, which maps a linearization process onto the two-dimensional layout of the apartment. The speaker thus conducts the hearer on a sort of an imaginary tour. This tour is seen as a speech act that provides a minimal set of paths by which each room could be entered. Among the regular principles that constrain the order of description of rooms (and, consequently, syntactic choice) are the following: (a) the imaginary tour begins at the front door of the apartment; (b) if the visitor comes to a one-room branch, he does not enter it; (c) if he comes to a branch with rooms beyond the first room, he always enters; (d) when he reaches the end of a branch and there are other branches to be traversed, he does not turn around and go back; instead he is moved back "instantaneously" to the fork point where the other branches originate.

The path to be traversed is a branching network, consisting of an entrance point, markers of directionality, and rooms to be identified. The departure point is the entrance door, and displacement is executed from room to room. This strategy sharply reduces the number of options for starting the description, and it also permits nonambiguous use of markers "left" and "right." Orientation is inferred from common knowledge that people have of their displacements in such spaces. In general, when you enter a room, this means that, while entering it, you are facing it and proceeding forward, so that your visual system is directly facing the room. In general, people will first describe a branch that opens on one room only rather than a branch that opens on several rooms. When there are several branches, they select one, describe it, and then "jump" back to the beginning of this branch. Starting again from this point, they select another branch, and so on, until all branches are exhausted. The tour ends in the last described room. Transition from one room to another is not random, but is commanded by their connectivity. To summarize, an important feature of descriptions of apartments is that linearization is implemented in the form of a simulated tour.

In the description of individual rooms (including description of furniture arrangement), Ullmer-Ehrich (1982) showed that most speakers segment rooms into subareas, each of which is described in turn. Descriptions thus reflect subdivisions of the room. Room descriptions, then, take the form of an imaginary "gaze tour" (distinct from imaginary "walking tours" used for describing apartments)—that is, people describe rooms as though they were gazing along the walls.

Speakers use two different linearization principles in organizing a gaze tour. On the higher level of linearization, *connected linearized descriptions* proceed continuously along the walls. When giving a connected description, the speaker does not jump around to nonadjacent subareas. *Disconnected descriptions,* on the other hand, do involve such jumps. Speakers who give such descriptions organize their gaze tour through the room via two or three parallel lines, each line going from one of the walls straight through the room to the opposite wall. On the lower level of linearization, connected descriptions are characterized first by the introduction of one piece of furniture. Then a second, neighboring piece is located with respect to the first one, a third piece with respect to the second, etc., which corresponds to a *sequencing* linearization mode. In disconnected descriptions, only one piece of furniture serves as a reference point for locating all other pieces belonging to the respective subarea. This corresponds to the application of a *grouping* principle.

Ehrich and Koster (1983) showed that the selection of one of these two procedures is determined by the presence (or absence) of functional relations among the objects of a given subarea. Functionally defined areas (for instance, a study area, consisting of a desk, a lamp, and a chair) are more likely to be described according to the grouping principle, whereas the description of nonfunctional sets of furniture follows the sequencing linearization mode. Furthermore, in the grouping mode of description, the size of objects is taken into account. A large object (a table) is more likely to be selected than a small one (a vase) as the central item of the described subarea. Ehrich and Koster, in addition, provided evidence for microstructural properties of room descriptions (in particular, the order of mention of locating and located objects, and the use of definite determiners).

The constraints regulating the structuring of room descriptions were explored further by Shanon (1984). These constraints were shown to be governed by principles of pragmatic and semantic coherence. Room descriptions, obviously, are not unordered lists of objects. Rather, they are constrained by the structural organization of the described scene. In the case of rooms, the constraints are defined in terms of conceptual categories dividing the semantic domain of the room. Shanon proposed that the optimal categorization of rooms implies the following six levels: (1) the room proper; (2) parts of the room (walls, floor, and ceiling); (3) windows and doors; (4) major pieces of furniture; (5) objects with a definite place of their own; and (6) objects without a definite place of their own. The levels are ordered. They mark a progression in increasing order of translocability.

In the description of rooms, the items of the first three levels are mentioned prior to those of the three lower-level categories. This constraint generates hierarchically ordered descriptions, which consist of progressions from the general to the particular. This structure is correlated with a progression from large, unmovable objects to small, movable ones. Regular profiles of description are thus evidenced. For instance, speakers quite consistently select higher-order items, which are likely to be used as reference items for the localization of lower-order items. A reference item and a located item can both be situated at the same level of the hierarchy (e.g., "The sofa is on the right of the desk"), but an item cannot be located by reference to another lower-order item ("The desk is below the lamp").

Descriptions of large-scale spatial environments were analyzed by Taylor and Tversky (1992b). In their experiment, subjects were presented with maps of different environments (city, amusement park, convention center) and were asked to recall them in the form of written descriptions, as well as in the form of drawings. Analysis of descriptions revealed hierarchical structures based on spatial and functional features of the environments and on conventions for sequencing the landmarks. For instance, subjects consistently recalled landmarks in decreasing order of size (e.g., in the description of the town, they first mentioned large natural features such as mountains and rivers, then major highways, then individual buildings). For the amusement park, subjects tended to proceed top–down and left–right, a strategy also observed by Denis and Denhiere (1990). Subjects also tended to use breadth-first hierarchies (by first mentioning the major subareas of an environment) more often than depth-first hierarchies (by describing one subarea entirely, then another, and then the third).

In addition, Taylor and Tversky collected evidence indicating that the order of description is quite similar to the organization revealed when subjects are required to draw maps. In particular, subjects tend to recall landmarks in the same order for both tasks. The clustering of landmarks in recall also shows high concordance between the two tasks, although within clusters, order of landmarks was more consistent in descriptions than in drawings. In short, a number of commonalities of organization between descriptions and depictions suggest that both activities are governed by similar communicative intentions. Just as the goal of drawing is to re-create a map, an actual one, so the goal of descriptions is to re-create a map, in this case, in the mind of another person.

To summarize the issues discussed in this section, the processes implemented in the generation of descriptive discourse produce linguistic outputs whose structure provides at least partial information on these processes. All of the studies reported above have in common the fact that they account for processes that produce linguistic outputs and that initially operate on inputs that are *cognitive* in nature (whatever their more precise characterization, as mental maps, visual images, etc.). These internal representations are memory evocations of spatial objects or configurations previously experienced. It is difficult to characterize the nature of the representations used as inputs for descriptive processes, but what can be stated is that these representations are *not* linguistic in nature and undoubtedly are *not* structured like language. Their structure is supposed to be similar to the structure of corresponding objects. They are closer to *depictions* than to descriptions (cf. Taylor & Tversky, 1992b). However, "the act of describing is not based on a naive-realistic mapping of things and words. Rather, descriptions presuppose a *cognitive structuring* of the world" (Shanon, 1984, p. 225, our italics).

Among the key processes at work on the cognitive representation used as an input for description, *segmentation* is probably the first critical one. Described objects are viewed as sets of more elementary subparts. Segmentation is often articulated with implementation of the principle of hierarchical organization, which is illustrated by subjects' tendency to subdivide the configuration, to assert and name its subsets, and then to describe each subset one after the other.

Another key process is that of *selection,* which means that most descriptions implicitly assume that some features have lower relevance than others, and therefore are not worth being explicitly entered in the descriptive sequence. Rather than providing addressees with extensive, detailed nomenclatures, it is part of describers' communicative efficiency to restrict the description to relevant items only. This procedure of selection implies the fixation of a threshold for relevance, but this level can be modified as a function of the requirements of the situation. In the description of most spatial environments, for example, it is appropriate not to mention all items actually present in these environments.

The third key feature of description, which has been repeatedly emphasized by researchers, is *linearization.* The output of any descriptive activity is an inherently linear linguistic sequence. This constraint correlatively implies the fourth key feature, which is the *ordering* of selected information. The researchers cited above are especially committed to the analysis of resulting sequences because of their expectation that order of description can reveal the mental organization of described environments or objects. However, it is worth mentioning that order of description also reveals some aspects of describers' cognitive capacities, as well as their willingness to take into account cognitive capacities of their addressees.

All these factors underscore the idea that descriptions are *not* disorganized lists of elements. Descriptions are constrained by the structural organization of described objects. The obvious trend from the studies reported above speaks in favor of the existence of descriptive *structures*. The concept introduced is that of *descriptive schemata* associated with the description of specific objects or classes of objects. An additional important consideration is that schemata activated by describers are expected to belong also to the addressees and help them to integrate incoming information. Various descriptive schemata are available that constitute indispensable shared knowledge, a requisite for felicitous communication. Descriptive strategies are based on schemata that are at work both in production and in comprehension. Here, the notion of *expectation* is probably central on the receiver side. Better processing will occur when any element provided to the addressee fills his current expectation. Not only do listeners or readers expect pieces of information at critical points of the descriptive discourse, but they also expect descriptive macro-operations to be easily identifiable, while probably tolerating some degrees of freedom on local sequences. Essentially, what they expect is structural *coherence*.

Particularly interesting are descriptions that leave the describer totally free of her production. These are what we may call *unconstrained descriptions,* which are usually characterized by the wide variety of resulting descriptive structures. This is the main point discussed in the next section. We will also consider the case of descriptions on which some external constraint is bearing—for instance, a constraint regarding the starting point. This sort of constraint typically restricts the number of effectively observed descriptive strategies. At the same time, its interest is to reveal how describers take the constraint into account and consequently reorganize their discourse. Much interest has been devoted to the cognitive factors regulating the production of constrained discourse. A later section reviews findings from several research programs, one of which in addition takes into account the impact of visuospatial capacities of subjects on the description of spatial configurations.

The Production of Unconstrained Descriptions

Suppose that a speaker has to describe a territory unknown to her addressee and that her task is to provide him with information regarding the relative positions of main geographical landmarks. The analysis of descriptions reveals that the speaker has to make several successive decisions regarding how to initialize her discourse, which kind of perspective she will prescribe to her addressee, and which particular sequence will be followed in reporting the different landmarks.

The studies reported below were concerned with the investigation of these processes, especially the procedures followed by subjects to *order* the geographical features in their descriptions when they are free of any external constraint regarding this order. Subjects were presented with the map of a fictitious island. The map was approximately square-shaped, and nine landmarks were distributed on it according to a 3 × 3 grid. This structure was thought to be open to a variety of scanning modes (horizontal, vertical, circular, etc.). To avoid problems associated with landmark identification (and its variability across subjects), the corresponding label was written under each landmark (cf. Fig. 4.23).

Subjects were invited to produce written descriptions of the map, without time limitations. Instructions stressed that the description should provide information to a person who did not know anything about the island and only had available a blank map of it. This person was supposed to acquire exact geographical knowledge of the island. Our main objective was to identify the putative descriptive superstructures reflected by specific modes of sequentialization of landmarks. The analysis of protocols relied on an ATN-based (Augmented Transition Network) system designed to construct a representation of each description and to classify it according to a typology (cf. Carité, 1992).[2]

In the first study, we collected descriptions from 79 subjects. We first looked at what seemed to be the preliminary step of the description—that is, how describers provide their addressees with a framework with spatial cues which will serve later to locate the landmarks. The initial descriptive act is thus designed to construct a lattice over which features will be distributed later. Note that there are large interindividual differences in the care taken by describers in the prelimi-

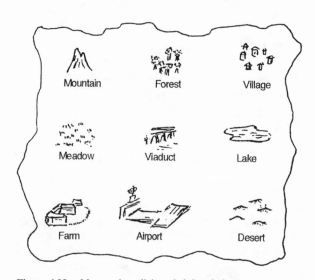

Figure 4.23.   Map used to elicit verbal descriptions.

nary framework description. In our sample, only 54 percent of the subjects provided even a minimal introduction describing the overall structure of the island.

A further decision is then made by the describer. The decision consists in choosing between the production of a discourse that aims at having the addressee construct a *survey* representation of the territory or places the addressee virtually on the ground and requires him to follow a *route* through the territory. This choice is crucial and has expected consequences at both the cognitive and linguistic levels. First, the two types of descriptions are likely to elicit different perspectives on the part of the addressee. Survey descriptions generally take a fixed perspective, whereas route descriptions take the perspective of a moving observer. As a consequence, discourse organizations are different. Survey descriptions are more likely to be hierarchically structured; route descriptions follow a sequence determined by the specific path followed. Consequently, in this latter case, it is more likely that descriptions exhibit referential continuity. Finally, spatial terminology is not the same in the two kinds of descriptions. Survey descriptions will mainly use canonical directional terminology (names of cardinal points). Route descriptions are more likely to use egocentric terminology related to the observers' changing positions.

It is legitimate to presume that these two linguistic forms will generate different types of representations with the potential consequence of unequal difficulty in processing the descriptions and performing cognitive decisions on the representations constructed (cf. Tversky, 1991). These hypotheses, however, are likely to be reconsidered given the results of the Taylor and Tversky (1992a) study, which revealed remarkable capacity of most readers to switch from one form of representation to the other.

The majority of respondents in our study (84%) produced survey descriptions of the nine landmarks on the map. Another point of interest is that the use of names of cardinal points was not strongly associated with survey descriptions. In fact, many survey descriptions used the terms "right," "left," etc., without necessarily referring to positions of an observer on the ground, but referring to positions of the person facing the map. Overall, the use of names of cardinal points was attested only in 47 percent of the protocols.

When the describer has opted for one of these descriptive modes, a further decision has to be made regarding the order in which the features present in the configuration will be entered into the description. As was mentioned above, description is a type of discourse on which minimal constraints bear as regards the order in which the different parts of the scene are mentioned. The description of the island theoretically can start from any of its landmarks. Once the first landmark has been entered into the description, it remains in principle possible to enter any of the remaining landmarks in the description. Consequently, the number of different (and likely) descriptive sequences is very large. The present study was precisely designed to check for this. Actually, if we consider the whole set of 79 protocols collected in this study, 39 different descriptive patterns were identified. Variability across subjects is thus very large. In addition, as will be shown below, frequencies of occurrence of these descriptive patterns are quite variable. More importantly, considerable variety exists in the structural quality of descriptions, from highly structured descriptions—well adjusted to cognitive capacities and assumed knowledge of the addressees, with minimal redundancy, in short "friendly" descriptions—to poorly structured ones, with a number of discontinuities or indeterminacies, not taking into account addressees' expectations.

Figure 4.24 shows the classification stemming from the analysis of protocols by the ATN system. The first group of sequences is that of *linear sequences*, whose prototype is *horizontal linear description* according to which the describer iteratively scans the three "lines" of the configuration. This sequential mode was adopted by 46.8 percent of the subjects, who scanned successively the first, second, then third line, each from left to right. To this dominant strategy type can be related variants of horizontal linear strategies, like those where lines are described starting with the bottom one, or the sinusoidal variant (in 5.1% of the protocols). Taking all these variants altogether, horizontal linear descriptions appeared to be largely dominant; they represented 59.5 percent of the entire sample. Much less frequent were the different variants of *vertical linear descriptions*, where the three "columns" are described one after the other. This type of description was illustrated in only 6.3 percent of the protocols. More frequent were *circular descriptions*, which were present in 12.7 percent of the protocols. These descriptions had several variants (clockwise or counterclockwise, starting from the central landmark or arriving at this landmark, etc.).

In a small percentage of the protocols (6.3%), the description seemed to be governed by a *categorial* principle. The subjects structured their descriptions as a function of three classes of sites: (a) the four sites at the corners of the island; (b) the four sites at the four cardinal points; and (c) the site at the center. Several types of sequencing were produced, that is, different orders of mention of the three groups of sites. The most frequent in our sample were those where the subject first described the center, then the cardinal points, then the corners. Another variant consisted of subjects first describing the corners, then the center, then the cardinal points. Finally, there was a group of descriptions (7.6%) where some sort of systematicity could be identified, without clearly belonging to one of the above-mentioned types, and another set of protocols (7.6%) that did not reveal any systematicity of the descriptive sequence.

These results largely confirm the assumptions on which this investigation was grounded: To produce a description is an activity in which the low degree of constraints bearing on sequentialization results in a considerable variety of descriptive orders. Among these orders, a great majority of orders emerge showing clear signs of systematicity. Systematicity is manifested in some privileged or-

Linear horizontal descriptions: **59.5%**

Example:

1	2	3
4	5	6
7	8	9

Linear vertical descriptions: **6.3%**

Example:

1	4	7
2	5	8
3	6	9

Circular descriptions: **12.7%**

Example:

1	2	3
8	9	4
7	6	5

Categorial descriptions: **6.3%**

Example:

1	5	2
6	9	7
4	8	3

Other systematic descriptions: **7.6%**

Example:

1	2	3
4	6	8
5	7	9

Non-systematic descriptions: **7.6%**

Example:

1	3	4
2	7	9
5	6	8

Figure 4.24. Classifications of descriptive sequences.

ders where sequentialization is implemented in the form of some scanning of the configuration. This scanning is not obligatorily associated with the simulation of a walking tour. Rather, it is a sort of "reading path," with consistent scanning of landmarks associated with a criterion of maximal proximity or connectedness. This strategy, however, does not preclude the occurrence of "jumps," similar to line-to-line jumps during reading (cf. Taylor & Tversky, 1992b). These descriptions with jumps are even more frequently produced than are descriptions totally respectful of continuity (sinusoidal or circular descriptions).

Description, on the whole, is an activity where systematicity can easily be evidenced. It produces structured outputs, which are far from random, and nevertheless show many variants. This situation raises the issue of the compatibility of describers' and addressees' mutual descriptive schemata. In the comprehension of texts, emphasis has been repeatedly placed on the fact that communication between narrator and reader is based on their sharing of the same narrative cognitive structures, and that this community of schemata guarantees mutual understanding. Even for a relatively simple configuration like the one used here, describers adopt quite diverse schemata. A question follows: Does the fact that a describer uses a very specific descriptive strategy imply that she is not able to use other strategies? In fact, if people are capable of producing various schemata, it is also likely that they have preferred sequences. This is equally true for the receiver of the description. Thus, it is reasonable to expect that conditions for communication will be optimal when people share schemata that allow them to construct common representations.

Among the elements that describers place and order in their descriptive sequence, the feature used as the starting point is of special interest. The site of this feature has consequences on the specific sequence that will be produced. Two contrasting hypotheses may be considered here. The first one is that what the describer chooses is a descriptive structure, and this structure commands the choice of the starting point. The alternate hypothesis is that subjects first choose a starting point, and from this point the sequencing of the remaining elements is decided. The following results suggest that structure is primordial, but that manipulation of the semantic content of landmarks is likely to affect the choice of the starting point.

In the previously reported study, we calculated the frequency with which each landmark was used as the starting point of the description. Figure 4.25 shows these frequencies. The landmark located in the upper-leftmost site (Mountain) was used as starting point by 67.1 percent of subjects. An appreciable number of choices were also made for the landmark located at the center (Viaduct), namely 16.5 percent. The other seven landmarks were much less frequently chosen, and three of them were never chosen. Among the subjects who chose Mountain as a starting point, a very large majority (90.5%) proceeded then with systematic linear description, either horizontal (83.0%) or vertical (7.5%). Among those who

.671	.038	.051
	.165	
.038	.038	

Figure 4.25. Frequency of using each landmark as a starting point for the description.

chose Viaduct, the probability of continuing with circular description was 46.2 percent, whereas it was 23.1 percent for a categorial description and 30.8 percent for any other form of systematic description.

To test the impact of factors other than the mode of sequentialization on the choice of the starting point, we conducted a further study, with a new group of subjects ($N = 83$), by simply changing the landmark located in the central position. The same island was used again, except that Meadow and Viaduct were reversed. The remaining landmarks of the configuration were kept in the same positions, as is shown in Figure 4.26. Analyses of landmarks as starting points revealed obvious changes in the results. Figure 4.27 shows frequencies for using each landmark as a starting point. Frequency for the uppermost, leftmost landmark, which is Mountain, decreased to 42.2 percent, whereas frequency for the central landmark increased to 30.1 percent. Thus, the probability for using the central item as the starting point is almost twice as much as before, when Meadow is placed at the center of the island. The intrinsic nature of this item apparently confers upon it a special attractive value for starting the description at least when it is at the center. Changes of starting points have consequences for the frequency of occurrence of the different types of descriptive strategies. In particular, horizontal linear descriptions decreased from 59.5 percent to 44.6 percent; there were no longer any vertical linear descriptions; finally, the most dramatic effect was the occurrence of new sorts of systematic descriptions starting from the center (16.9%, whereas the corresponding value was only 5.1% in the original study).

Other factors likely to affect descriptive sequences and items used as starting points can also be looked for if we consider the nature of the objectives served by the description. Who is the addressee? What are his cognitive capacities? What kind of task will he have to perform once he has read or listened to the description? In order to catch if only an aspect of this influence, we conducted a third study, using the same map as before (Meadow at the center), but providing

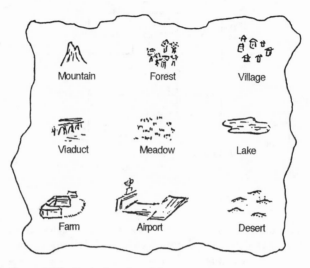

Figure 4.26. Revised version of the map.

describers with instructions designed to bias their choice of Meadow as the starting point more strongly than before. For this purpose, subjects were again instructed that they had to describe the island to someone who was expected to have exact knowledge of its geography. Instructions simply added that the reason this person had to acquire such knowledge was that the person would have to make a parachute jump onto the island.

It turned out that this simple additional instruction had a strong effect on choice of the starting point (Fig. 4.28). A total of 71 subjects participated in this new study. Choice of Meadow, central item of the configuration, now reached 46.5 percent; that is, by comparison with the previous study, the probability of

.422	.048	.096
	.301	
.060	.072	

Figure 4.27. Frequency of using each landmark as a starting point for a description of the revised map.

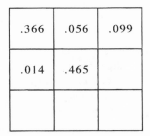

.366	.056	.099
.014	.465	

Figure 4.28. Frequency of using each landmark as a starting point for a description of the revised map with additional instructions.

starting the description by this specific feature increased by more than 50 percent. This item was even more frequently chosen than Mountain as a starting point. Obviously, the semantic factors manipulated here through the nature of landmarks, the type of instructions, and their interactions, all altered considerably the types of sequencing used to describe the island. In particular, the frequency of horizontal linear descriptions dropped to 32.4 percent, and the frequency of systematic descriptions (other than circular or categorial) starting from the center reached 26.8 percent. It would probably not be valid to conclude from these findings that descriptive activity is heavily dependent on semantic factors. However, researchers should not ignore the fact that the content of to-be-described objects, as well as the ultimate goal of the description, can appreciably affect the implementation of descriptive strategies.

Other factors should be considered as well. In particular, what are the characteristic features of an "apt describer"? There exist large differences among people as regards the quality of their descriptions. Some descriptions exhibit structural properties that seem to make them quite easy to understand, without requiring that the readers pause and reread a passage, or that the listeners ask for a repetition. Some descriptions, on the other hand, seem to be badly structured, apparently not obeying any plan or strategy. Could it be that some people are, in general, better describers than others? If such is the case, should we identify some basic cognitive capacities likely to account for individual differences in descriptive performance?

To answer these questions, a study was conducted in which 40 subjects produced written descriptions of the island used in the original study (Viaduct at the center). We analyzed their protocols and looked for features supposed to reflect good-quality descriptions. Independent judges were then asked to rate the 40 protocols for intrinsic quality, and our criteria were compared with judges' ratings. Finally, subjects completed a test of verbal production capacities (MINC) and a visuospatial test (MPFB) so that we could check whether scores on these tests would predict subjects' descriptive capacities to some extent.

The first criterion we considered was the presence or absence of an introduction to the description before subjects started enumerating the landmarks. Three cases were identified: (a) presence of a structuring introduction, that is, an introduction intended to prepare the addressee to integrate the remaining description in a frame with spatial cues (e.g., "The island is square-shaped. It can be divided into three rows and three columns, resulting in nine cells. In the cell which is located in the north-west, there is a mountain . . .") ($N = 10$); (b) presence of a minimal introduction (e.g., "I am going to describe you an island. At the extreme north-west, there is a mountain . . .") ($N = 14$); and (c) no introduction at all (e.g., "In the north-west, there is a mountain . . .") ($N = 16$).

The second criterion concerned the mode of sequentialization of the description. Four levels were considered: (1) highly systematic descriptions, following a linear sequence, without any deviation from linearity ($N = 12$); (2) systematic descriptions, which followed a linear sequence with moderate deviations from linearity ($N = 7$); (3) nonlinear systematic descriptions ($N = 12$); and (4) nonsystematic descriptions ($N = 9$). It turns out that the type of introduction and the mode of sequentialization were not independent. Subjects who produced a sequence of type (1) tended to produce an introduction of type (a); type (2) sequencing was associated with type (b) introductions; and types (3) and (4) sequencing were associated with the absence of any introduction (c). Thus, features selected as potential criteria of "good descriptions" seemed to exhibit some reasonable consistency.

Five judges rated the 40 protocols on a 7-point rating scale. They were asked to evaluate the communicative efficiency of each description. Their evaluations were largely distributed over the whole range of values, and they showed high interjudge reliability. The important point is that judges' ratings confirmed the validity of our criteria. For instance, if we contrast the subgroup of subjects who produced introduction (a) vs. (c), judges' ratings were 5.92 and 3.80, respectively. If we compare subjects who produced sequencing (1) vs. (4), ratings were 5.75 and 2.60, respectively. The contrast is even more marked when criteria (a) and (1) are associated, as compared to criteria (c) and (4), since ratings were 5.96 and 2.27, respectively. All of these differences were statistically significant.

Finally, we contrasted the upper and lower thirds of subjects ($N = 14$ in each case) by using the distribution of judges' ratings. This manipulation was intended to contrast "good" vs. "poor" describers. Whereas verbal capacities did not discriminate the two subgroups significantly (7.28 vs. 8.28, respectively), a significant difference emerged between them when we took into account their visuospatial capacities (20.57 vs. 16.42, respectively). Thus, verbal capacities, as measured by the test used here, did not appear to influence greatly the quality of descriptions. Other measures of verbal capacities, however, should be used, in particular those from tests expected to tap syntactic aspects of production.

It is interesting to note that visuospatial capacities were related to subjects' descriptive capacities. If these data are confirmed, they would suggest that an apt describer is not only a person with capacities for correct linguistic expression, but also a person who possesses adequate capacities of mental representation of the spatial entities to describe. The structural quality of the representation a describer constructs of the to-be-described object may thus influence the implementation of the linguistic device intended to make the addressee build his mental representation of the object.

The Production of Constrained Descriptions

The descriptive tasks analyzed above are illustrative of situations devoid of any constraint with regard to the starting point of the description or its sequence. We also have to consider situations with constraints, and in particular those concerning the starting point of the description. Which cognitive factors might then be expected to influence the ordering of discourse?

Suppose that a speaker has to describe the urban scene shown in Fig. 4.29, with the single constraint of starting the description from the bus terminal. From the terminal, it is possible either to describe first the buildings distributed along Madison Street, then those found when starting on Spring Street, or alternately to describe first Spring Street, then Madison Street. Both descriptions are quite

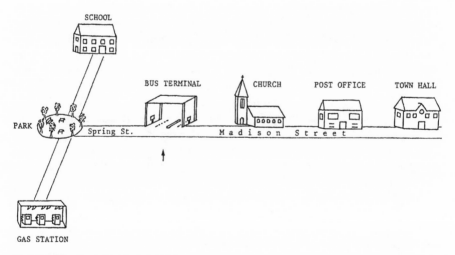

Figure 4.29. Example of urban scene.

correct, but they reflect different directional choices which may create differential cognitive load for the describer (and maybe also for the addressee). Differential cognitive load is not defined here in terms of the total number of items that need to be described on each side of the bus terminal (since the numbers on each side are the same), but in terms of the number of items on one side that have to be maintained in working memory during the description of the other side.

As a matter of fact, when a description starts from the bus terminal, whatever the direction taken first, the describer has to keep in memory that when she has completed the description of the first branch, her description of the second branch will have to start again from the bus terminal. If the speaker first describes the right branch, she has to maintain in memory the bus terminal as the backtrack point. But if she first describes the left branch, she will maintain the same item in memory for the same purpose as before, but also, at a given time, she will have to maintain the park (during the description of the school, for instance) as the backtrack point before the description of the gas station.

The experiments conducted by Levelt (1982a, 1982b) on the description of patterns of colored circles connected by horizontal and vertical lines showed that speakers' directional choices do not occur randomly, and that describers prefer strategies which minimize the number of items they have to store simultaneously in working memory (or the duration of such storage). This corresponds to what Levelt calls the *principle of minimal effort,* based on short-term memory economy. Not only do these supposedly optimal strategies minimize the load on speakers' working memory, but also on listeners' memory. These strategies may reflect to some extent speakers' concerns about the limitations of the processing capacities of their addressees.

Levelt identified three main types of regularities for three classes of networks. An example of the first class of networks is shown in Figure 4.30a. Two branches, a short one and a longer one, lead off from the green circle. The duration of maintenance of the starting point in working memory (during the description of the first branch) will vary as a function of which branch is described first. Duration of storage before returning to the green circle to describe the other branch is longer if the longer branch is described first. Thus, it should be cognitively more economical to describe the shorter branch first, since duration of storage will be shorter. The data collected by Levelt (1982a) confirmed that when subjects are required to start their description from the green circle, the probability is larger than 50 percent that they will describe the shorter branch before the longer one.

Figure 4.30b presents an example of the second class of networks. Here, subjects are required to start their descriptions from the red circle. From there, two branches head in opposite directions. A linear branch extends to one side, and a more complex T-shaped branch (which leads to a further intersection) is on the other side. The linear branch and the T-shaped branch have the same number of

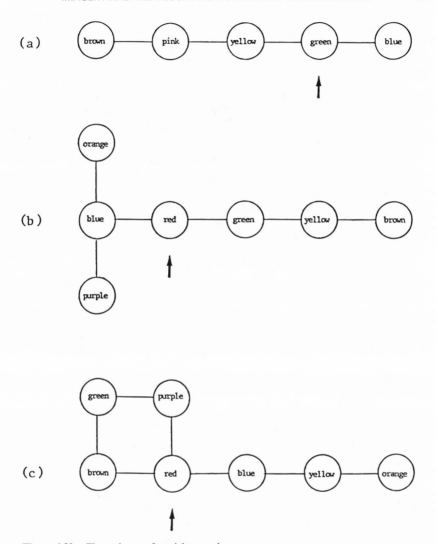

Figure 4.30. Three classes of spatial networks.

circles, and they only differ in terms of their structural complexity. Consequently, less information needs to be stored transiently in working memory during the description of the first branch when it is the linear branch. In this latter case, subjects only have to keep track of one circle, the red one, which is the "backtrack point," before describing the other branch. If subjects start their description with the complex branch, they have to store both the red and the blue circle. In fact, results showed that when subjects start their descriptions from the red circle, the probability is larger than 50 percent that they describe the branch without any embedded choice points before the branch with one or several embedded choice points.

The third class of networks is illustrated in Figure 4.30c. Three branches lead off from the red circle. One branch is linear, and the other two branches form a square-shaped loop. The most appropriate strategy, here, consists of describing the loop first, then the linear branch. Using this strategy, subjects avoid having to store any backtrack point, and they simply follow a linear path. Note that when subjects start their descriptions from the red circle, they have to choose among three possible directions. Thus, the probability that they will describe the loop before the linear branch should be larger than 67 percent. This tendency, in fact, was only observed for a subset of subjects (Levelt, 1982a).

Further experiments used the same kind of materials, but new variants on the network structures were introduced to explore several factors more systematically (cf. Robin, 1992; Robin & Denis, 1991). One manipulation consisted of varying the differential information load between the two branches of a network. For example, in the first type of network, one branch was only made up of one circle, while the other branch could have one, two, or three circles. Adding circles to one side of the network was expected to increase the cognitive load involved in the processing of the longer branch and consequently to increase the likelihood that describers resort to the principle of minimal effort. Hence, the probability that subjects would describe the shorter branch first should be higher. The data confirmed these expectations, as is shown in Figure 4.31. Similar outcomes were obtained for variants of these networks, where the two branches were connected to each other orthogonally.

One highly interesting pattern of results emerged from the analysis of description latencies. For example, from network 1.1.0, to network 1.1.1, and finally to network 1.1.2, the time to start describing steadily increased. Thus, as networks were more demanding in terms of the amount of cognitive resources required to implement nonoptimal strategies, response latencies were longer. The same pattern emerged for the other sets of networks. Apparently, when subjects were engaged in the process of deciding whether to start their description in one direction or another, processing times varied as a function of the quantity of information to be processed. Larger amounts of to-be-processed information were reflected in greater amounts of time.

Probably the most relevant finding in the analysis of latencies is what differentiates subjects who eventually used the optimal descriptive strategy (shorter branch first). For each network, we selected the group of subjects who consistently chose the optimal strategy for both versions (that is, the version shown in Figure 4.31 and its mirror counterpart). These subjects were considered *consistent strategy-appliers*. The remaining subjects were qualified *nonconsistent appli-*

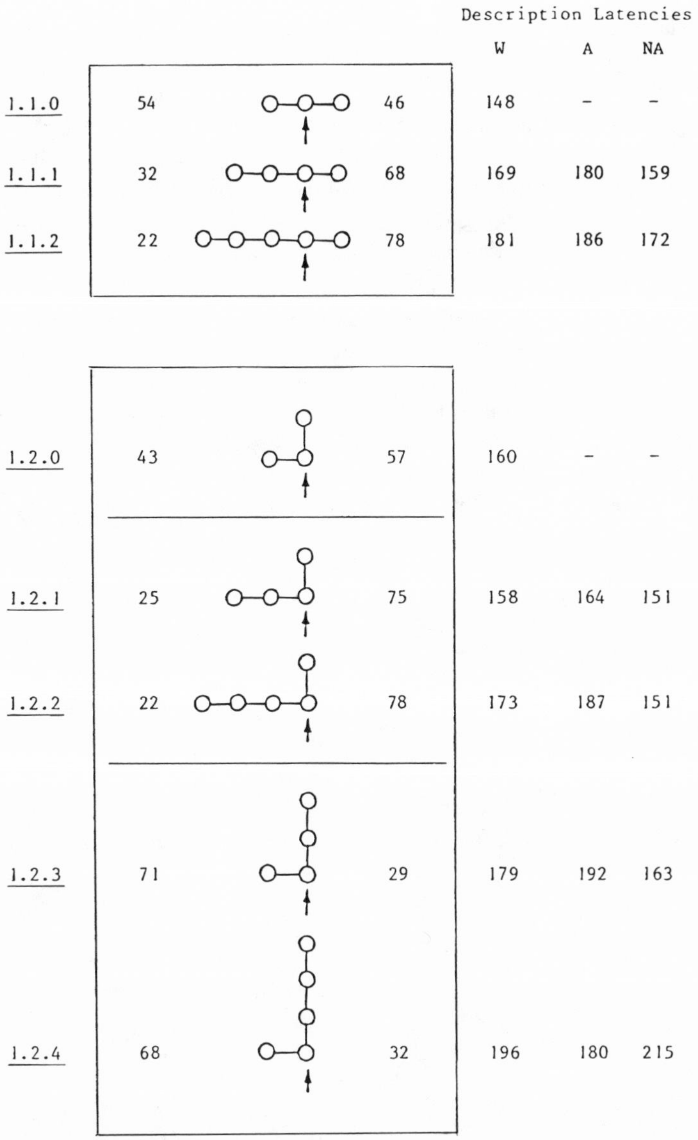

Figure 4.31. Class 1 networks: Short versus long linear branches (arrows indicate starting points for descriptions). Proportions of subjects making each directional choice are given for each network (average proportion for each network and its mirror version). Mean description latencies (in centiseconds) for the whole sample (W), consistent strategy-appliers (A), and nonconsistent appliers (NA) are shown to the right of the figure.

ers. What emerged from this analysis was that the consistent strategy-appliers had overall significantly *longer* description latencies than did nonappliers for all the networks of this class (with the single exception of network 1.2.4). A likely explanation of these time patterns is that application of the optimal strategy is dependent on more extensive analysis of the network before responding.

Another variant on Levelt's paradigm involved altering the visual presentation of some branches by making them visually more complex. For instance, instead of being a straight line, the linear branch in the second and third class of networks was distorted. This manipulation was expected to affect the probability of occurrence of typical descriptive strategies. We assumed, in particular, that subjects would tend to describe the other branch first, since it might appear to be comparatively less complex. Figure 4.32 shows that in comparison to networks 2.1 and 2.2, the probability of describing the linear branch first decreased for networks 2.3 and 2.4, yielding in the second case the reverse of the theoretically optimal strategy. In the case of networks 2.3 and 2.4, not only was the relative (perceived) complexity of the complex branch lower than before, but the fact

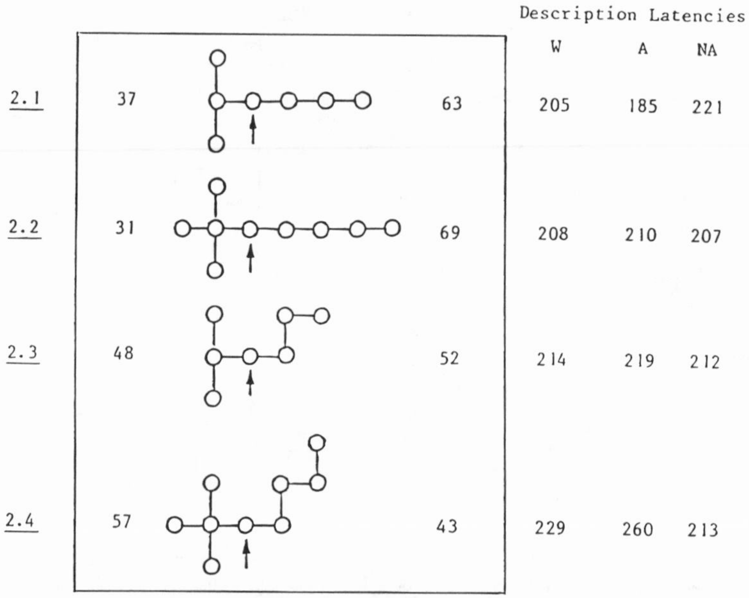

Figure 4.32. Class 2 networks: Linear versus embedded branches (arrows indicate starting points for descriptions). Proportions of subjects making each directional choice are given for each network (average proportion for each network and its mirror version). Mean description latencies (in centiseconds) for the whole sample (W), consistent strategy-appliers (A), and nonconsistent appliers (NA) are shown to the right of the figure.

that its structure was an appealing Gestalt increased the probability that it would be described first. Subjects apparently did not only judge branch complexity in terms of the number of embedded points, but also in terms of structural complexity (or amount of distortion) of the linear branch.

For the second class of networks, distorting the linear branch increased response latencies, which suggests that greater visual complexity of the pattern tended to delay the onset of description. However, no reliable difference emerged from the comparison of appliers and nonappliers. The only exception was network 2.4, where the subjects who consistently applied the dominant strategy (in this case, describing the embedded branch first) had longer onset delays before starting their descriptions. This result is in line with the data collected for the first class of networks.

According to Levelt, the strategy expected to be dominant for the third class of networks consists of describing the loop first, then the linear branch. In fact, the occurrence of this strategy is dependent on the length of the linear branch. For network 3.1, where this branch contains only one circle, a minority of subjects described the loop first (see Fig. 4.33). The probability of describing the loop first substantially increased for network 3.2, where the addition of further circles to the linear branch was intended to increase its load. However, the pro-

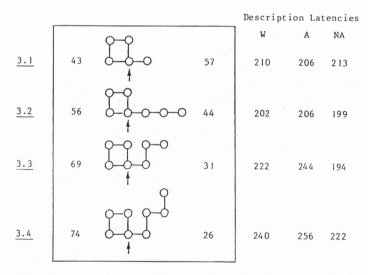

Figure 4.33. Class 3 networks: Loop versus linear branches (arrows indicate starting points for descriptions). Proportions of subjects making each directional choice are given for each network (average proportion for each network and its mirror version). Mean description latencies (in centiseconds) for the whole sample (W), consistent strategy-appliers (A), and nonconsistent appliers (NA) are shown to the right of the figure.

portion of subjects who chose the loop-first strategy still remained moderate. The manipulation of the linear branch in network 3.3 (from a straight to an angled line) further increased the probability that subjects would first engage in description of the loop. The occurrence of this strategy further increased when both visual complexity and load of the linear branch (in terms of number of circles) were increased (network 3.4).

Response latencies were similar for networks 3.1 and 3.2, and they clearly increased when the linear branch of network 3.3 was an angled line, and then again when one further circle was added in network 3.4. Thus, as patterns made the optimal strategy more useful, the time required for elaborating the response was longer. In addition, latencies were longer for subjects who used the loop-first strategy.

Implementation of descriptive strategies thus appears to be governed by several cognitive factors. The occurrence of descriptive strategies can be predicted on the basis of an analysis of the cognitive load associated with the processing of different parts of the to-be-described object. Further, analysis of response latencies provides converging evidence as more demanding networks involve longer onset delays before starting descriptions. The data also provide clear indications that more processing time is involved before producing a response that is in accordance with the optimal (dominant) strategy. The response latency findings may reflect the fact that subjects perform some implicit computation before responding, and that the more computation, the better adapted the outputs. Apparently, the subjects who tend to be consistent strategy appliers also tend to engage in deeper analyses of the networks before describing them.

In an extension of this experiment, we compared descriptive strategies used to describe visually presented networks and those used to describe *mental images* of previously memorized networks. When subjects described their mental images, their strategies exhibited strong similarities with those involved in the description of physically present configurations. These findings are compatible with the hypothesis that similar processes are used to access perceptual events and visual images of spatial configurations. Furthermore, while descriptive strategies were similar for perceived and imagined configurations, description latencies were overall longer in the imaginal than in the perceptual condition, which probably indicates that a greater amount of cognitive effort was required when subjects had to describe visual images than when they described perceptually presented networks.

Additional analyses provided information regarding within-subject consistency in strategies used for describing perceived or imagined networks. High consistency was found for those networks for which a clear dominant strategy was evidenced in the perceptual condition. For example, there was a consistent tendency for subjects who used the dominant strategy in the first class of networks (i.e., describe the shorter branch first) to use this strategy again in the imaginal condition (cf. Robin & Denis, 1991). Finally, no reliable differences were found between high and low imagers as regards their inclination to use dominant descriptive strategies. The only difference between the two groups was that high imagers had consistently shorter description latencies than did low imagers (and they reliably devoted more time to study networks during the memorization phase) (cf. Robin, 1992).

In Levelt's account of descriptive strategies, descriptions are essentially considered as "tours." Linearization strategy consists in making a tour similar to those reported for descriptions of apartments or rooms (cf. Linde & Labov, 1975; Ullmer-Ehrich, 1982). Levelt (1982b) reported that subjects divide into two main linearization types, which he terms "jumpers" and "movers." The essential difference between them lies in the way they deal with backtracking to choice points. Jumpers first select one branch and describe it entirely; then they leap back to the choice point in order to describe the other branch. Movers do not leap back, but move step by step back, along the branch already described, until they again reach the choice point. Tour-like linearization is essentially based on the principle of connectivity—that is, "wherever possible, choose as the next node to be described one that has a direct connection to the current node" (Levelt, 1989, p. 140).

However, an extension of Levelt's approach was proposed more recently by Bisseret and Montarnal (1993), who argued for the existence of other strategies than those which depend on tour-like linearization. Their subjects exhibited what Bisseret and Montarnal call analytical (or breaking down) strategies. These strategies consist in executing hierarchical analysis of networks. Networks are seen as sets of subparts, which can themselves be analyzed into more elementary items. Subparts may sometimes be labeled (for instance, "On the left side, there is a tilted T," or "On the right, there is a cross"). Other strategies are also reflected by subjects' descriptions. One of them consists in describing the distribution of circles and lines of the networks across a virtual $i \times j$ matrix. The value of these strategies is that they are freed from the principle of maximal connectivity. Therefore, they cannot be interpreted in terms of tour linearization.

Bisseret and Montarnal also showed that the frequency of occurrence of these strategies increased in a condition where Levelt's networks were used in description tasks without any constraint on the starting point. The dominance of tour-like descriptions thus may to some extent depend on the constraints associated with the task and materials originally used by Levelt. In another study, Montarnal (1993) showed that the various descriptive strategies evidenced were found in both oral and written descriptions. The dominant directional choices for the three types of networks also were confirmed in both oral and writing conditions.

Another indication of the robustness of preferred directional choices originally evidenced by Levelt (1982a) was obtained in a recent study where we asked subjects to describe two sets of pictures: (1) networks made of colored circles

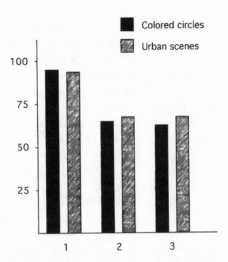

Figure 4.34. Proportion of subjects exhibiting the dominant directional choice for each class of networks with each set of pictures: colored circles versus urban scenes.

connected by horizontal and vertical lines, and (2) urban scenes where colored circles were replaced by buildings and lines by streets (similar to those shown on Fig. 4.29). The question was whether realistic, semantically rich visual scenes would produce the same results as those obtained with rather abstract, meaningless patterns. The results indicated that subjects showed quite similar strategies in the description of both realistic and abstract materials (Fig. 4.34). The cognitive constraints that affect describers' linguistic choices thus appear to be quite general, and in particular to be effective when the configurations to describe are visuospatial urban scenes. This finding should encourage researchers in this domain to identify other possible constraints of this type, with the objective of promoting descriptive conditions with minimal cognitive load and maximal communicative efficiency.

CONCLUSIONS AND EXTENSIONS

This chapter described a variety of empirical work that attests to the fact that people are capable of constructing visuospatial mental representations, like visual images or cognitive maps, from verbal descriptions of spatial configurations. The experiments described demonstrate that these representations contain information in which the structure is, to a large extent, similar to perceptual information. The validity of this phenomenon was established mainly through studies of mental scanning and mental comparison. Our findings show that it is particularly well demonstrated when configurations have rather low degrees of complexity and are described according to sequences that allow people to integrate on-line information in an efficient way (such as sequences preserving referential continuity). The structure of the description affects the structural qualities of the representation constructed by the subject, but it is also important to note that there are large individual differences. In particular, visuospatial imagery strongly facilitates cognitive processing in these situations.

A wide variety of descriptive strategies is available to subjects describing a visuospatial scene or situation, but the structural quality and communicative value of those strategies can vary widely. In most cases, descriptive strategies reveal describers' intentions to facilitate addressees' on-line integration of elements of the described configuration. People have at their disposal a set of discursive procedures that allow them to provide their addressees with a global view of the configuration, and then to deliver more detailed pieces of information in a systematic fashion. These strategies are largely dependent on the structure of the described object, as well as on the objective associated with the descriptive situation.

Taking into account addressees' domain-relevant knowledge is also crucial. In description tasks in which there are constraints on the starting point, speakers order their discourses in such a way that memory load of their addressees is lowered. "Apt" describers are not only characterized by adequate linguistic aptitudes but also by their capacity of constructing a coherent visuospatial representation of the object to be described.

All of the data presented converge on the notion that spatial cognition and language, despite essential structural differences, may interact in the human cognitive system, and most certainly do have intimate functional relationships. People apparently create the same sorts of internal mental representations from verbal descriptions as they do from direct perceptual observations. Such a view was acknowledged by Talmy (1983), who proposed that linguistic descriptions of space are represented in terms of nonpropositional spatial schemas. These schemas are composed of perceptual representations of basic elements such as points and planes.

A similar view was suggested, more recently, by David Bryant (1992). According to Bryant, both perceptual and linguistic spatial information are represented by the same cognitive system. The "spatial representational system" (SRS) creates spatial models from disparate sources of input and is independent of those memory systems involved in other domains of knowledge. The primary role of SRS is to organize spatial information in a form that can be accessed by either perceptual or linguistic mechanisms. The SRS provides coordinate representations that are analogous to the structure of real space and reflect all possible relations between objects encoded in the coordinate space.

The conclusion that there is a common form of spatial representation for perceived and described environments is especially relevant in light of current linguistic research on the expression of space in various human languages. Klein (1982, 1993), Vandeloise (1986), Borillo (1991), and others have provided fine-grained analyses of the repertoires available for expressing spatial relations. Their works stress the importance for speakers of sharing identical (or sufficiently similar) representations of the domain of space. In addition, it is crucial for felicitous social interactions that speakers share knowledge of specific lexical meanings of spatial expressions and have also capacities for setting up common deictic space. These factors are especially important in collaborative dialogue about spatial objects or configurations (cf. Deutsch & Pechmann, 1982; Garrod & Anderson, 1987; Hupet, Seron, & Chantraine, 1991; Isaacs & Clark, 1987; Schober, 1993) and the description of routes in unfamiliar environments (cf. Gryl, 1993; Lloyd, 1991; Riesbeck, 1980; Waller & Harris, 1988; Wunderlich & Reinelt, 1982).

These issues are central in the understanding of human communication, but their investigation is also a source of inspiration in the study of interactions between humans and artificial systems, especially when one considers the increasing need for devices designed to assist people's orientation in unfamiliar environments. How should one integrate in an artificial system both knowledge and functions that would endow the system with capacities similar to those of human speakers (and maybe, in some cases, even more powerful capacities)? Beyond the relevance of this question from an ergonomic point of view, simulating natural processes has a heuristic value for the understanding of human cognition: It forces scientists to construct more explicit and realistic models of processes under study.

How can an artificial system be designed which transforms visuospatial information into linguistic expressions? How can this system answer questions on relative positions of landmarks and on the most convenient ways to connect them? How should spatial information be represented in the system? Which kinds of procedures should be implemented to access and utilize this information, and then express it in the form of outputs as close as possible to natural language? These questions, obviously, require solving a number of problems.

The first and probably the most difficult one concerns the analysis of visual scenes and their interpretation—that is, relating them to symbolic descriptions. Another crucial problem is to select appropriate formalisms for representing visuospatial information in computers, and to identify the best ways for manipulating these representations to achieve functionality associated with natural (mental) visuospatial representations (see Glasgow, 1993; Glasgow & Papadias, 1992).

These studies have to be closely connected, in particular with semantic analyses of spatial expressions and formal approaches to spatial reasoning (cf. Aurnague & Vieu, 1993; Briffault, 1992; Freksa & Zimmermann, 1993; Ligozat, 1993; Wazinski & Herzog, 1992). Finally, there is a set of problems involved in finding appropriate procedures for endowing artificial systems with the capacity for generating linguistic outputs. Some encouraging attempts for the design of generators of texts describing visual scenes have been reported (e.g., Conklin & McDonald, 1982; Denis, Robin, Zock, & Laroui, 1994; Wahlster, 1989).

Obviously, solving these problems can only be envisaged if connections are established among cognitive psychologists, linguists, and computer scientists, as well as experts in environmental cognition (e.g., Axia, Baroni, & Mainardi Peron, 1988; Garling & Golledge, 1989). This chapter, I hope, provides sufficient evidence that imagery and language have a number of important interfaces with spatial cognition, and that in exploring this domain, cognitive psychology has much to contribute in the context of interdisciplinary research.

ACKNOWLEDGMENTS

The author's research reported in this chapter was supported by the CNRS and by a DRET Grant (89-242). The author is grateful to André Bisseret, Luc Carité, Marie-Paule Daniel, Peggy Intons-Peterson, Phil Johnson-Laird, Marc Marschark, Barbara Tversky, Manuel de Vega, and Hubert Zimmer for insightful commentaries and suggestions during the preparation of this chapter. Thanks to Maryvonne Carfantan for her help in the preparation of the manuscript. Figure 4.1 was designed by Massimiliano Canestrari.

NOTES

1. To avoid the problems associated with the use of masculine and feminine pronouns, the convention that Subject A is a female speaker and Subject B a male listener has been adopted throughout the chapter.

2. The system interprets descriptions given by subjects in natural language. The software includes: (a) a dictionary containing syntactic, semantic, and pragmatic information necessary for the interpretation of descriptions; (b) an automaton, which uses dictionary information during the analysis of descriptions in order to build a representation of them; and (c) a repertory of typical descriptive sequences established from subjects' productions in a pilot study. The role of the ATN is to determine the specific sequence according to which landmarks are described by each subject and to group them into classes of sequences. The software checks for the matching between the subject's description and the configuration; it then attempts to match the sequence used with the sequences available in the repertory. In case of matching failure, the new sequence is incorporated in the repertory. Sequences are then grouped together as a function of a typology.

REFERENCES

Adam, J.-M. (1986). Prolégomènes à une définition linguistique de la description. *Travaux du Centre de Recherches Sémiologiques,* No. 52, 147–188.

Adam, J.-M., & Petitjean, A. (1989). *Le texte descriptif.* Paris: Nathan.

Aurnague, M., & Vieu, L. (1993). A three-level approach to the semantics of space. In C. Zelinsky-Wibbelt (Ed.), *The semantics of prepositions: From mental processing to natural language processing* (pp. 393–439). Berlin: Mouton de Gruyter.

Axia, G., Baroni, M. R., & Mainardi Peron, E. (1988). Representation of familiar places in children and adults: Verbal reports as a method of studying environmental knowledge. *Journal of Environmental Psychology, 8,* 123–139.

Baddeley, A. D. (1986). *Working memory.* Oxford: Clarendon Press.

Bisseret, A., & Montarnal, C. (1993). *Stratégies de linéarisation lors de descriptions textuelles de configurations spatiales. Rapport de recherche No. 1927,* INRIA, Grenoble, France.

Borillo, M. (1991). Sémantique de l'espace et raisonnement spatial. In *Actes du Colloque "Sciences de la Cognition"* (pp. 125–128). Paris: Ministère de la Recherche et de la Technologie.

Bower, G. H., & Morrow, D. G. (1990). Mental models in narrative comprehension. *Science, 247,* 44–48.

Briffault, X. (1992). *Modélisation informatique de l'expression de la localisation en langage naturel.* Unpublished doctoral dissertation, Université Pierre-et-Marie-Curie, Paris.

Bryant, D. J. (1992). A spatial representation system in humans. *Psycoloquy, 3* (16) space.1.

Bryant, D. J., Tversky, B., & Franklin, N. (1992). Internal and external spatial frameworks for representing described scenes. *Journal of Memory and Language, 31,* 74–98.

Byrne, R. M. J., & Johnson-Laird, P. N. (1989). Spatial reasoning. *Journal of Memory and Language, 28,* 564–575.

Byrne, R. W. (1979). Memory for urban geography. *Quarterly Journal of Experimental Psychology, 31,* 147–154.

Carité, L. (1992). Analyse automatique de descriptions spatiales. *Annexe au Rapport sur les travaux exécutés dans le cadre du contrat DRET 89–242,* "Elaboration et manipulation de cartes cognitives: Rôle de l'imagerie et des processus verbaux."

Conklin, E. J., & McDonald, D. D. (1982, June). Salience: The key to the selection problem in natural language generation. *Proceedings of the 20th Annual Meeting of the Association for Computational Linguistics* (pp. 129–135), Toronto.

Dean, R. S., & Enemoh, P. A. C. (1983). Pictorial organization in prose learning. *Contemporary Educational Psychology, 8,* 20–27.

Dean, R. S., & Kulhavy, R. W. (1981). Influence of spatial organization in prose learning. *Journal of Educational Psychology, 73,* 57–64.

Denis, M. (1991). *Image and cognition.* New York: Harvester Wheatsheaf.

Denis, M. (1993). Visual images as models of described environments. In D. Burger & J.-C. Sperandio (Eds.), *Non-visual human-computer interactions: Prospects for the visually handicapped* (pp. 3–12). Paris: Editions INSERM/John Libbey Eurotext.

Denis, M., & Carfantan, M. (1985). People's knowledge about images. *Cognition, 20,* 49–60.

Denis, M., & Carfantan, M. (1990). Enhancing people's knowledge about images. In P. J. Hampson, D. E. Marks, & J. T. E. Richardson (Eds.), *Imagery: Current developments* (pp. 197–222). London: Routledge.

Denis, M., & Cocude, M. (1989). Scanning visual images generated from verbal descriptions. *European Journal of Cognitive Psychology, 1,* 293–307.

Denis, M., & Cocude, M. (1992). Structural properties of visual images constructed from poorly or well-structured verbal descriptions. *Memory & Cognition, 20,* 497–506.

Denis, M., & Denhière, G. (1990). Comprehension and recall of spatial descriptions. *European Bulletin of Cognitive Psychology, 10,* 115–143.

Denis, M., Robin, F., Zock, M., & Laroui, A. (1994). Identifying and simulating cognitive strategies for the description of spatial networks. In W. Schnotz & R. W. Kulhavy (Eds.), *Comprehension of graphics* (pp. 77–94). Amsterdam: North-Holland.

Denis, M., & de Vega, M. (1993). Modèles mentaux et imagerie mentale. In M.-F. Ehrlich, H. Tardieu, & M. Cavazza (Eds.), *Les modèles mentaux: Approche cognitive des représentations* (pp. 79–100). Paris: Masson.

Denis, M., & Zimmer, H. D. (1992). Analog properties of cognitive maps constructed from verbal descriptions. *Psychological Research, 54,* 286–298.

Deutsch, W., & Pechmann, T. (1982). Social interaction and the development of definite descriptions. *Cognition, 11,* 159–184.

de Vega, M. (1994). Characters and their perspectives in narratives describing spatial environments. *Psychological Research, 56,* 116–126.

van Dijk, T. A., & Kintsch, W. (1983). *Strategies of discourse comprehension.* New York: Academic Press.

Ehrich, V., & Koster, C. (1983). Discourse organization and sentence form: The structure of room descriptions in Dutch. *Discourse Processes, 6,* 169–195.

Ehrlich, K., & Johnson-Laird, P. N. (1982). Spatial descriptions and referential continuity. *Journal of Verbal Learning and Verbal Behavior, 21,* 296–306.

Einstein, G. O., McDaniel, M. A., Owen, P. D., & Coté, N. C. (1990). Encoding and recall of texts: The importance of material appropriate processing. *Journal of Memory and Language, 29,* 566–581.

Engelkamp, J., & Denis, M. (1990). Sind mentale Repräsentationen multimodal? *Schweizerische Zeitschrift fur Psychologie, 49,* 222–233.

Finke, R. A., Pinker, S., & Farah, M. J. (1989). Reinterpreting visual patterns in mental imagery. *Cognitive Science, 13,* 51–78.

Foos, P. W. (1980). Constructing cognitive maps from sentences. *Journal of Experimental Psychology: Human Learning and Memory, 6,* 25–38.

Foos, P. W., Smith, K. H., Sabol, M. A., & Mynatt, B. T. (1976). Constructive processes in simple linear-order problems. *Journal of Experimental Psychology: Human Learning and Memory, 2,* 759–766.

Franklin, N., & Tversky, B. (1990). Searching imagined environments. *Journal of Experimental Psychology: General, 119,* 63–76.

Franklin, N., Tversky, B., & Coon, V. (1992). Switching points of view in spatial mental models. *Memory & Cognition, 20,* 507–518.

Freksa, C., & Zimmerman, K. (1993, August). *On the utilization of spatial structures for cognitively plausible and efficient reasoning.* Paper presented at IJCAI 93, Workshop "Spatial and Temporal Reasoning," Chambéry, France.

Gärling, T., & Golledge, R. G. (1989). Environmental perception and cognition. In E. H. Zube & G. T. Moore (Eds.), *Advances in environment, behavior, and design* (Vol. 2, pp. 203–236). New York: Plenum.

Garrod, S., & Anderson, A. (1987). Saying what you mean in dialogue: A study in conceptual and semantic co-ordination. *Cognition, 27,* 181–218.

Glasgow, J. I. (1993). The imagery debate revisited: A computational perspective. *Computational Intelligence, 9,* 309–333.

Glasgow, J. I., & Papadias, D. (1992). Computational imagery. *Cognitive Science, 16,* 355–394.

Glenberg, A. M., & Langston, W. E. (1992). Comprehension of illustrated text: Pictures help to build mental models. *Journal of Memory and Language, 31,* 129–151.

Gryl, A. (1993, September). *Analysis of cognitive processes used in route descriptions.* Paper presented at the European Conference on Spatial Information Theory, Marciana Marina, Italy.

Hupet, M., Seron, X., & Chantraine, Y. (1991). The effects of the codability and discriminability of the referents on the collaborative referring procedure. *British Journal of Psychology, 82,* 449–462.

Intons-Peterson, M. J., & Roskos-Ewoldsen, B. B. (1989). Sensory-perceptual qualities of images. *Journal of Experimental Psychology: Learning, Memory, and Cognition, 15,* 188–199.

Isaacs, E. A., & Clark, H. H. (1987). References in conversation between experts and novices. *Journal of Experimental Psychology: General, 116,* 26–37.

Jarvella, R. J., & Deutsch, W. (1987). An asymmetry in producing versus understanding descriptions of visual arrays. In A. Allport, D. G. MacKay, W. Prinz, & E. Scheerer (Eds.), *Language perception and production: Relationships between listening, speaking, reading and writing* (pp. 41–59). London: Academic Press.

Johnson-Laird, P. N. (1983). *Mental models: Towards a cognitive science of language, inference, and consciousness.* Cambridge: Cambridge University Press.

Johnson-Laird, P. N. (1989). Mental models. In M. I. Posner (Ed.), *Foundations of cognitive science* (pp. 469–499). Cambridge, MA: MIT Press.

Johnson-Laird, P. N., & Byrne, R. M. J. (1991). *Deduction.* Hillsdale, NJ: Erlbaum.

Kintsch, W. (1974). *The representation of meaning in memory.* Hillsdale, NJ: Erlbaum.

Kintsch, W., & Young, S. R. (1984). Selective recall of decision-relevant information from texts. *Memory & Cognition, 12,* 112–117.

Klein, W. (1982). Local deixis in route directions. In R. J. Jarvella & W. Klein (Eds.), *Speech, place, and action* (pp. 161–182). Chichester: John Wiley.

Klein, W. (1993). L'expression de la spatialité dans le langage humain. In M. Denis & M. Carfantan (Eds.), *Actes du Colloque Interdisciplinaire du Comité National "Images et Langages"* (pp. 73–85). Paris: CNRS.

Kosslyn, S. M. (1980). *Image and mind.* Cambridge, MA: Harvard University Press.

Kosslyn, S. M., Ball, T. M., & Reiser, B. J. (1978). Visual images preserve metric spatial information: Evidence from studies of image scanning. *Journal of Experimental Psychology: Human Perception and Performance, 4,* 47–60.

Kosslyn, S. M., Brunn, J., Cave, K. R., & Wallach, R. W. (1984). Individual differences in mental imagery: A computational analysis. *Cognition, 18,* 195–243.

Kosslyn, S. M., Reiser, B. J., Farah, M. J., & Fliegel, S. L. (1983). Generating visual images: Units and relations. *Journal of Experimental Psychology: General, 112,* 278–303.

Kulhavy, R. W., Lee, J. B., & Caterino, L. C. (1985). Conjoint retention of maps and related discourse. *Contemporary Educational Psychology, 10,* 28–37.

Kulhavy, R. W., Stock, W. A., Verdi, M. P., Rittschof, K. A., & Savenye, W. (1993). Why maps improve memory for text: The influence of structural information on working memory operations. *European Journal of Cognitive Psychology, 5,* 375–392.

Levelt, W. J. M. (1982a). Linearization in describing spatial networks. In S. Peters & E. Saarinen (Eds.), *Processes, beliefs, and questions* (pp. 199–220). Dordrecht: Reidel.

Levelt, W. J. M. (1982b). Cognitive styles in the use of spatial direction terms. In R. J. Jarvella & W. Klein (Eds.), *Speech, place, and action* (pp. 251–268). Chichester: John Wiley.

Levelt, W. J. M. (1989). *Speaking: From intention to articulation.* Cambridge, MA: MIT Press.

Ligozat, G. F. (1993). Qualitative triangulation for spatial reasoning. In A. U. Frank & I. Campari (Eds.), *Spatial information theory: A theoretical basis for GIS* (pp. 54–68). Berlin: Springer-Verlag.

Likert, R., & Quasha, W. H. (1941). *Revised Minnesota Paper Form Board (Series AA).* New York: The Psychological Corporation.

Linde, C., & Labov, W. (1975). Spatial networks as a site for the study of language and thought. *Language, 51,* 924–939.

Lloyd, P. (1991). Strategies used to communicate route directions by telephone: A comparison of the performance of 7-year-olds, 10-year-olds and adults. *Journal of Child Language, 18,* 171–189.

Mani, K., & Johnson-Laird, P. N. (1982). The mental representation of spatial descriptions. *Memory & Cognition, 10,* 181–187.

Marschark, M. (1983). Semantic congruity in symbolic comparisons: Salience, expectancy, and associative priming. *Memory & Cognition, 11,* 192–199.

McDaniel, M. A., Einstein, G. O., Dunay, P. K., & Cobb, R. E. (1986). Encoding difficulty and memory: Toward a unifying theory. *Journal of Memory and Language, 25,* 645–656.

Moar, I., & Bower, G. H. (1983). Inconsistency in spatial knowledge. *Memory & Cognition, 11*, 107–113.

Montarnal, C. (1993). Descriptions de configurations spatiales: Comparaison oral/écrit. In M. Denis & M. Carfantan (Eds.), *Actes du Colloque Interdisciplinaire du Comité National "Images et Langages"* (pp. 87–97). Paris: CNRS.

Morrow, D. G., Bower, G. H., & Greenspan, S. L. (1989). Updating situation models during narrative comprehension. *Journal of Memory and Language, 28*, 292–312.

Morrow, D. G., Greenspan, S. L., & Bower, G. H. (1987). Accessibility and situation models in narrative comprehension. *Journal of Memory and Language, 26*, 165–187.

Moyer, R. S. (1973). Comparing objects in memory: Evidence suggesting an internal psychophysics. *Perception and Psychophysics, 13*, 180–184.

Paivio, A. (1975). Perceptual comparisons through the mind's eye. *Memory & Cognition, 3*, 635–647.

Paivio, A. (1986). *Mental representations: A dual-coding approach.* New York: Oxford University Press.

Paivio, A. (1991). *Images in mind: The evolution of a theory.* New York: Harvester Wheatsheaf.

Paris, C. L., & McKeown, K. R. (1987). Discourse strategies for describing complex physical objects. In G. Kempen (Ed.), *Natural language generation: New results in artificial intelligence, psychology and linguistics* (pp. 97–115). Dordrecht: Martinus Nijhoff.

Perrig, W., & Kintsch, W. (1985). Propositional and situational representations of text. *Journal of Memory and Language, 24*, 503–518.

Potts, G. R., & Scholz, K. W. (1975). The internal representation of a three-term series problem. *Journal of Verbal Learning and Verbal Behavior, 14*, 439–451.

Pylyshyn, Z. W. (1981). The imagery debate: Analogue media versus tacit knowledge. *Psychological Review, 88*, 16–45.

Riesbeck, C. K. (1980). "You can't miss it!": Judging the clarity of directions. *Cognitive Science, 4*, 285–303.

Robin, F. (1992). *Stratégies cognitives dans la description de configurations spatiales.* Unpublished doctoral dissertation, Université René-Descartes, Paris.

Robin, F., & Denis, M. (1991). Description of perceived or imagined spatial networks. In R. H. Logie & M. Denis (Eds.), *Mental images in human cognition* (pp. 141–152). Amsterdam: North-Holland.

Rumelhart, D. E., & Norman, D. A. (1988). Representation in memory. In R. C. Atkinson, R. J. Herrnstein, G. Lindzey, & R. D. Luce (Eds.), *Stevens' handbook of experimental psychology* (2nd ed.): *Vol. 2: Learning and cognition* (pp. 511–587). New York: John Wiley.

Schober, M. F. (1993). Spatial perspective-taking in conversation. *Cognition, 47*, 1–24.

Schriefers, H., & Pechmann, T. (1988). Incremental production of referential noun-phrases by human speakers. In M. Zock & G. Sabah (Eds.), *Advances in natural language generation: An interdisciplinary perspective* (Vol. 1, pp. 172–179). London: Pinter.

Schwartz, N. H., & Kulhavy, R. W. (1981). Map features and the recall of discourse. *Contemporary Educational Psychology, 6,* 151–158.

Shanon, B. (1984). Room descriptions. *Discourse Processes, 7,* 225–255.

Talmy, L. (1983). How language structures space. In H. L. Pick, Jr., & L. P. Acredolo (Eds.), *Spatial orientation: Theory, research, and applications* (pp. 225–282). New York: Plenum.

Taylor, H. A., & Tversky, B. (1992a). Spatial mental models derived from survey and route descriptions. *Journal of Memory and Language, 31,* 261–292.

Taylor, H. A., & Tversky, B. (1992b). Descriptions and depictions of environments. *Memory & Cognition, 20,* 483–496.

Tversky, B. (1991). Spatial mental models. In G. H. Bower (Ed.), *The psychology of learning and motivation: Advances in research and theory* (Vol. 27, pp. 109–145). New York: Academic Press.

Ullmer-Ehrich, V. (1982). The structure of living space descriptions. In R. J. Jarvella & W. Klein (Eds.), *Speech, place, and action* (pp. 219–249). Chichester: John Wiley.

Vandeloise, C. (1986). *L'espace en français: Sémantique des prépositions spatiales.* Paris: Editions du Seuil.

Vandenberg, S. G., & Kuse, A. R. (1978). Mental Rotations, a group test of three-dimensional spatial visualization. *Perceptual and Motor Skills, 47,* 599–604.

Wagener, M., & Wender, K. F. (1985). Spatial representations and inference processes in memory for text. In G. Rickheit & H. Strohner (Eds.), *Inferences in text processing* (pp. 115–136). Amsterdam: North-Holland.

Wagener-Wender, M., & Wender, K. F. (1990). Expectations, mental representations, and spatial inferences. In A. C. Graesser & G. H. Bower (Eds.), *The psychology of learning and motivation* (Vol. 25, pp. 137–157). New York: Academic Press.

Wahlster, W. (1989). One word says more than a thousand pictures: On the automatic verbalization of the results of image sequence analysis systems. *Computers and Artificial Intelligence, 8,* 479–492.

Waller, G., & Harris, P. L. (1988). Who's going where? Children's route descriptions for peers and younger children. *British Journal of Developmental Psychology, 6,* 137–143.

Wazinski, P., & Herzog, G. (1992, August). Coping with topological and directional relations based on three-dimensional geometric representations. Paper presented at the Tenth European Conference on Artificial Intelligence, Workshop "Spatial Concepts: Connecting Cognitive Theories with Formal Representations," Vienna, Austria.

Wunderlich, D., & Reinelt, R. (1982). How to get there from here. In R. J. Jarvella & W. Klein (Eds.), *Speech, place, and action* (pp. 183–201). Chichester: John Wiley.

CHAPTER 5

Representations of Visuospatial Cognition: A Discussion

Manuel de Vega, Marc Marschark,
Margaret Jean Intons-Peterson, Philip N. Johnson-Laird,
and Michel Denis

At the outset of this collaboration, the contributors to this volume all met on Tenerife, in the Canary Islands, at a meeting organized by the University of La Laguna. The following discussion includes conversation drawn from that meeting, as well as later exchanges, as we grappled with trying to understand the points of agreement and disagreement in each other's perspectives. Our goal was not to try to provide definitive answers to the questions that have been raised throughout the long tradition of research on visuospatial cognition, nor did we anticipate arriving at any consensus. We did expect, however, that after the presentations by our three invited speakers, we would be in a better position to discuss our points of agreement and disagreement concerning the nature and functions of visuospatial cognition. In this regard, we were surely successful. We leave to our readers whether the articulation of such diverse perspectives provides any better understanding of the phenomena of interest or is better seen as merely the beginning of a longer process that will accomplish that end. One thing that is certain, however, is that what came out of this collaboration is more—and quite different—from what we had expected.

From the outset, all of the contributors to this volume agreed that people use visuospatial representations in a variety of cognitive tasks, both inside and outside of the laboratory. As should be evident from the preceding chapters, we also agree that these visuospatial representations have some analogical or perceptual-like quality, and that they cannot be reduced to any kind of linguistic or propositional code. Michel Denis, for example, stresses that mental images resemble the structure of the entities they represent, rather than having an arbitrary syntax; Philip Johnson-Laird describes visuospatial images as representations of the perceivable aspects of a situation from an observer's point of view; and Margaret Jean Intons-Peterson argues that imagery is a sensory-perceptual memory with spatial extent. These assumptions entail somewhat different foci, but they are similar in the primacy of their analogical flavor. Far from being a reprise of the classical debate about the ontological status of mental imagery, this volume, at first blush, appears to have all of its authors lined up on the same side.

Despite our apparent agreement, examination of the three primary chapters reveals that the authors differ substantially in the content and goals of their arguments as well as in their theoretical views (a point later noted by Intons-Peterson). Even at the time of our "roundtable" meeting, the diversity of views within the group was apparent. In that context, Marc Marschark was the first to suggest that the similarity in the participants' positions might be more apparent than real, when he argued that they seemed to be talking about rather different levels of analysis. Margaret Jean Intons-Peterson responded:

[In fact], my knowledge-weighted model of imagery is closer to the work of Denis than to that of Johnson-Laird, but both Denis and I have limited our focus more than Johnson-Laird. This does not mean that the three views are incompatible. To the contrary, all of our work may be treated as dealing with subclassifications of human cognition.

In her chapter, Intons-Peterson sought to clarify the interface between imagery and language. Her theoretical focus derives largely from issues relating to memory performance, and those origins are evident in the way that her theoretical framework for mental imagery, in her words, "embraces linguistic components, rather than minimizing them." In examining a variety of research findings across several paradigms, this approach allowed Intons-Peterson to integrate diverse findings relevant to the role of knowledge in imagery, the functional parallelism between perception and imagery, the neuropsychology of imagery, the role of imagery in creative thinking, and, finally, the possibilities for a connectionist approach to understanding mental imagery.

Michel Denis also explored the functional interface between language and mental imagery, but his focus resided in the domains of interpersonal communication and individual differences. His central question, as he put it, was "how can imagistic and linguistic representations 'cooperate' when one cognitive system has to interact with another one with the purpose of conveying information about spatial entities?" Denis provided several answers to this question, considering both the point of view of the comprehender, who hears or reads descriptions of spatial scenes, and the point of view of the describer, who tries to communicate how such a scene appears. On the comprehender's side, Denis demonstrated through studies of mental scanning and mental comparison that subjects use verbal descriptions of maps to build detailed images that preserve metric distances. On the other side, a describer appears to follow a variety of conversational conventions to facilitate the comprehender's on-line integration of the described scene.

In contrast to Denis's emphasis on visuospatial codes and Intons-Peterson's integration (rather than separation) of verbal and imaginal representations, Philip Johnson-Laird provided evidence for a triple-code hypothesis of mental representation. To the classical dual view of propositions and images as the two primary forms of mental representation, Johnson-Laird added mental models as a third alternative with its own distinctive features. In his view, mental models share with images an analogical character that contrasts with the arbitrary nature of the symbols and syntax of propositions. Unlike images, however, Johnson-Laird argued that mental models "contain abstract elements that cannot be visualized, and they correspond not to a single situation, but to a class of situations or, in some cases, to a set of such classes." To support his position, Johnson-Laird reexamined evidence accumulated from a decade of problem-solving research, primarily with regard to deductive reasoning. The result of that reexamination (and occasional reinterpretation) was strong support for the triple-code approach.

As Intons-Peterson noted, her position and that of Denis appear to mesh fairly well. Both investigators focused on the functional relationships between language and imagery, and they were primarily concerned with the perceptual nature of visuospatial imagery. For both, the theoretical roots of their imagery work appear intertwined with Paivio's (1971, 1986) dual-coding model (see also, Denis, 1979), as well as in the "spatial tradition" of imagery research (see Intons-Peterson, this volume). Their perspectives on mental imagery have been enriched and elaborated, however, by the incorporation of new findings coming from recent research in their own and others' laboratories. Johnson-Laird, meanwhile, clearly takes issue with the dual-coding perspective in his integration of mental models with the current view of the role of mental imagery in human cognition. Perhaps surprisingly, Denis supported the distinction of mental models and mental images, "in spite of their functional similarity" and, with Johnson-Laird, sought to establish the similarities and differences between mental models and imagery processes.

The diversity of topics and levels of analysis inherent in these three positions creates a serious challenge to any attempt to reconcile them within a single, coherent schema. From the perspective of the contributors, however, the differences among these positions are just as interesting as their similarities. As Michel Denis noted, our purpose in this collaboration was to gain a better understanding of visuospatial cognition, not by "homogenizing" our points of view, but by assembling and clarifying some of the major themes in the field. It therefore should not be surprising that some long-standing, controversial issues arose in all of the chapters and in our discussions. We now turn to consideration of those points.

HOW MANY CODES?

In the 1960s and 1970s Paivio's dual-coding model popularized the view of an analogical, visuospatial imagery code distinct from a verbal (linguistic) system. That view dominated research on comprehension and memory for well over a decade. During the 1970s, in the context of computational models of cognition, however, the debate arose concerning whether or not analogical representations were theoretically necessary to account for imagery-related effects in various tasks. Although Johnson-Laird's earlier work on verbal and nonverbal components of syllogistic reasoning well positioned him to mediate this "imagery debate," he took another approach. In his initial account, Johnson-Laird (1983, p. 157) suggested:

> There is plainly a relation between images and mental models, and I shall assume that images correspond to *views* of models: as a result either of perception or imagination, they represent the perceptible features of the corresponding real-world objects. In imagining, say a rotating object, the underlying mental model of the object is used to recover a representation of its surfaces, reflectances, and so forth—what the late David Marr . . . called the "2½-D sketch." Hence . . . when you form an image, you must compute the projective relations from the model to the 2½-D sketch: a model underlies an image.

More than a decade (and quite a bit of research) later, however, Johnson-Laird's chapter in this volume makes clear that he now holds the view that mental models and images are different and equally valid forms of mental representation. During our roundtable discussion, Michel Denis expressed his surprise at this theoretical shift, prompting this response from Johnson-Laird:

> Michel asked why I changed my view. . . . You know, if someone actually said, "we're going to execute you tomorrow unless you abandon this [new] view, or persuade us otherwise," I don't think I could come up with a good argument to distinguish between the two positions. So if nothing else, it's a kind of intuition . . . but notice that the structure of the argument I made was first to separate our propositional representations to leave the rest, and then to try to tease [images and models] apart. So I

certainly think that in some sense that structure is the right way to think about it: Images are closer to models and models are closer to images than either of them is to propositional representations. . . . [At the same time], the case for models being distinct from images comes from two simple observations: First, as I discuss in my chapter, Shepard's mental-rotation studies show that subjects rotate three-dimensional representations and project images from them. So the distinction between a model and an image is certainly to be found in Metzler and Shepard. [See also his discussion of 3-D models below.] It also speaks to the ability of congenitally blind individuals in mental-rotation tasks: they are rotating models, not images. Second, there is considerable evidence that the representations underlying reasoning often depends on information that cannot be visualized, for example, negation [see Johnson-Laird, this volume].

In principle, having two analogical codes rather than just one seems a loss of parsimony, which demands some justification. Both Denis and Johnson-Laird outline some criteria that would allow the distinction between imagery and mental models in their respective chapters. Interestingly, those criteria fall largely along the lines of the previously noted "long-standing, controversial issues" surrounding mental imagery itself.

SPATIAL RESOLUTION

Mental images are usually thought of as fine-grained representations that preserve perceptual properties of the objects or events they represent. Mental models, in contrast, like "schematic images," analogically preserve only some gross structural parameters of the situation, such as correspondence among sets of individual tokens (see Denis, this volume; Denis & de Vega, 1993). In our discussion, Marschark suggested that there may be schematic images that are formed very quickly (less than a second) and are sufficient for many imagery tasks, while more detailed images take 3 to 4 seconds to form (cf. Paivio, 1971) and may have more specific "cognitive functions." Whether schematic images are "filled-in" over (a brief) time to produce detailed images or whether the two are different sorts of representation, with different origins and properties, has not been determined. The kinds of performance taken as evidence for the psychological reality of visuospatial images in laboratory studies, in any case, clearly depend on the latter type of richly detailed imagery. These representations can be used "on-line" and preserve perceptual parameters such as metric distances, orientations, and kinematic transformations of depicted objects.

The high-resolution nature of some images is clearly demonstrated by Denis through scanning experiments in which subjects accurately preserved time-distance relations in "moving" between landmarks of a described island. Degree of spatial resolution cannot be considered a sharp criterion for distinguishing between imagery and models, however, and in his chapter, Denis argues for a continuum of analogical representation from the extreme of finely detailed images to stylized mental models (see also Denis & de Vega, 1993).

AWARENESS

Perhaps above all else, there is a phenomenological quality of images that is absent from mental models. Images typically entail a vivid subjective experience, whereas mental models are less accessible to subjects' consciousness. During the roundtable discussion, controversy arose over the status of awareness within imagery theory. The most radical position was that of Johnson-Laird.

> JOHNSON-LAIRD: One of the things about images is that, almost by definition, one is conscious of them. That is to say, I don't know whether you would imagine that there could be unconscious images . . . whereas one of the things that I've always said about models is that people are aware of the content in the model and not the model itself, because if they were [aware], there wouldn't be all this argument about what is the proper structure.

Awareness, precisely because of its subjective nature, however, seems a weak criterion for distinguishing between images and mental models.

> MARSCHARK: There are also people, like Paivio, who believe in unconscious images. [From their view] if you have analogue properties in the behavioral data then it must have been done with an analogue representation, even if you're not aware of it.

Further, it is possible to be aware of some aspects of images and not of others. Subjects, for example, may have "access" to the initial and final states in a mental rotation while not being conscious of the intermediate states.

> DENIS: There are aspects [of representations] which are functional in imagery but are not accessed by consciousness. . . . You may admit the idea of conscious images with some aspects or features of the image being functional without being experienced as such.

Like spatial resolution, however, awareness is not an all-or-none property of mental representation. The vividness of our phenomenological experiences is surely a matter of degree, and the line between the content of models and the models themselves needs to be made a priori, not in terms of its availability to introspection. Part of the problem, all of the contributors agree, is that individuals differ in their reports of image vividness (which can be seen as one measure of awareness), and even high-imagery subjects probably are not totally aware of all of the metric and kinematic details that potentially could be part of their images.

SPATIAL VERSUS NONSPATIAL INFORMATION

Throughout this book it has been argued that both mental models and mental imagery can reflect spatial information in an analogical manner. However, mental models—unlike mental images—also can represent nonspatial information. This statement is rather obvious if we consider deductive reasoning, because the concepts in the premises are sometimes abstract—or even meaningless—and therefore nonvisualizable. Even when the content of premises involves visual referents, Johnson-Laird claims that models—unlike images—serve to represent nonvisual properties such as negation and quantifiers. Consider the example of negation that he mentioned above. In his chapter, Johnson-Laird argues:

> The theory postulates that models contain elements representing negation. Negation, however, is an abstract notion that cannot be visualized. Individuals might have an image, say, of a large cross superimposed on the image of the relevant situation, but, as Wittgenstein (1953) pointed out, the image itself does not do the work of negation. It depends on the procedures for interpreting the image—that is, for mapping a negative sentence into the image, and for mapping the image back into a negative sentence. Most people, however, do not report using such images as a regular basis for understanding negative sentences.

Mental models, on the other hand, are "condensed" representations in comparison to spatial images. According to Johnson-Laird, when mental models are used in deductive reasoning, they represent a "class of situations" rather than a single situation. Mental images, in contrast, represent individual objects or scenes. If we accept both the analogical and the abstract qualities of mental models, it appears that they should provide more efficient support for reasoning and comprehension than mental imagery.

This conclusion conflicts with the facilitation produced by external visual aids both in reasoning (Johnson-Laird, this volume) and comprehension (Glenberg & Langston, 1992). Johnson-Laird, for example, found that subjects benefited from using diagrams (geometric shapes) arbitrarily assigned to relations between premises (e.g., inclusive disjunction, exclusive disjunctions). The use of diagrams (which presumably induces mental images) improved subjects' performance in reasoning relative to standard verbal materials. This facilitation probably reflects the reduction in working memory load through the symbolic function attributed to images (Johnson-Laird, this volume).

In the same vein, Glenberg and Langston (1992) demonstrated that diagrams facilitated the comprehension and retention of texts, even when the texts described sequential procedures rather than visuospatial contents. As in Johnson-Laird's present experiment, subjects in the Glenberg and Langston study used diagrams as "symbolic mental models" to understand abstract relationships. The moral of those experiments appears to be that subjects can use imagery-like processes (mental rotation, representation of scenes, etc.) under the control of abstract mental models in order to accomplish reasoning and comprehension.

Despite the similarity of mental models and visuospatial images in some respects, it is clear that the two forms of representation are quite different. In fact, some of the proposed features of mental models appear rather close to characteristics traditionally attributed to propositional representations. For example, both mental models and propositions are seen as appropriate for the natural representation of abstract relations, whereas images generally are not. Both mental models and propositions are essentially "unconscious" codes, whereas images typically are accessible to awareness. Finally, de Vega and Denis suggested that both propositions and models appear to be constructed relatively automatically, without effort, relative to the effort entailed in constructing, maintaining (refreshing), and manipulating visuospatial images. Johnson-Laird, however, was "slightly skeptical" of that view, suggesting instead that "it's just that one normally uses materials that are within the abilities of the individuals tested."

These similarities between mental models and propositional representations led Manuel de Vega to suggest that the representational status of mental models may be midway between images and propositions, sharing characteristics of both. For example, there is a clear difference between mental models and propositions in terms of their underlying structure. According to Johnson-Laird, propositions involve an arbitrary syntax (that is still unexplained) "based on the relation between a predicate and its argument." Denis, meanwhile noted that mental models are representations based on the "semantics of resemblance." Just as schematic diagrams represent the structure of an object or situation, a mental model functionally contains the structure of what it represents: Tokens represent individual entities, properties of tokens represent properties of individuals, and so on (Johnson-Laird, this volume).

In his chapter, Johnson-Laird provides a wide range of empirical evidence intended to differentiate mental models from propositions. Mani and Johnson-Laird (1982), for example, showed that subjects are more likely to retain verbatim details of an indeterminate text (i.e., one compatible with more than one layout) as compared to a determinate text (i.e., one compatible with only a single layout). Conversely, subjects were better able to recognize a layout under the determinate condition than the indeterminate one.

JOHNSON-LAIRD: A plausible interpretation of these results is that subjects attempted to envisage the layout corresponding to a determinate description—

they constructed an image or a more abstract model of the situation—whereas they abandoned this attempt with indeterminate descriptions, which are consistent with more than one layout, and instead tried to hold onto a propositional representation of the description.

This interpretation reflects an important point of agreement among the three contributors: A propositional format is likely to be the best form of representation for some kinds of information.

During our discussions, both de Vega and Intons-Peterson suggested the possibility that propositional representations might function primarily as a sort of auxiliary code. One function of such a code is to "back up" information from linear inputs in order to retain verbatim details before building a representation of the situation. During language comprehension, for example, the propositional system allows a "first pass" computation of concepts and relations described by the text (e.g., Kintsch & van Dijk, 1978). This notion was not acceptable to others, however.

DENIS: My perception of the meaning of "auxiliary" is that of something optional, nonmandatory. In fact, I think there is agreement that propositions are obligatory and that mental models more frequently play an optional (but so helpful!) role. If what is meant by "auxiliary" is closer to "helpful," then I agree that propositions are especially helpful in the case where mental models are not well-suited to the processing of some sorts of texts.

Consistent with Denis's sentiment, there seems to be a consensus that neither full comprehension of texts nor deductive reasoning relies exclusively on propositional codes. Comprehenders often need a more explicit representation of the referent situation in order to reach full understanding of a text or to derive conclusions from a set of premises (assuming that a full semantic analysis is necessary in a particular context). Recent research in both language comprehension (e.g., Glenberg, Meyer, & Lindem, 1987) and deductive reasoning (see Johnson-Laird & Byrne, 1991) has generally adopted the mental-model terminology in referring to subject-generated representations of situations. When comprehenders are asked to make judgments of relative location or relative distance based on learned verbal descriptions, however, their mental representations appear to be more similar to the traditional notion of visual images rather than to mental models (see Denis, this volume). Still at issue is whether such differences entail distinct modes of representation at encoding, or whether alternative forms of representation can be constructed from the same information, depending on the current task situation.

Another auxiliary function of propositions, according to Intons-Peterson, is that they can guide the retrieval of visuospatial images from long-term memory into working memory (see also Marschark, Richman, Yuille, & Hunt, 1987). The use of mental images in ongoing tasks thus could benefit from the semantic (propositional) organization of long-term memory. A semantic, conceptual, or amodal long-term memory would provide an optimally flexible interface for both verbal and nonverbal information (regardless of its modality), and various studies appear to support this position (see Marschark et al., 1987; Nelson, Reed, & McEvoy, 1977; Potter, Kroll, Yachzel, Carpenter & Sherman, 1986).

SIMILARITY OF PERCEPTION AND VISUOSPATIAL REPRESENTATIONS

The apparent similarity between perception and visuospatial imagery has been a focus for research ever since the mid-1960s (see Carmichael, Hogan, & Walter, 1932). By definition, mental imagery is a perceptual-like code. In the case of visuospatial imagery, that code involves properties such as having subjective visual and spatial extent and the parallel availability of contained information. However, explaining this similarity beyond naive intuitions is not a simple matter.

A wide range of empirical evidence shows that visuospatial images are akin to perceptions of real-world stimuli, as both imagery and perception produce similar performance in many tasks (see Intons-Peterson, this volume). For example, the mental image of a rotating object is functionally similar to the perception of the real rotating object, insofar as the reaction times for the imaginal task parallel the function obtained in a comparable perceptual task. Additional evidence for an intimate relation between imagery and perception comes from neuropsychological studies suggesting that perception and imagery partially share the same neural circuitry (Farah, 1988; Kosslyn, 1987).

Along the same lines, experiments described by Denis and Intons-Peterson in the present volume are guided by the heuristic of an imagery-perception parallelism. This parallelism sometimes is exploited as a methodological device: To the extent that mental images result in performance that resembles visual perceptual performance (or not), the imagery system can considered visuospatial (or not). Intons-Peterson's experiments on image reconstrual and imaginal recomposition, for example, allow the contrast of performance in an imaginal task with that in an equivalent perceptual task (see Cornoldi, Logie, Brandimonte, Kaufmann, and Reisberg, 1995). Denis, in contrast, uses scanning experiments to demonstrate that mental images of described maps are functionally equivalent to their perceptual counterparts.

Despite the impressive accumulation of data on perception-imagery parallelism, the issue is far from clear and remains open to several possible interpretations (see reviews by Finke, 1985; Finke & Shepard, 1986; Intons-Peterson &

McDaniel, 1991; and Intons-Peterson, this volume). In response to Intons-Peterson's discussion of image interpretation, for example, Johnson-Laird offered an alternative view.

> JOHNSON-LAIRD: You write, "when we are deciding whether an object we saw . . . was a cup, glass, or bowl, we retrieve an image of the object for comparison with a generic (canonical) image of the various categorical possibilities." I would argue (following Marr) that we have a catalogue of 3-D models rather than canonical images, and that we can project images from such models. Also, visual images have a point of view whereas 3-D models do not—hence, there is the need to make a projection in order to experience them as images. [See also Denis, this volume, p. 132.]

Several other implications of the suggested imagery-perception link are of particular interest to this collaboration and thus worthy of discussion as we continue to consider some of the issues surrounding visuospatial imagery as a mode of mental representation.

THE VISUAL NATURE OF IMAGES

This volume, as the title indicates, deals with mental representations that are subjectively "visual" and "spatial" in nature. Although several investigators are now examining imagery in other modalities (e.g., motor, kinesthetic, auditory, olfactory), the overwhelming majority of the studies that have attempted to elucidate issues surrounding mental imagery have been in the visuospatial domain (i.e., the effects of varying the visual imageability of materials, instructions to image, high versus low visual imagery ability).

Given the analogical nature of imagery, it seems reasonable to assume that images of visual objects would entail visual qualities. This assumption has been challenged, however, by studies involving visuospatial imagery in congenitally blind persons (e.g., Cornoldi, de Beni, Roncari, & Romano, 1989; for a review, see Ernest, 1987). Several studies have indicated that totally, congenitally blind people—that is, who have had no visual experience—nonetheless demonstrate substantially the same pattern of results that have been taken as evidence of visuospatial imagery in sighted persons. Blind people, for example, show the typical angular disparity-reaction time relation in a mental-rotation tasks (e.g., Carpenter & Eisenberg, 1978; Marmor & Zaback, 1976).

There are several possible interpretations of these and similar findings (see Cornoldi et al., 1989), but it is clear that people can have mental representation of visuospatial displays without any visual substrate. Further, a wealth of evidence demonstrates that those representations cannot be attributed solely to spatial information derived from tactile, kinesthetic, or verbal experience. Consequently, the benchmarks of imaginal processing, such as mental rotation and mental scanning, must be compatible with some amodal, or at least nonvisual, form of representation that preserves metric information (Carreiras & Codina, 1992; Yates, 1985). At the same time, such an assertion seems incompatible with the introspections of sighted people, for whom images are phenomenologically rooted in the visual modality.

It is important, however, that we avoid radical conclusions from the studies with blind persons. The visual substrate may well play an important role in the images of sighted people, whereas the images of the blind might be constructed from other sources of information (spatial, kinesthetic, verbal, haptic), which might be less efficient in terms of the speed or accuracy of performance even while producing generally parallel performance. Similar results (and interpretation) with regard to auditory imagery in profoundly deaf individuals (e.g., Leybaert, 1993; Marschark, Cornoldi, & Porter, 1995) appear to support both the notion of amodal long-term memory representation and the flexibility of on-line, apparently sensory information.

SPATIAL EXTENT OF IMAGES

Some approaches to visuospatial imagery are guided by what we might call the "screen" metaphor, which is essentially a qualified version of the classical "picture in the head" metaphor. The most explicit version of the screen metaphor was provided by Kosslyn (1978; Kosslyn, Ball, & Reiser, 1978). According to that framework, images have metric structures, which entail distances, sizes, and mental transformations analogous to the corresponding physical properties. The picture-like nature of images leads to the assumption of a "visual field" for images, described in terms of "spatial resolution," "visual angle," and the like (Finke & Kosslyn, 1980).

In many ways, the contributors to this volume appear to adopt an implicit screen metaphor. Denis and Intons-Peterson, for example, claim that distances are preserved in images as indicated by scanning experiments (see also, Denis & Cocude, 1989). Denis and Johnson-Laird both identify the spatial nature of images with their visual quality.

DENIS: In some circumstances, it may be desirable to incorporate the metric structure of the represented world. . . ; visual imagery is especially useful in such a case. Indeed, visual imagery is a process which usually constructs representations with a very high degree of analogy (with an exact metric of distances and accurate expressions of relative positions).

JOHNSON-LAIRD: A visual image . . . gives the appearance of something, a seen object or something, from a particular point of view, and it does have some depth information in it.

Intons-Peterson went one step further, interpreting the studies with the blind as evidence that images are "memories with spatial extent," regardless of whether they are actually based on visual input (a point that Johnson-Laird and Marschark found troubling). This dissociation between the metric and the visual properties of images is a novelty, as until now most people had treated both characteristics as essentially the same. More importantly, her elaboration of this point brings the issue into line with earlier points about the number of codes likely to influence cognition and the ways in which we go about elucidating them.

INTONS-PETERSON: It is easy to be led into thinking that linguistic input, spatial images, and mental models exhaust the types of representations in human cognition. So they might. This surmise is unlikely to be true, however, for the following reasons: The first is that [all three of us] have concentrated on visuospatial imagery. There are other forms of imagery, such as auditory, gustatory, olfactory, and so forth. These forms may be spatial in nature—and auditory imagery appears to have spatial aspects—but the sensory-perceptual ones differ in part from their visuospatial cousins.

One other caution [concerning the link of perception and imagery] addresses the contention that similar outcomes imply similar underlying mechanisms. They might, but similarity of outcome is no guarantee of similar processing or representations. . . . Until we are able to track the neurochemical mechanisms underlying perceptual and imaginal performance (still neuroscience fantasy, unfortunately), the most we will be able to say is that responses in the two situations are highly similar. It is more likely that responses will be similar in some ways and differ somewhat in others, such as comparisons based on imagery taking longer than those based on actual perception. In these cases, we may have plausible tentative explanations for the differences, but these explanations are not definitive.

THE NEGLECT OF PERSPECTIVE

The screen metaphor lacks an important feature of human spatial cognition: Many of our perceptions and memories of the environment are perspective-oriented. Perhaps for the sake of methodological simplicity, most imagery experiments have dealt with representations of two-dimensional displays. Even when three-dimensional displays are used, they are placed or described in front of rather than surrounding experimental subjects (e.g., Pinker, 1980). One consequence of this bias is that the notion of perspective, and especially of egocentric perspective, has been neglected in the bulk of imagery research.

The present contributions do not address the perspective issue directly, as most of the experiments described entail two-dimensional internal and external displays involving scanning, reconstrual, mental addition, or verbal descriptions. Nevertheless, the issue is a relevant one that the authors recognize as needing clarification. Johnson-Laird, for example, explicitly suggested that images are constructed to represent a particular point of view. Denis makes a similar suggestion in his comparison of mental models and images.

DENIS: While the possibility remains that visual imagery can be used in order to instantiate a model by imposing a specific "view" on it, mental modeling cannot be viewed as being uniquely associated with a model of representation-like imagery, which mandatorily generates perspective-bound mental representations. . . . [At the same time] looking from particular perspectives, images can serve genuine symbolic functions.

The importance of egocentric perspective in spatial cognition has been stressed in a variety of studies (e.g., Denis, this volume; Denis & de Vega, 1993; de Vega, 1994; Franklin & Tversky, 1990). In many everyday situations, fine-grained metric parameters about size and distance are less important than gross egocentric, topological parameters that are labeled as "in front of you," "to your left," "over your head," and so on (see Denis, this volume). Comprehenders who receive verbal descriptions of three-dimensional scenes (i.e., given from a second-person perspective) are able to build egocentric frameworks, the dimensions of which have biased accessibility. In particular, objects placed in the head-feet dimension are the most accessible, followed by the front-back dimension, and then the right-left dimension. In addition, along the front-back dimension, the front is more accessible than the back (Franklin & Tversky, 1990). This dimensional nonequivalence presumably derives from asymmetries in the physical world, as a consequence of the design of our bodies and resulting perceptual and motor experience (Clark, 1973).

Importantly, egocentric frameworks are not static representations, because subjects are able to shift their perspective mentally or to describe alternative perspectives within the same framework (de Vega, 1994). This finding means that, contrary to the classical object-centered mental-rotation studies based on the screen metaphor, we are able to rotate entire spatial frameworks in addition to rotating objects within those frameworks.

ROLE OF KNOWLEDGE

What is the role of world knowledge in analogical representations? Pylyshyn (1981) argued that because visuospatial imagery is penetrable to beliefs, goals, and tacit knowledge, it could not be the ultimate form of mental representation. Johnson-Laird (1983, p. 152) took issue with that argument, stating that

> whether anything from ulcers to short-term memory fails to be "cognitively penetrable" might be difficult to determine. The real trouble is that Pylyshyn has pitched the battle in the wrong place. To see why, one only has to consider how a thoroughgoing materialist might react to Pylyshyn's recourse to beliefs, goal, and tacit knowledge. Such notions, the materialist might say, are epiphenomenal and not part of the functional architecture of the machine because they are "imagistically penetrable," i.e., the way in which they govern behavior can be influenced in a rationally explainable way by images. The moral is plain: images and beliefs are both high-level constructs, and it is a mistake to argue that they are epiphenomenal just because they can "penetrate" each other.

Consistent with this view, none of the present contributors seemed particularly impressed by Pylyshyn's theoretical argument, and all considered the issue of relations between knowledge and analogical representations a matter of empirical inquiry. Denis, Johnson-Laird, and Intons-Peterson all explored the link between language and visuospatial cognition (albeit from quite different empirical perspectives), and the only evidence against such a connection was Denis's null effect concerning the salience of landmarks on mental scanning times, an issue that we deal with below.

Intons-Peterson (this volume), for example, showed that visuospatial representations are sensitive to knowledge of real-world physical properties, such as object weight. In one set of experiments she reported that mental travel is slower when subjects imagine carrying heavier rather than lighter objects. In another set of experiments, she found that the time for mental recomposition and identification from imagined fragments increases as a function of the way in which objects are partitioned. Meaningful divisions (or those with Gestalt closure) are easier to reassemble mentally than are random divisions. According to Intons-Peterson, the influence of knowledge (and language) on visuospatial representation is so ubiquitous that the interface between knowledge and imagery should be taken as a primary characteristic of analogical representations (hence her *knowledge-weighted* framework).

Intons-Peterson's findings indicate that knowledge-weighting can facilitate performance. In deductive reasoning, however, relevant knowledge does not always enhance performance. According to Johnson-Laird,

When people reason, they tend to be "inferential satisficers," that is, if they reach a conclusion that is plausible because it fits their general knowledge, they are likely to stop reasoning. They may therefore accept an invalid conclusion because it is congenial to them. But, if they reach a conclusion that is implausible, they will tend to search more assiduously for a model of the premises that will refute it.

This situation presents two possibilities: In some cases, knowledge may facilitate reasoning, as incorrect conclusions will not fit with previous knowledge and reasoners will search for alternative models that eventually allow refutation of the conclusion. In other cases, the same mechanism of knowledge assessment can produce logically incorrect conclusions when they are plausible (Johnson-Laird, this volume; Oakhill, Johnson-Laird, & Garnham, 1989). Johnson-Laird shows that one theoretical advantage of mental models over purely propositional theories of reasoning is that they predict and explain the sorts of errors that subjects produce in reasoning tasks, whereas competing theories do not. Not all are satisfied, however.

INTONS-PETERSON: Johnson-Laird's model assumes that subjects "attempt to check that there are no alternative models that are true to their premises but that refute their conclusion. If there are none, then their conclusion is valid." I assume that the word "attempt" must be emphasized. In other words, that subjects may try to generate alternative models, but that there are no guarantees that they are successful or that they generate all possibilities. Hence, errors may occur. In fact, many of the predictions made by Johnson-Laird follow from assumptions about memory failures. The difficulty is that logically untrained individuals may not systematically seek alternative models and even those who do may not exhaust the possibilities. I assume that his theory is to be restricted to people trained in logic, but I'm not sure what the boundary conditions are with respect to individual differences [including] the stopping rules presumably employed when people attempt to identify alternatives.

JOHNSON-LAIRD: People do indeed overlook alternative models, both in the laboratory and in real life. Laboratory studies show that certain inferences are almost impossible for most people precisely for this reason. They also show that there are vast individual differences in reasoning performance [see, e.g. Johnson-Laird, 1983, pp. 118–119, for some typical data]. [You are asking], in effect, what causes these differences, that is, what determines when an individual stops searching for alternative models? The short answer is: No one knows. In my view, one important factor is likely to be working-memory capacity, and a recent study provides some evidence for this hypothesis [see

Bara, Bucciarelli, & Johnson-Laird, in press]. Likewise, the effects of diagrams in helping reasoning also support it. Yet, there are likely to be other, as yet unknown, factors too.

If there is no doubt that subjects can use their knowledge to modulate visuospatial images and evaluate the plausibility of their models, it is less clear whether that knowledge is used mandatorily or optionally. That is, the notion of cognitive penetrability assumes that tacit knowledge influences cognitive processes, such as imagery, automatically and potentially without subject control or awareness. Denis, however, showed that imagery scanning times were not affected by experimenter-supplied semantic or episodic information intended to modify the relative salience of landmarks. The null effects of salience in those tasks suggest that images may lack cognitive penetrability in some situations, or as Denis suggested, "that subjects are able to withdraw themselves from the influence of irrelevant factors."

Denis's view appears to conflict with Intons-Peterson's experiments involving mental travel, which, superficially, appear similar to his mental scanning task. Intons-Peterson's results were taken to indicate that subjects cannot ignore their knowledge about the physical world.

INTONS-PETERSON: I don't think images exist in a vacuum; obviously they make contact with other components, residents if you will, of long-term memory.

An important difference in the two methodologies, however, was that the salient information was provided by the experimenter in the Denis experiments but was subject-generated, tacit knowledge in the Intons-Peterson experiments. Thus, the ability of Denis's subjects to ignore biasing information about landmarks may be due to the episodic nature of such information. General world knowledge (i.e., from long-term memory) may operate more automatically in modulating imaginal and other cognitive processes, consistent with Intons-Peterson's findings.

INDIVIDUAL DIFFERENCES IN VISUOSPATIAL ABILITY

Imagery is usually associated with vivid subjective experience, and hence, as discussed above, awareness is usually considered as a distinctive trait of mental imagery relative to other mental codes. Not all people, however, describe their images as having the same degree of vividness, and introspection suggests variability in the vividness and detail of mental imagery across both situations and individuals. The mental-rotation paradigm provides a good example.

JOHNSON-LAIRD: I would guess that there are people who really do have a vivid image that they are consciously aware of rotating, if you do the experiment in the right way. There are others, such as myself, who, no way am I going to be able to do that.

The issue of individual differences in visuospatial imagery becomes particularly important when we try to establish operational measures of it and try to evaluate the performance of high- and low-scoring individuals on related tasks. This concern has arisen in several places within this volume, and it emerged as a primary point of debate during our face-to-face discussion.

Of central interest to all of the contributors was the methodological issue of accepting self-reports (usually via questionnaires) as a measure of individual differences in imagery. All the contributors agreed that the subjective nature of these questionnaires makes them suspect as measures of imagery ability. Questionnaires are easy to use, and their acceptance as measures of individual differences is often, as Intons-Peterson suggested, just a matter of expediency. At the same time, questionnaires like the *Vividness of Visual Imagery Questionnaire* and the *Individual Differences Questionnaire* do have some predictive power with regard to behavioral performance and even with regard to neuropsychological indices such as evoked potentials.

DENIS: [Such questionnaires] are not totally without use. They separate people who qualify themselves as high imagers and people who qualify themselves as low imagers and it turns out that there is something valid in this separation.

However, neither predictive power nor expediency is sufficient to give validity to self-reports. As Johnson-Laird pointed out, it is possible that questionnaires are predictive without our having any clear notion of what they are measuring (see also, Marschark et al., 1987). His critical argument proceeded on logical grounds:

JOHNSON-LAIRD: I always find it ironical that people doing individual differences research, if they use the questionnaire method, somehow feel that it's the questionnaire that's predicting the experimental result, whereas it seems to me that the experimental result is telling you what the questionnaire is actually measuring, if you're lucky.

The measurement problem, to a great extent, has been overcome in recent years by using performance in visuospatial tasks as measures of imagery ability, rather than relying on solely self-report questionnaires. Two such tests are the *Minnesota Paper Form Board,* which requires the mental reassembly of the parts of a figure, and the *Flags Test,* which requires mental rotation and comparisons. Performance on such tests generally is positively related to subjects' performance in visuospatial tasks, even if they fail to predict performance in other domains of mental imagery, such as memory for words (e.g., Katz, 1983). Denis, for example, presents results showing that subjects who report being high in visuospatial imagery ability produced shorter scanning times and a higher correlation of time and distance than did subjects reportedly low in visuospatial ability. Moreover, visuospatial capacities were related to subjects' performance on the task of describing visual scenes. Specifically, Denis found that high visuospatial subjects produced descriptions with better structures than did low visuospatial subjects, whereas verbal skills did not predict performance.

The loci of individual differences in imagery remain unclear, although all of the contributors speculate about their possible mechanisms. Both Denis and Intons-Peterson agreed with Marschark's earlier point that constructing or retrieving images may be a slow process of "filling in" visuospatial details on an initial "sketch." According to Intons-Peterson, high-imagers and low-imagers differ in their thresholds for classifying the result as an image.

DENIS: When you construct an image it is not constructed at once, but you engage in the process of more and more sharpness, more and more coherence, better or more veridical relationships between items. So, I am fighting against the idea of images as entities that are constructed at once and which can be used at any time since they are constructed. They are events which can undergo better structure, and in this respect probably high versus low imagers are people who take more or less time and effort to engage in this sharpness process.

It is clear that individual differences in visuospatial abilities sorely need clarification. Kosslyn, Brunn, Cave, and Wallach (1984) provided one comprehensive account in this regard, based on a componential analysis of visuospatial performance in a variety of "on-line" imagery-related tasks. Their computational model was later replaced by the neurologically based model of Kosslyn, Van Kleek, and Kirby (1990), although the more rigorously defined parameters of the latter model accounted for little more variance than did the completely "ad hoc" model.

Kosslyn's work did point the way for researchers in this area, emphasizing the need to provide an integrated account of imagery abilities that includes performance across a variety of tasks and subtasks as well as recognition of neurological and perceptual constraints on models of visuospatial abilities. His models also indicated the need to link visuospatial processing capabilities with the inferred effects of visual imagery on memory and comprehension performance.

Still at issue is whether such skills are better dealt with in terms of the general cognitive bases of individual differences or via more articulate modules or mechanisms that distinguish various subskills in that domain (see Kosslyn et al., 1984). In addition, de Vega has suggested that an important component of this broad investigation will be our understanding of those tasks in which visuospatial processing could affect performance but does not (see examples in the previous chapters of this volume).

LANGUAGE AND VISUOSPATIAL REPRESENTATION

Michel Denis has suggested that the linkage between language and spatial representation is the primary point that provided an interface for the three contributors. Johnson-Laird, however, was concerned about the limits of the generalization.

DENIS: It is particularly important that this is an imagery framework that embraces linguistic components. . . . I think it is useful to underline that a satisfying model of imagery demands both verbal and spatial approaches to encompass the available data [see Intons-Peterson, this volume]. I like the notion that images are "language-sensitive."

JOHNSON-LAIRD: I was not completely convinced by [Intons-Peterson's arguments] that all imagery paradigms admit some linguistic influence. Our study of reasoning from diagrams led to better performance than reasoning from verbal premises—a result that should also rule out worries about subvocalization [see Johnson-Laird, this volume]. I suppose it depends what you mean by "linguistic influence." Do Shepard's rotation studies admit of such an influence?

INTONS-PETERSON: Yes, in the sense that the rotation operation needs some kind of linguistic initiation to describe the task to the imagers. Once imaginal processes are underway, they may or may not be linguistically modified, depending on the task. If the imaginal task is one that relies on the knowledge of the real world, this knowledge may well affect the image constructed. But, at this point, I do not want to adopt a dogmatic stance that all images are always linguistically sensitive and modifiable.

Denis, meanwhile, elaborated the language sensitivity of visuospatial representations as they relate to the construction of mental maps during naturalistic communication. His research has provided a first glimpse of how people manage to build detailed functional images from verbal descriptions and the elaboration of verbal descriptions as a function of visuospatial displays that are either perceived or imagined. Intons-Peterson, however, suggested that additional research is necessary to relate the functional nature of the descriptions generated by the speaker and spatial relations elaborated by the addressee. Thus, de Vega and Intons-Peterson considered a common question:

DE VEGA: Have you tested whether the most popular, that is, the most frequent, descriptions are also the most efficient in terms of being understood by the addressee?

INTONS-PETERSON: When people attempt to describe a situation, they use a number of strategies. A little more than half of them include an initial overview of the situation. As Michel Denis has noted, describers may—and do— use different strategies. The question is whether the listener can adapt to different strategies and be able to produce a reasonable configuration. In his words, the conceptual structure may be instantiated in different linguistic structures. Are the linguistic structures equally effective facilitators of configuration construction? Denis does not describe research on this issue . . . [but] it would be very interesting to know about the accuracy of spatial scenes constructed from various kinds of linguistic descriptions of spatial scenes.

DENIS: We have not tested this formally up to now, but it is my intuition that probably one of the factors that regulates the choice of one branch or another branch [in the mental travel through an experimental layout] is . . . the fact that the speaker takes into account the cognitive capacities of the addressee. So I think probably the same factors are involved on both the production side and the comprehension side.

The links between language and visuospatial representations have been explored recently with regard to topological language (e.g., Franklin & Tversky, 1990) as well as visual reinterpretation (see Cornoldi et al., 1995). On the basis of such studies, it might be suggested that visual imagery must be contextually dependent on a variety of egocentric variables, including perspective and conceptual knowledge. One intuitively appealing approach would be to consider such sources of information as separate but interconnected systems in the same way as Paivio (1971) formulated the link of imagery and verbal processes. This kind of linkage has been challenged by Bryant (1992), however, who argued that there is an amodal spatial representation system that is linked to both perceptual and linguistic systems. Similar arguments have been about an amodal semantic system underlying both imagery and verbal systems (Marschark et al., 1987; Potter et al., 1986).

LEVELS OF THEORETICAL ANALYSIS

For any given domain of cognitive phenomena there are several levels of analysis that are complementary and constrain each other (Anderson, 1990; Cosmides, 1989; Marr, 1982; Pylyshyn, 1986). In Anderson's (1990) terminology, for example, we could identify "rational," "algorithmic," "computational," and "hardware" levels of analysis. The *rational* level (equivalent to Marr's computational theory) is that which describes the goal of the computation—the nature of the problem to be solved by a cognitive system. At this level, evolutionary considerations are usually relevant: Cognitive mechanisms were not designed randomly, but they have been optimized by evolution to fit some environmental demands. This level has been neglected by most students of cognitive psychology, although Marr emphasized that the nature of the problem to be solved imposes constraints (as well as guidelines) on the psychological theory.

The *algorithmic* level describes the functional architecture of the system, employing the vocabulary of representations, processes, modules and the like. The computational level (the level of actual implementation) involves the elaboration of effective procedures that simulate computationally a psychological theory. Finally, the *hardware* level corresponds to the description of the neurological support of cognitive functions.

These various levels of theory may "cooperate" in constraining each other. For instance, a theory at the psychological-algorithmic level of analysis may take into account the adaptive goals of the computations, the relevant data form neuroscience (hardware level), and use implementations as a sort of formal test of theoretical "fit."

Most of the literature on visuospatial cognition cited in this book, including the contributors' own research, has adopted a disciplinary perspective of cognitive psychology. That is, mental images and mental models are generally described in the vocabulary of "representations," "processes," and the like, corresponding to Anderson's algorithmic level of analysis. In her chapter, however, Intons-Peterson also considers the importance of the computational implementation and the hardware-neurological levels (Johnson-Laird and Denis also have done so elsewhere). Concerning implementation, she is particularly interested in the potential of a connectionist approach to visuospatial imagery. A few attempts have been made to produce such models relevant to visuospatial representation (e.g., Kosslyn, Chabris, Marsolek, & Koenig, 1992; Sergent, 1991), and Intons-Peterson seems cautious about the possibilities of connectionism when she describes its pros and cons in her chapter. Her position about connectionist is rather eclectic, accepting that parallel processing should be combined with serial and localized representations:

INTONS-PETERSON: One clear advantage flows from some basic assumptions about connectionist architecture, namely that representations are distributed and parallel. It now is clearly the case that at least higher mental processes are not strictly localized; rather, they appear to be fairly widely distributed across the brain. Moreover, given this distribution, substantial processing must be done in parallel to achieve the response times characteristic of humans. These assumptions may be combined with those of localized representation and serial processing, as may be needed to accommodate early stages of processes and efferent responses.

Johnson-Laird and Denis do not discuss connectionism or any other kind of computational-level theory in their chapters. However, during our meetings, Johnson-Laird expressed skepticism about the possibilities of connectionism:

JOHNSON-LAIRD: In essence, my views are that the most interesting thing about connectionism is this notion of a distributed representation. . . . [T]he learning algorithms that people have come up with don't interest me so much. Nobody has got a learning algorithm—though many people claim they have—that will learn even a context-free grammar, so at the moment I see a big gap between connectionism and dealing with natural language, but someone may come up with a different, more powerful learning algorithm. . . . It's an interesting idea, but extremely difficult to see how you can test the general idea. I once was standing with Dave Rumelhart and John Anderson and I said to them both, "We can test your specific theories but how can we test whether ACT as a general theory about architecture is the right one as opposed to the connectionist architecture." Neither of them had an answer.

Relevant to the hardware or neuropsychological level of analysis, Intons-Peterson provides an extensive review of the literature and commentary on some methodological problems in many current neuropsychological studies. Of particular importance, she calls attention to the difficulty of localizing imagery processes in one or the other hemispheres of the brain when experiments involve verbal materials that "probably bias processing toward left-hemisphere involvement." Another problem concerns the interpretation of metabolic methods of hemispheric localization. Contrary to the typical interpretation of such studies, whereby more metabolic activity is taken as an indicator of more cognitive activity, Intons-Peterson suggested that "It seems plausible that skilled activity would require less energy than unskilled" (see also Sergent, 1991). Given our current level of knowledge, Intons-Peterson concludes that implementation and hardware levels of analysis have to play a secondary role to psychological, empirical validation:

INTONS-PETERSON: I want to stress that connectionist and neuropsychological models are useful only to the extent that they satisfactorily define empirical results. Then, the assumptions underlying the model can be scrutinized carefully.

Concerning the rational (evolutionary) level of theorizing, there has been very little discussion in the domain of visuospatial cognition. Perhaps the most explicit formulation of a rational theory in this area was developed by Shepard (1984), who explained mental kinematics (responsible for mental rotation in imagery and apparent motion in perception) as a built-in mechanism resulting from the evolutionary development of the visual system. This mechanism would entail the internalization of constraints of kinematic geometry, its primary purpose being to optimize activity in "degraded" situations such as when the environment yields incomplete information (e.g., owing to darkness or obstruction), when there is insufficient time for complete analysis (e.g., in dangerous or time-cost trade-off situations), or following damage to the brain or the perceptual apparatus. Shepard's speculation seems theoretically useful as it allows a unified understanding of perception and imagery, and it gives a functional purpose to the apparently "modular" mechanism of mental rotation. Despite its potential interest, however, similar rational-evolutionary analyses of other visuospatial phenomena apparently have not been developed.

CONCLUDING REMARKS

The presentations of Johnson-Laird, Intons-Peterson, and Denis have provided extensive support for the notion that human cognition involves one or more specialized systems for dealing with visuospatial information. The authors' current research illustrates several trends in the study of visuospatial cognition in the 1990s, and clear progress from earlier theoretical and methodological approaches that were more limited in their scope.

Perhaps the most salient advance, common to all three contributors, is the integration of visuospatial representation with complex human capacities including comprehension, reasoning, and navigation. This perspective goes far beyond the earlier focus on memory for isolated words and pictures and recognizes that mental imagery may not be a unitary system. The abandonment of more simplistic views of imagery will result in a better understanding of the mechanisms of visuospatial processing and their place within the full constellation of human cognitive functioning. Preliminary findings, such as those reported here, suggest that some power will be removed from the concept of the mental image, placing it in domains such as semantic processing or alternative knowledge structures. Consistent with this shift, Johnson-Laird demonstrated that mental models appear to be the "raw material" for deductive reasoning, whereas propositions and images play a secondary role. Most importantly, mental models provide an a priori framework that explains both correct and incorrect reasoning, thus accounting for more variance in related tasks, both literally and metaphorically.

Denis and Intons-Peterson have both demonstrated and clarified some of the intricate relations between language and visuospatial representation. According to Intons-Peterson, visual images can combine both visual-sensory qualities and language (i.e., conceptual) sensitivity. This sensitivity extends from the phonological level to the conceptual-semantic level, and boldly rejects arguments that mental representations must be cognitively impenetrable for them to be ontologically primary (cf. Pylyshyn, 1981). Denis, meanwhile, has provided evidence that mental images built from verbal descriptions are functionally equivalent to those derived from direct perception, at least in the kinds of tasks that he has employed. Most importantly, he has begun an important exploration of the descriptions that are generated from visual scenes in order to communicate their structure to others.

The title of this volume signals the visual bias of most current research on nonverbal mental representation. There is a growing interest in nonvisual imagery, however, especially in the areas of motor imagery (e.g., Engelkamp, 1991; Helstrup, 1989) and auditory imagery (e.g., Marschark et al., 1995; Reisberg, 1992). Intons-Peterson has been at the forefront of this exploration of imagery in other modalities, and in her chapter she described some interesting experiments involving images of sounds and odors. Such images are notoriously difficult to describe, at least in part because the vocabulary for these modalities is poorer and less accurate than the visual vocabulary.[1] The reason for that difference remains unclear—but potentially exciting for a broad segment of cognitive psychology. Beyond being interesting in their own right, further research on mental representation in these nonvisual modalities will be theoretically and methodologically useful for understanding visuospatial imagery, because they are likely to be less "contaminated" by verbal-semantic factors (see Intons-Peterson, this volume).

Research presented by the contributors in this volume blends the use of older and newer experimental paradigms. This shift in paradigms is not just a methodological one, however. Several empirical questions and procedures closely associated with earlier work in visuospatial cognition now appear almost exhausted in their capacity to yield new theoretical information. We know, for example, that imagery most often improves free recall of isolated words in lists and in paired-associate learning of concrete and abstract words (cf. Marschark & Hunt, 1989). Further studies of this sort appear unnecessary unless they can contribute to our understanding of the role of imagery in more naturalistic and more complex task situations.

Other "traditional" experimental procedures continue to yield fruitful findings.

Denis's scanning experiments, for example, are directly inspired by Kosslyn, Ball, and Reiser's (1978) experiments, although Denis introduced verbal input rather than real maps as experimental materials. In the same vein, mental-rotation procedures similar to those created by Shepard (e.g., Shepard & Metzler, 1978) are still broadly used in variety of research venues, although their utility also has been questioned (Yuille, 1983).

It would not be the least bit exaggerating to suggest that the research on visuospatial imagery and the links between imagery and language has shaped much of cognitive psychology as we know it today. Indeed, visual imagery has played a key role in practical, empirical, and theoretical aspects of memory for centuries (see Paivio, 1971). More recent and well-focused investigations in the domain of mental imagery have produced new and exciting findings that have helped to shape our understanding of visuospatial cognition, working memory, long-term memory, and reasoning. The chapters of this volume allow the reader to trace the history of such research from verbal learning to language comprehension and memory to chronometric studies of image generation and manipulation to complex problem solving. In this progression, we can see the history of modern cognitive psychology and its likely shape in the future.

Finally, new research findings presented here in the areas of image reconstrual and recomposition, imaginal subtraction, and imaginal priming reveal one direction that the field will take in the coming years. With less concern about the ontological status of visuospatial images, there also will be a renewed focus on the role of related processes in language comprehension, language production, and higher-level processes. In the latter category, we foresee elaboration of mixed models of thinking and reasoning, without the constraints imposed by more reductionist theories that required homogeneity of representation and homogeneity of theoretical explanation. It is toward that more complex and more realistic level of discourse that our collaboration has propelled us.

NOTES

1. In fact, one of Allan Paivio's favorite informal arguments in favor of analogue imagery is that, in his view, the smell of a rose cannot be represented as a verbal or propositional string.

REFERENCES

Anderson, J. R. (1990). *The adaptive character of thought.* Hillsdale, NJ: Erlbaum.

Bara, B., Bucciarelli, M., & Johnson-Laird, P. N. (in press). The development of syllogistic reasoning. *American Journal of Psychology.*

Bryant, D. J. (1992). A spatial representation system in humans. *Psychology, 3,* (16), space. 1.

Carmichael, L., Hogan, H. P., & Walter, A. A. (1932). An experimental study of the effect of language on the reproduction of visually perceived form. *Journal of Experimental Psychology, 15,* 73–86.

Carreiras, M., & Codina, B. (1992). Spatial cognition of the blind and sighted: Visual and amodal hypotheses. *Cahiers de Psychologie Cognitive/European Bulletin of Cognitive Psychology, 12,* 51–78.

Carpenter, P. A., & Eisenberg, P. (1978). Mental rotation and the frame of reference in blind and sighted individuals. *Perception and Psychophysics, 23* 117–124.

Clark, H. H. (1973). Space, time, semantics, and the child. In T. E. Moore (Ed.), *Cognitive development and the acquisition of language* (pp. 27–64). New York: John Wiley.

Cornoldi, C., de Beni, R., Roncari, S., & Romano, S. (1989). The effects of imagery instructions on total congenital blind recall. *The European Journal of Cognitive Psychology, 7,* 321–331.

Cornoldi, C., Logie, R., Bradimonte, M., Kaufmann, G., & Reisberg, D. (1995). *Stretching the imagination: Representation and transformation in mental imagery.* New York: Oxford University Press.

Cosmides, L. (1989). The logic of social exchange: Has natural selection shaped how humans reason? Studies with the Wason selection task. *Cognition, 31,* 187–276.

Denis, M. (1979). *Les images mentales.* Paris: Presses Universitaires de France.

Denis, M., & Cocude, M. (1989). Scanning visual images generated from verbal descriptions. *The European Journal of Cognitive Psychology, 1,* 293–308.

Denis, M., & de Vega, M. (1993). Modèles mentaux et imagerie mentale. In M-F. Ehrlich, H. Tardieu, & M. Cavazza (Eds.), *Les modèles mentaux: Approache cognitive des representations* (pp. 79–100). Paris: Masson.

de Vega, M. (1994). Characters and their perspectives in narratives describing spatial environments. *Psychological Research, 56,* 116–126.

Engelkamp, J. (1991). Memory of action events: Some implications for memory theory and for imagery. In C. Cornoldi & M. A. McDaniel (Eds.), *Imagery and cognition* (pp. 183–220). New York: Springer-Verlag.

Farah, M. J. (1988). Is visual imagery really visual? Overlooked evidence from neuropsychology. *Psychological Review, 95,* 307–317.

Ernest, C. (1987). Imagery and memory in the blind: A review. In M. A. McDaniel & M. Pressley (Eds.), *Imagery and related mnemonic processes: Theories, individual differences, and applications,* (pp. 218–238). New York: Springer-Verlag.

Finke, R. A. (1985). Theories relating mental imagery to perception. *Psychological Bulletin, 98,* 236–260.

Finke, R. A., & Kosslyn, S. M. (1980). Mental imagery acuity in the peripheral visual field. *Journal of Experimental Psychology: Human Perception and Performance, 6,* 244–264.

Finke, R. A., & Shepard, R. N. (1986). Visual functions of mental imagery. In K. R. Boff, L. Kaufman, & J. Thomas (Eds.), *Handbook of perception and human performance* (Vol. 2, pp. 1–55). New York: John Wiley.

Franklin, N., & Tversky, B. (1990). Searching imagined environments. *Journal of Experimental Psychology: General, 119,* 63–76.

Glenberg, A. M., & Langston, W. E. (1992). Comprehension of illustrated text: Pictures help to build mental models. *Journal of Memory and Language, 31,* 129–151.

Glenberg, A. M., Meyer, M., & Lindem, K. (1987). Mental models contribute to foregrounding during text comprehension. *Journal of Memory and Language, 26,* 69–83.

Helstrup, T. (1989). Loci for act recall: Contextual influence on processing of action events. *Psychological Research, 51,* 168–175.

Intons-Peterson, M. J., & McDaniel, M. A. (1991). Symmetries and asymmetries between imagery and perception. In C. Cornoldi and M. A. McDaniel (Eds.), *Imagery and cognition* (pp. 47–76). New York: Springer-Verlag.

Johnson-Laird, P. N. (1983). *Mental models.* Cambridge: Cambridge University Press.

Johnson-Laird, P. N., & Byrne, R. M. J. (1991). *Deduction.* Hillsdale, NJ: Erlbaum.

Katz, A. (1983). What does it mean to be a high imager? In J. C. Yuille (Ed.), *Imagery, cognition, and memory* (pp. 39–64). Hillsdale, NJ: Erlbaum.

Kintsch, W., & van Dijk, T. A. (1978). Toward a model of text comprehension and production. *Psychological Review, 85,* 363–394.

Kosslyn, S. M. (1978). Measuring the visual angle of the mind's eye. *Cognitive Psychology, 10,* 356–389.

Kosslyn, S. M. (1987). Seeing and imagining in the cerebral hemispheres: A computational approach. *Psychological Review, 94,* 148–175.

Kosslyn, S. M., Ball, T. M., & Reiser, B. J. (1978). Visual images preserve metric spatial information. Evidence from studies of image scanning. *Journal of Experimental Psychology: Human Perception and Performance, 4,* 47–60.

Kosslyn, S. M., Brunn, J., Cave, K. R., & Wallach, R. W. (1984). Individual differences in mental imagery ability: A computational analysis. *Cognition, 18,* 195–243.

Kosslyn, S. M., Chabris, C. F., Marsolek, C. J., & Koenig, O. (1992). Categorical versus coordinate spatial relations: Computational analyses and computer simulations. *Journal of Experimental Psychology: Human Perception and Performance, 18,* 562–577.

Kosslyn, S. M., Van Kleek, M. H., & Kirby, K. N. (1990). A neurologically plausible model of individual differences in visual mental imagery. In P. J. Hampson, D. F. Marks, & J. T. E. Richardson (Eds.), *Imagery: Current developments* (pp. 39–77). London: Routledge.

Leybaert, J. (1993). Reading in the deaf: The roles of phonological codes. In M. Marschark & M. D. Clark (Eds.), *Psychological perspectives on deafness* (pp. 269–310). Hillsdale, NJ: Erlbaum.

Mani, K., & Johnson-Laird, P. N. (1982). The mental representation of spatial descriptions. *Memory & Cognition, 10,* 181–187.

Marmor, G. S., & Zabeck, L. A. (1976). Mental rotation in the blind: Does mental rotation depend on visual imagery? *Journal of Experimental Psychology: Human Perception and Performance, 2,* 515–521.

Marr, D. (1982). *Vision.* San Francisco: W. H. Freeman.

Marschark, M., Cornoldi, C., & Porter, T. (1995). *The role of auditory imagery in memory by people who are deaf.* Manuscript submitted for publication.

Marschark, M., & Hunt, R. R. (1989). A re-examination of the role of imagery in learning and memory. *Journal of Experimental Psychology: Learning, Memory and Cognition, 15,* 710–720.

Marschark, M., Richman, C. L., Yuille, J. C., & Hunt, R. R. (1987). The role of imagery in memory: On shared and distinctive information. *Psychological Bulletin, 102,* 28–41.

Nelson, D. L., Reed, V. S., & McEvoy, C. L. (1977). Learning to order pictures and words: A model of sensory and semantic encoding. *Journal of Experimental Psychology: Human Learning and Memory, 3,* 523–528.

Oakhill, J. V., Johnson-Laird, P. N., & Garnham, A. (1989). Believability and syllogistic reasoning. *Cognition, 31,* 117–140.

Paivio, A. (1971). *Imagery and verbal processes.* New York: Holt, Rinehart and Winston.

Paivio, A. (1986). *Mental representation: A dual-coding approach.* New York: Oxford University Press.

Pinker, S. (1980). Mental imagery and the third dimension. *Journal of Experimental Psychology: General, 109,* 354–371.

Potter, M. C., Kroll, J. F., Yachzel, B., Carpenter, E., & Sherman, J. (1986). Pictures in sentences: Understanding without words. *Journal of Experimental Psychology: General, 115,* 281–294.

Pylyshyn, Z. (1981). The imagery debate: Analogue media versus tacit knowledge. *Psychological Review, 88,* 16–45.

Pylyshyn, Z. (1986). *Computation and Cognition: Toward a foundation for cognitive science.* Cambridge, MA: MIT Press.

Reisberg, D. (Ed.). (1992). *Auditory imagery.* Hillsdale, NJ: Erlbaum.

Sergent, J. (1991). Judgments of relative position and distance on representations of spatial relations. *Journal of Experimental Psychology: Human Perception and Performance, 91,* 762–780.

Shepard, R. N. (1984). Ecological constraints on internal representation: Resonant kinematics of perceiving, imagining, thinking, and dreaming. *Psychological Review, 91,* 417–447.

Shepard, R. N., & Metzler, J. (1978). Mental rotation of three-dimensional objects. *Science, 171,* 701–703.

Yates, J. (1985). The content of awareness is a model of the world. *Psychological Review, 92,* 249–284.

Yuille, J. C. (1983). The crisis in theories of mental imagery. In J. C. Yuille (Ed.), *Imagery, cognition, and memory* (pp. 263–284). Hillsdale, NJ: Erlbaum.

Index